THE PRESIDENTS
AND
CIVIL DISORDER

BY
BENNETT MILTON RICH

THE BROOKINGS INSTITUTION
WASHINGTON, D.C.
1941

PREFACE

The Presidents and Civil Disorder is a study of the role of the chief executive in domestic disturbances involving the armed forces of the United States. It is an account of the activities of the presidents, or their agents, in circumstances where federal troops were requested or actually used. No effort has been made to examine in detail all of the disorders in which federal troops have been involved. The Reconstruction Period, for example, because of the abnormal conditions existing then, has not been considered. The study does take into account, however, the major disturbances since the federal government was established and others which have some special significance.

A considerable quantity of primary source material was available for study, such as letters to or from the presidents, reports to the presidents or their agents, and reports of congressional or departmental investigations. In addition to published materials, pertinent manuscripts have been examined in the William L. Clements Library, Ann Arbor, Michigan, the Hayes Memorial Library, Fremont, Ohio, the Library of Congress, the Library of the Office of the Judge Advocate General, and the United States Archives. The War Department very graciously granted access to its files on disorders for all disturbances through 1914.

I wish to thank the University of Michigan and The Brookings Institution for the privilege of spending the academic year 1940-41 as a Michigan-Brookings Fellow at The Brookings Institution. Although this study was begun several months before, and finished sometime after, the period of the fellowship, it could not have been completed had it not been for the special opportunities afforded by the fellowship.

I should like to express my appreciation to those members of the staff of The Brookings Institution who assisted in the work incident to the publication of this study: especially to Dr. F. F. Blachly and Dr. Meyer Jacobstein, who aided in obtaining access to pertinent materials and who later read the manuscript; to Dr.

Fred W. Powell, who read the manuscript and made a number of helpful suggestions; and to Dr. Laurence F. Schmeckebier, whose advice was frequently sought concerning problems pertaining to the preparation and publication of the study.

I wish to thank Major General E. S. Adams, Adjutant General, for making available the War Department records dealing with disorders through 1914, and Colonel Archibald King and Lieutenant Colonel Archer L. Lerch, of the Judge Advocate General's Office, for their assistance and advice.

In addition to the persons mentioned above, I am grateful to many others who assisted in obtaining material for this study.

I am indebted most of all to Professor Everett S. Brown, of the University of Michigan, whose continued encouragement and scholarly guidance I very deeply appreciate.

For all statements of fact and all expressions of opinion, I alone am responsible.

BENNETT M. RICH

University of Pennsylvania
   November 1941

CONTENTS

INTRODUCTION

The problem of maintaining domestic peace is as old as government itself. American colonial history, from the rebellion of Nathaniel Bacon to that of Daniel Shays, gave ample warning to the framers of the Constitution that adequate provision must be made for protecting the federal system from internal violence. The point was made in the Constitutional Convention that unless the "General Government" was empowered "to suppress rebellions against particular states . . . it must remain a passive Spectator of its own subversion."[1] As a consequence of this fear, a procedure was set up by which federal assistance could be given troubled states. The constitutional provisions empowering such aid and the provisions relating to the enforcement of federal law were early supplemented by congressional legislation which authorized the president to use force, if necessary, to prevent, or to subdue, domestic violence. It is the purpose of this study to show what the presidents have done during the past century and a half when the ever-potential threat of domestic disorder became an unfortunate reality.

[1] Max Farrand, *The Records of the Federal Convention of 1787*, Vol. II, p. 47.

CHAPTER I

WASHINGTON AND THE WHISKEY INSURRECTION

There have been many instances of domestic disorder since the Whiskey Insurrection in 1794. However, none better illustrates the concern of the first citizen of the land for all his people. Washington was determined that the law should be obeyed. He was equally determined that those charged with the task of suppressing the insurrection should not, in their zeal, be instruments of oppression.

In 1786 when Washington had given advice about the proper method of handling Shays Rebellion, his tone had been very belligerent. Of the "present tumults" in Massachusetts he wrote:

Know precisely what the insurgents aim at. If they have *real* grievances, redress them if possible; or acknowledge the justice of them, and your inability to do it in the present moment. If they have not, employ the force of government against them at once. . . . Let the reins of government then be braced and held with a steady hand, and every violation of the constitution reprehended.[1]

As president of the United States, Washington's ultimate aim was in every sense consistent with the policy here recommended. His procedure for overcoming resistance, however, far from being one of sudden suppression, was one of reasonable, though firm, patience and moderation.

CAUSES OF DISSATISFACTION

The excise tax, a part of Hamilton's financial program, had aroused opposition in many parts of the country. In Pennsylvania, where resistance was most formidable, the lower house of the legislature, at the time Congress was debating the measure, passed resolutions condemning the "collection of revenue by means of excise."[2]

[1] Washington to Henry Lee, Oct. 31, 1786. *The Writings of George Washington* (W. C. Ford, ed.), Vol. XI, pp. 77-78.
[2] *Pennsylvania Archives*, 2d series, Vol. IV, p. 19. For years the state had been

To the people in the four western counties of the state, a tax on liquors was especially distasteful. The cost of shipping their farm produce in freight wagons to the eastern cities was prohibitive, and, as a consequence, their only recourse was to reduce their grains to a more portable form. The excise was, to them, simply a tax on their livelihood, another element of cost to reduce what was already an exceedingly small margin of profit. Furthermore, since the tax · was on the process of distilling rather than on the retailer or consumer, the people believed the government was discriminating against them to the benefit of those in the east who were better able to pay.

It was to the principle of the tax as well as to its size that objection was made.[3] As one petitioner expressed it, "Why we should be made subject to a duty for drinking our grain more than eating it, seems a matter of astonishment to every reflecting mind.[4] Why, also, the argument went, should they meekly accept the imposition of a tax from a government that, after all, had done very little for them. The inhabitants of the western area were dissatisfied with the manner in which the frontier wars had been conducted. In addition, they claimed that "the General Government had been inattentive to the execution of the treaty of peace respecting the western posts, and remiss in asserting the claims to the navigation of the Mississippi."[5]

PROCLAMATION OF SEPTEMBER 15, 1792

Opposition to the new law first gained public attention as a result of protest meetings in the summer of 1791 at Brownsville,

attempting, with little success, to collect an excise tax on liquors. It was not, in fact, until *after* the passage of the federal law that the state act was repealed. See Leland D. Baldwin, *Whiskey Rebels*, pp. 56-60.

[3] By the act of Mar. 3, 1791 (1 Stat. L. 199), the yearly duty amounted to 60 cents for every gallon of capacity of a private still. The act of May 8, 1792 (1 Stat. L. 267) reduced the tax to 54 cents with the option of paying 7 cents on every gallon produced. This amount was equal to one-quarter of the retail price in the west but only one-eighth of the selling price in the east. "Thus the ad valorem rate of the tax was highest in the region where specie for tax payments was scarcest." Solon J. Buck and Elizabeth H. Buck, *The Planting of Civilization in Western Pennsylvania*, p. 467.

[4] Baldwin, *Whiskey Rebels*, p. 26.

[5] "Report of the United States Commissioners to President Washington," *Pennsylvania Archives*, 2d series, Vol. IV, p. 350.

Washington, and Pittsburgh. In September, Robert Johnson, the collector for Washington and Allegheny Counties, was tarred and feathered. At Washington, in August of the following year, the revenue office in the house of William Faulkner was forced open, "the excise notice was torn down and the sign of the President's head . . . was filled with bullet holes, the rioters saying that that was the man who had signed the excise act."[6] Of greater importance, so far as public opinion was concerned, was a second conference at Pittsburgh, August 21, 1792, when a group of men from various parts of the four counties drew up a report strongly condemning the excise and in effect threatening complete ostracism to anyone accepting the office of collector.[7]

During the previous month, President Washington, on a trip from Philadelphia to his home at Mount Vernon, had made inquiries along the route concerning "the sentiments which are entertained of public measures." He listed the complaints and wrote Hamilton asking for his "ideas upon the discontents here enumerated." One of the criticisms the President had encountered was that the nation had been compelled "even to resort to an excise law, of odious character with the people, partial in its operation, unproductive, unless enforced by arbitrary and vexatious means, and committing the authority of the government in parts where resistance is most probable and coercion least practicable."[8] Hamilton replied that opposition had developed in some parts of North and South Carolina, Kentucky, and the four western counties of Pennsylvania, but that "as to the idea of a war upon the citizens to collect the impost duties, it can only be regarded as a figure of rhetoric."[9]

This reassuring letter had hardly arrived when news of the Pittsburgh meeting, coupled with reports of discontent from the supervisors in North and South Carolina, made necessary some action by the government. Washington wrote that if there were clear evidence of opposition to the law, he would "exert all the legal powers with which the executive is invested to check so dar-

[6] Baldwin, *Whiskey Rebels*, p. 85.
[7] *Pennsylvania Archives*, 2d series, Vol. IV, pp. 30-31.
[8] Washington, *Writings* (Ford, ed.), Vol. XI, p. 148.
[9] *The Works of Alexander Hamilton* (John C. Hamilton, ed.), Vol. IV, p. 253.

ing and unwarrantable a spirit."[10] Attorney General Edmund Randolph advised, however, that there was insufficient evidence to prosecute the offenders. Upon the recommendation of Hamilton, Washington took official notice of the opposition by issuing the proclamation of September 15, 1792.[11] Its contents are well summarized in one paragraph:

... I ... most earnestly admonish and exhort all persons whom it may concern to refrain and desist from all unlawful combinations and proceedings whatsoever, having for object or tending to obstruct the operation of the laws aforesaid; inasmuch as all lawful ways and means will be strictly put in execution for bringing to justice the infractors thereof, and securing obedience thereto.[12]

That Washington was at least considering the ultimate use of troops is indicated in his letter to Hamilton the day after he signed the proclamation:

I have no doubt but that the Proclamation will undergo many strictures; and as the effect proposed may not be answered by it, it will be necessary to look forward in time to ulterior arrangements. And here not only the constitution and laws must strictly govern, but the employing of the regular troops avoided, if it be possible to effect order without their aid; otherwise there would be a cry at once, "The cat is let out; we now see for what purpose an army was raised." Yet if no other means will effectually answer, and the constitution and laws will authorize these, they must be used as the dernier resort.[13]

Hamilton replied that he thought the proclamation would answer a very valuable purpose. "I do not despair," he continued, "that with a proper countenance, the ordinary course of legal coercion will be found adequate."[14]

---

[10] To Hamilton, Sept. 7, 1792. *Writings* (Ford, ed.), Vol. XII, p. 182.

[11] Although dated September 15, the proclamation, which was drafted by Hamilton, was not issued until September 29. In the meantime it was dispatched to Monticello for the signature of Thomas Jefferson, Secretary of State. It is worth noting that this first proclamation was sent not only to the governor of Pennsylvania but also to the governors of North and South Carolina.

[12] James D. Richardson, *A Compilation of the Messages and Papers of the Presidents*, official edition, Vol. I, p. 125. All citations to Richardson's *Messages and Papers of the Presidents* are to the original official edition, published in 1896 as House Miscellaneous Document 210, 53 Cong. 2 sess., and also without document number. There are numerous later commercial editions which vary in the pagination.

[13] *Writings* (Ford, ed.), Vol. XII, p. 187.

[14] Hamilton, *Works*, Vol. IV, p. 315.

Washington was not one to sidestep the problem of enforcement merely by disregarding the law. On the contrary, he directed the Attorney General to attend the circuit court in order to see that the proceedings against those indicted for opposing the excise laws were "conducted in a manner to which no exception can be taken with propriety: and for the further purpose, also, of giving to this measure of Government a more solemn and serious aspect."[15] To impress the inhabitants of the western counties with the authority of the government, he also directed that hereafter all indictments be served in person by the federal marshal of the Pennsylvania district.[16]

ATTACK ON BOWER HILL

For a time the enforcement problem was practically forgotten. Hamilton apparently had prophesied correctly. During the remainder of 1792 and all of 1793, comparatively few instances of opposition were manifest. But in the spring of 1794 attacks on the collectors of Westmoreland and Fayette Counties gave notice of renewed opposition on a much wider scale. Once again, public attention was focused on the excise.

The agitation of the newly formed Democratic societies, the selection of collectors, some of whom did not command popular respect, and the approach of the time (June) when the law specified that stills were to be reported, were contributing factors to the period of crisis. The immediate cause of the insurrection was none of these, but an effort to bring into court those who had not reported their stills in 1793. To the inhabitants west of the mountains, a most annoying provision of the law was the requirement for appearance in a federal court. The time and expense involved in transportation to the nearest court, which was in Philadelphia, and the costs incident to the litigation itself, seemed an unbearable burden. Objection was so general that the law was eased by the act of June

---

[15] Oct. 1, 1792, *The Writings of George Washington from the Original Manuscript Sources, 1745-1799* (John C. Fitzpatrick, ed.), Vol. XXXII, pp. 171-72. Through the courtesy of Mrs. Arthur Claggett at the Library of Congress, the writer had access to the unpublished volumes of the Fitzpatrick edition. Uncertainty as to the time of publication of this more complete work made it advisable to cite the Ford edition where possible.

[16] Nov. 24, 1792. The same, p. 236.

5, 1794, which provided that the judicial courts of the states might take cognizance of suits arising out of the excise law.[17] In the meantime, writs commanding appearance at Philadelphia had been issued under the old law, although not served until a month after the new law was in effect.[18]

It was the attempt to serve these court processes by United States Marshal David Lenox, in company with General John Neville, the local inspector, that brought on the famous attack on Neville's Bower Hill home, July 17, 1794. This was the most violent disturbance of the insurrection. At the inspector's request, a small detachment of regular troops from the garrison at Pittsburgh had come to his aid, but they were compelled to surrender by the much larger attacking body, a considerable number of whom were Pennsylvania militiamen. The leader of the militia, Major James McFarlane, who had fought in the Revolution, was killed in the conflict. Neville's house and the buildings on his estate were burned.[19]

The incident at Bower Hill aroused great public excitement. The mail from Pittsburgh was robbed to determine the feelings of certain prominent Pittsburghers toward the excise. Numerous meetings occurred, culminating in a great gathering August 12, at Braddock's field, eight miles from Pittsburgh. Estimates of the number there ranged from 1,500 to 7,000. Despite agitation by the more radical element for a demonstration of their power, sane counsel prevailed and, instead of the feared attack on the fort at Pittsburgh and the sacking of the town, the assembly dispersed after an orderly march through the city.

USE OF FORCE THREATENED

The attack on Neville's home stirred the President to action. With no precedent to guide him, and presumably not wishing to antagonize the state government by any hasty step, Washington took the eminently sane course of calling a conference of the high

---

[17] 1 Stat. L. 378.

[18] See Baldwin for statement of the argument that Hamilton by this means deliberately provoked the crisis. *Whiskey Rebels*, pp. 110-12.

[19] The prominent part played by the militia was due to their having gathered nearby for a military meeting to draft men for service against the Indians. *Pennsylvania Archives*, 2d series, Vol. IV, p. 11.

officials of both governments. On the first Saturday in August, Washington and his Cabinet met with Governor Thomas Mifflin, the Chief Justice, the Secretary of the Commonwealth, and the Attorney General. The minutes of the meeting are incomplete, but it is apparent that the officials of the state were reluctant to initiate military measures. As a result, no co-operative plan of action was formulated.[20]

The results of the meeting were very disappointing to the President. All hopes for action by the state disappeared three days later when Governor Mifflin wrote that in his opinion it would be improper to use the military power of the state unless the judicial authority had been proved incompetent. However, the Governor did assure the President that he would promptly and faithfully discharge any duty imposed upon him.[21]

Undecided as to the most advisable course to pursue, the President again asked Hamilton for his opinion. In contrast to his previous position, Hamilton now urged force, "an imposing one, such if practicable, as will deter from opposition, save the effusion of the blood of citizens, and serve the object to be accomplished." He feared there might be 9,000 men in arms, with the possibility of a larger number if augmented from the neighboring counties of Virginia, and he recommended that 12,000 militia should prepare to march.[22] Washington called out 12,950 men, an action which indicates, in striking fashion, the great influence of his Secretary.

Some time before conferring with the state officials, Washington had turned over to Associate Justice James Wilson the evidence which had been collected showing resistance to the laws. On August 4, Wilson certified to the President that the "laws of the United States are opposed, and the execution thereof obstructed by combinations too powerful to be suppressed by the ordinary course of Judicial proceedings or by the powers vested in the Marshal of that district."[23] This was the go-ahead signal for the President since, according to the law of May 2, 1792, he could not call forth the militia until notification by "an associate justice or the district

[20] The same, pp. 144-46.
[21] The same, pp. 104-09.
[22] Hamilton, *Works*, Vol. IV, p. 577.
[23] *Pennsylvania Archives*, 2d series, Vol. IV, pp. 82-83.

judge" of the failure by judicial proceedings to halt obstructions to the laws of the United States.[24]

Three days after the issuance of Judge Wilson's certificate, a second proclamation was published. The first, issued two years before, had merely exhorted obedience to the laws. The second was decidedly different in tone. This time force was to be used. The President stated why, in his opinion, force was necessary, and cited the law under which he was acting.[25] In accordance with that law, he called on the insurgents "on or before the first day of September next, to disperse and retire peaceably to their respective abodes."[26]

The proclamation was sent to Governor Mifflin and in an accompanying letter Henry Knox, Secretary of War, stated that the President

has directed me to request your Excellency forthwith to issue your orders for organizing and holding in readiness to march at a moment's warning, a Corps of the Militia of Pennsylvania, amounting to five thousand two hundred non-commissioned officers and privates, with a due proportion of commissioned officers, . . . armed and equipped as completely as possible, with the articles in possession of the State of Pennsylvania, or of the individuals who shall compose the corps.[27]

To this force were to be added 2,100 from New Jersey, 2,350 from Maryland, and 3,300 from Virginia. This letter brought an instant response from the Governor, who issued orders to Adjutant General Josiah Harmar to call into service the number of men requested by the President.[28]

LAST-MINUTE EFFORTS AT CONCILIATION

While preparing to use force, Washington decided "to make one more experiment of a conciliatory appeal to the reason, virtue, and patriotism" of the insurrectionists.[29] To this end, he ap-

[24] 1 Stat. L. 264.
[25] The same.
[26] *Pennsylvania Archives*, 2d series, Vol. IV, pp. 124-27.
[27] The same, p. 122.
[28] The same, p. 129. It was decided in a Cabinet meeting at the President's home on Aug. 24, 1799, to "call for a further number sufficient to complete the whole to 15,000 non-commissioned officers and privates"—1,500 from Virginia and 500 each from Maryland and New Jersey. Library of Congress, *Pennsylvania Insurrection*, Vol. I, Mss.
[29] Randolph to Mifflin, Aug. 7, 1794. The same, p. 121. This act of the President, according to Hugh H. Brackenridge, "saved the country from civil war.

pointed a commission of three men to go to the western counties: James Ross, United States Senator from Pennsylvania, Jasper Yeates, Associate Justice of the Pennsylvania Supreme Court, and William Bradford, Attorney General of the United States. They were instructed to grant concessions even to the waiving of duties of former years "if they could thereby secure compliance for the current year." To give added weight to the necessity of negotiating a settlement, the commissioners were authorized to say that orders had already been issued for assembling the militia and for making ready its movement.[30]

The commission, in company with two representatives of Governor Mifflin, held several meetings with delegates from the western counties during the last week of August and the first days of September. Provision was made for a popular referendum on the question of submission, but the vigorous, even violent, activity of the opposition at several of the polling places brought results deemed unsatisfactory by the commission. They reported to Washington that "some more competent force is necessary to cause the laws to be duly executed, and to ensure to the officers and well disposed citizens that protection which it is the duty of Government to afford."[31]

While the commissioners were preparing to go west, the President suffered a period of great anxiety. He called a Cabinet meeting for August 9, to discuss the insurrection. Inspector Neville and Marshal Lenox were in the Capital, and Washington directed Randolph to bring the two officials to the meeting.[32] Three days later the President issued instructions to re-enforce the garrison at Pittsburgh from the post at Fort Franklin, 70 miles to the north.[33] Influenced no doubt by reports of the march on Pittsburgh, Washington held up the pay for the army under General Wayne because

---

It gave the government a strength which nothing could resist. It silenced, at once, all clamour from below, and decided the people here. The reasonableness of the propositions, left the refractory without excuse; and brought forth the force of government with a warmth of heart, unchecked by an idea that all conciliatory means had not been tried." See Hugh H. Brackenridge, *Incidents of the Insurrection in the Western Parts of Pennsylvania in the Year 1794*, Vol. II, p. 83.

[30] *Pennsylvania Archives*, 2d series, Vol. IV, p. 139.
[31] The same, p. 358.
[32] Washington, *Writings* (Fitzpatrick, ed.), Vol. XXXIII, p. 462.
[33] The same, p. 468.

of the hazards of sending it through districts that were "in open rebellion."[34]

RAISING AN ARMY

In the meantime, preparations were afoot to get the troops organized and in readiness to assemble.[35] Governors Richard Howell of New Jersey, Henry Lee of Virginia, and Thomas Lee of Maryland experienced relatively little difficulty in raising the required number of troops. Governor Mifflin had acted immediately on the President's request, but he delayed for almost three weeks any effort at a follow-up of his orders. On August 27, the Governor wrote to General Harmar for a report on the success of the draft, but that officer had also been guilty of delay and in turn had to write his brigade inspectors for a report.[36] One month after his original order, Governor Mifflin wrote to the Adjutant General expressing his great mortification, upon examining the latter's report, at the unwillingness of some of the brigades to comply with the call.[37] Almost frantically he called for a renewed effort to fill the state's quota, if not with the supposedly organized militia, then with volunteer enlistments.[38] To give added force to the drive, the Governor went into a number of counties and spoke to the militia officers, demanding that they resign their commissions unless they were willing to serve.[39] Speed on the part of the state officials was imperative, since, on the same day that the Governor issued a schedule of the days he planned to meet the militia officers, a

[34] To Hamilton, August 21, the same, pp. 471-72.

[35] Randolph wrote a strong letter to the President in which he pointed out the hazards to be encountered in calling out the militia and advising further delay. For the letter, see Francis Wharton, *State Trials of the United States*, pp. 156-59.

[36] *Pennsylvania Archives*, 2d series, Vol. IV, p. 209.

[37] The lack of enthusiasm of the Dauphin County militia is evidenced by the following letter written by Brigade Inspector John Gloninger to Adjutant General Harmar, Aug. 29, 1794: "According to the information I have received from several parts of the County, it appears that the militia from this County are not willing to march to quell the insurrection in the Western part of Pennsylvania. They say that they are ready to march, according to the former Orders against a foreign enemy, but not against the citizens of their own State—so that from every circumstance I have great reason to believe they will not turn out on the last call." *The Papers of Brigadier General Josiah Harmar*, Mss., William L. Clements Library, Ann Arbor, Michigan.

[38] *Pennsylvania Archives*, 2d series, Vol. IV, p. 265.

[39] The same, p. 274.

message came from the President, via Hamilton, asking the Governor to assemble the state's quota immediately. Carlisle was given as the place of general rendezvous.[40] By draft, and by acceptance of volunteers, the filling of the quota was speeded. On September 17, instructions were issued by General Harmar to proceed toward Carlisle, where the Pennsylvanians were to meet the New Jersey troops.

While the troops were moving westward, and on the day after he had received the report of the United States commissioners, Washington issued a third proclamation directed at the insurrectionists. Declaring that "a force which according to every reasonable expectation is adequate to the exigency" was even then "already in motion to the scene of disaffection," he warned against giving aid or comfort to the insurgents and directed that all offenders be brought under the "cognizance of the laws."[41]

ORGANIZATION AND DISCIPLINE OF TROOPS

In his diary Washington records that he had determined to go to the place appointed for the rendezvous of the troops.[42] In company with his private secretary and with Hamilton, who had requested permission to accompany him, Washington left Philadelphia the last day of September and arrived at Carlisle on October 4.[43] The crowds in the street were silent as Washington passed through the town, but when he later reviewed the Pennsylvania troops, one soldier thought the "spectacle was grand, interesting, and affecting —every man, as he passed along, poured forth his wishes for the preservation of this most valuable of their fellow citizens."[44]

During his stay at Carlisle, Washington talked with two special representatives of the western area, Congressman William Findley, of Westmoreland County, and David Reddick of Washington County, who had been selected to make a final effort to stop the coming of the troops.[45] He told them that since the "greatest part

---

[40] The same, p. 267.
[41] Proclamation of Sept. 25, 1794, the same, p. 361. Usually referred to as the second proclamation, actually it was the third, counting that of Sept. 15, 1792.
[42] *The Diaries of George Washington*, Vol. IV, p. 209.
[43] Hamilton, *Works*, Vol. V, p. 30.
[44] "Notes on the March," *Pennsylvania Archives*, 2d series, Vol. IV, p. 428.
[45] The townships had elected representatives, the so-called Committee of Safety, to meet at Parkinson's Ferry (now Monongahela City), on October 2. This com-

of the expense had already been incurred," he intended to go on "in order to convince them [the insurgents] that the government could, and would enforce obedience to the laws not suffering them to be insulted with impunity."[46] To Edmund Randolph he wrote, "I believe they are scared."[47]

Washington did not assume command of the troops but for some days assisted Governor Mifflin in organizing the hastily assembled detachments from the various counties.[48] He did, however, determine the rank of the officers. Unless Washington himself went to the scene of the disorder, Governor Lee of Virginia was to be the first in command, with Governors Mifflin and Howell in second and third positions, and Major Generals Daniel Morgan or William Irvine in fourth position.[49]

The President's greatest service during his stay at Carlisle was to instill in the minds of the soldiers a much needed sense of responsibility for their conduct. Many of the troops had been persuaded to join the expedition by the oratorical efforts of state militia officers.[50] Once aroused, and with inadequate training for the task required of them, some were anxious for a little blood-letting. On the march to Carlisle, two persons had met death at the hands of the troops, and there had been numerous instances of damage to the property and dignity of the citizenry. "Those among themselves who had reasoned in favour of the subjection of the military to the civil law," records William Findley, who was in the encampment at Carlisle for some days,

or suggested that those who killed a citizen in cold blood should answer to the proper courts, and that the army were only employed to aid the Judiciary in the exercise of its proper functions, and not to usurp or exercise those functions themselves, were in as much danger, and equally the objects of threats, as the whiskey men, and in fact were called so.[51]

---

mittee selected delegates Findley and Reddick to meet with Washington. For the conference between the President and the delegates, see William Findley, *History of the Insurrection in the Four Western Counties of Pennsylvania*, pp. 178 ff.

[46] *The Diaries of George Washington*, Vol. IV, p. 215.

[47] *Writings* (Ford, ed.), Vol. XII, p. 473.

[48] *The Diaries of George Washington*, Vol. IV, p. 212.

[49] The same, p. 217.

[50] "Trifling incidents were magnified into crimes, and the most orderly citizens were characterized as offenders." Findley, *History of the Insurrection*, p. 160.

[51] The same, p. 143.

Washington labored constantly to remove this spirit from the minds of the soldiers.[52] He told delegates Findley and Reddick that the chief reason for his practice of mixing and conversing daily with the officers "was to impress the army with a proper sense of the importance of submitting to the laws, and that unless they did so, the last resort of a republican government would be defeated."[53] He also informed the delegates that his intended visit to other divisions of the army was for the same purpose.

At first the President was undecided how far he should accompany the troops, but after the western delegates had reported that opposition to the laws had almost completely disappeared, he seemed inclined to the belief that there was no necessity of his going farther west than Bedford and that a return to Philadelphia for the meeting of Congress would be the wiser procedure. On October 12, Washington left Carlisle, arriving at Bedford a week later. During his brief stay he wrote both a personal letter and, through Hamilton, general orders to Lee instructing him as to the conduct of the army. In the letter he made one special recommendation:

It is this, that every officer and soldier will constantly bear in mind that he comes to support the laws, and that it would be peculiarly unbecoming in him to be in any way the infractory of them. That the essential principles of a free government confine the province of the military when called forth on such occasions, to these two objects:

1st. To combat and subdue all who may be found in arms in opposition to the national will and authority.

2nd. To aid and support the civil magistrates in bringing offenders to justice.

The dispensation of justice belongs to the civil magistrate, and let it ever be our pride and our glory to leave the sacred deposit there unviolated.[54]

---

[52] "After the President had convinced the army, by his discourses, of the propriety, and enforced by his authority the necessity of the subordination of the military to the civil power, and after he had given an unequivocal testimony of his sincerity by obliging those who killed the two men, to enter recognizance with bail, so standing their trial at court, no more accidents of the kind happened." The same, p. 144.

[53] "The President was happily successful in reducing the licentious part of the army to subordination to the laws, and in inspiring the people in the western counties with such a measure of confidence, as prevented any conduct on their part, that could give the army any just cause of irritation." The same, p. 189.

[54] *Pennsylvania Archives*, 2d series, Vol. IV, pp. 418-19.

In the general orders were stated the specific reasons for calling forth the militia, namely, "to suppress combinations which exist in some of the western counties of Pennslyvania" and to "cause the laws to be executed."[55] He then added that the function of the military, in addition to overcoming armed opposition, was "to countenance and support the civil officers in the means of executing the laws." Upon arriving within the insurgent country, General Lee was to take care that "those persons in arms, if any, whom you may make prisoners . . . be delivered up to the civil magistrate" and to "make such dispensations as shall appear proper . . . to aid the civil officers in the execution of their respective duties." To aid the judicial process, the district judge and the district attorney were to accompany the army. General Lee was to instruct the latter to cause those arrested for capital offenses to be brought to the Philadelphia jail for safekeeping. Prosecutions for indictable offenses were to be handled in United States courts; for penalties on delinquents, in the courts of Pennsylvania.[56]

Washington suggested that Lee publish a proclamation "inviting all good citizens, friends of the Constitution and laws, to join the standard of the United States."[57] The proclamation was issued and the President's suggestion was put into concrete form through the requirement of an oath of allegiance to the Constitution.[58] Much to Lee's chagrin, the local magistrates took advantage of the occasion to charge a fee for administering the oath. Lee quickly ordered the discontinuance of the fee-extracting practice.

In spite of the President's instructions to Lee that the troops were at all times to maintain scrupulous regard for the rights of persons and property, there were occasions when the order was ignored by some of the inferior officers. The most serious mistreatment of the western inhabitants occurred on "the dismal night" of November 13, the date set for a general round-up of all suspects.

---

[55] At Carlisle Washington had been worried by the rumor that the troops were being taken west "to employ them against the British posts or against the savages." To quiet the rumor Governor Mifflin was directed to announce, in Washington's name, that the sole object was to suppress the insurrection. The same, p. 405.

[56] The same, pp. 412-13.

[57] The same, p. 412.

[58] The same, p. 445. The instructions of Washington contemplated no such action. Congressman Findley pointed out that "Lee must have known that a magistrate had no authority to administer an oath, that the law did not prescribe." *History of the Insurrection*, p. 322.

Witnesses as well as suspects suffered indignities and exposure. Many were later dismissed for want of sufficient evidence, but twenty of those arrested were marched under guard to Philadelphia. Some were released on bail; others languished in prison for months. The difficulty of securing witnesses from the west proved insurmountable and not one of the twenty was found guilty. Some of those who escaped the general round-up later surrendered to stand trial.[59]

THE END OF THE INSURRECTION

By the time the troops arrived, all resistance to the laws had ceased. Since the approaching winter would make the problems of transportation and supply even more difficult, orders were given by General Lee to begin the homeward journey.[60] The round-up of suspects took place on November 13; the order for the immediate return of the troops was given four days later.

Anticipating the army's brief stay, Washington had already given Hamilton instructions about the homeward journey. Frequent complaints had reached the President condemning the conduct of the army on the westward march. "In some places," he informed the Secretary, "I was told they did not leave a plate, a spoon, a glass or a knife; and this owing, in a great measure, as I was informed, to their being left without officers. At *most* if not *all* the encampments I found the fences in a manner burnt up." Apparently the Pennsylvania troops were most remiss in their conduct, for Hamilton was instructed to impress upon Governor Mifflin the necessity of preventing any recurrence of such behavior.[61] The President insisted that all the governors give the officers specific instructions to remain with the troops throughout the trip.[62]

Washington had previously instructed General Lee to arrange for an adequate force to remain in the western counties in order to

---

[59] Baldwin, *Whiskey Rebels*, pp. 244-47.
[60] *Pennsylvania Archives*, 2d series, Vol. IV, p. 455. Rain and snow, cold and hunger, made the journey over the mountains very arduous. See "Autobiography of William Michael (Part II)," in *Historical Papers and Addresses of the Lancaster County Historical Society*, Vol. XXV, No. 7, pp. 69-77.
[61] *Writings* (Ford, ed.), Vol. XII, pp. 480-81.
[62] The same, p. 483.

discourage any signs of renewed opposition to the laws.[63] No sooner did Lee reach the disturbed area than he began to recruit troops for the winter encampment.[64] Technically there was no authority for recruiting troops for the winter service. The act of May 2, 1792 provided that in the event the President called out the militia when Congress was not in session, their period of service would expire thirty days after the Congress was convened.[65] In his message of November 19, Washington pointed out this fact and suggested that Congress enact legislation which would enable him to station a force in the Monongahela country.[66] Ten days later Congress had passed, and the President had approved, an act to station as many as 2,500 men, if necessary, in the four western counties.[67] By this time, however, a large part of the army was on its way homeward and it was impossible, as well as unnecessary, to recruit such a large number.[68] Strangely enough, a portion of those on duty were recruited from the very inhabitants against whom the larger body had marched but a few weeks before.[69]

Acting under instructions from the President, General Lee issued a pardon to all but certain groups before he returned to the east. On July 10, 1795, Washington, by proclamation, enlarged the scope of the pardon to include every one concerned in the insurrection except those who were indicted or convicted of any offense against

[63] *Pennsylvania Archives*, 2d series, Vol. IV, p. 414.
[64] Hamilton, *Works*, Vol. V, p. 50. "To each non-commissioned officer and soldier of the infanry and artillery who may enlist in this corps [the one staying for the winter] will be given one suit of complete uniform with two shirts. To each dragoon will be furnished arms and equipment and there will also be allowed reasonable compensation per month for the use of his horse with a suit of clothes and two shirts." "General Orders, November 9, 1794, Headquarters near Parkinson's Ferry," *St. Clair and Harmar Orderly Book, 1791-1794*. Mss., Library of Congress.
[65] 1 Stat. L. 264.
[66] *Writings* (Ford, ed.), Vol. XII, p. 491.
[67] 1 Stat. L. 403. Major General Daniel Morgan was placed in command.
[68] Probably about 1,000 men remained during the winter. See *The Writings of Albert Gallatin* (Henry Adams, ed.), Vol. III, p. 35. Brackenridge states that 800 of the militia that crossed the mountain remained with Morgan, and that, in addition, a corps of cavalry was raised from the country itself. *Incidents of the Insurrection of the Western Parts of Pennsylvania in the Year 1794*, Vol. III, p. 30.
[69] It was not until Apr. 13, 1795, that Washington gave orders to reduce, by degrees, the force remaining in the western counties. Washington, *Writings* (Fitzpatrick, ed.), Vol. XXXIV, p. 176.

the United States.[70] The grand jury had indicted several of the prisoners for high treason. In the trials before the Circuit Court, the jury brought in a verdict of guilty in but two instances, and in only one of those was the question of what constituted treason argued at any length.[71] Did the crime of the insurgents meet with the first constitutional definition of treason, namely, levying war against the government?[72] In his charge to the jury, Justice Patterson said that the object of the insurrection "was to suppress the excise offices, and to prevent the execution of an act of Congress, by force and intimidation. . . . It is usurpation of the authority of government; it is high treason by levying of war. It [the object of the insurrection] was of a general nature, and of national concern."[73] Washington pardoned the two persons sentenced to death when he learned, through petitioners, that one of the prisoners was a "simpleton" and the other "insane."[74]

EFFECTIVENESS OF THE PRESIDENT'S PROCEDURE

The President's message to Congress of November 19, 1794, was concerned chiefly with the insurrection. He strongly condemned the "self created societies" which were, to his mind, largely responsible for the lack of respect toward the government. Once more he reviewed the events leading up to the calling of the troops. He stated that because of uncertainty as to the number of militia necessary to quell the insurrection, he had "put into motion fifteen thousand men, as being an army, which according to all human calculation, would be prompt and adequate in every view, and might perhaps, by rendering resistance desperate, prevent the diffusion of blood."[75]

[70] Richardson, *Messages and Papers of the Presidents*, Vol. I, p. 181.
[71] *United States* v. *Mitchell*, 2 Dallas 348 (1795); see also *United States* v. *Insurgents of Pennsylvania*, 2 Dallas 335 (1795); *United States* v. *Wright*, and *United States* v. *Stewart*, 2 Dallas 343 (1795); *United States* v. *Porter*, 2 Dallas 345 (1795); *United States* v. *Vigol*, 2 Dallas 346 (1795) (found guilty).
[72] Art. III, sec. 3.
[73] *United States* v. *Mitchell*, 2 Dallas 355 (1795).
[74] See Baldwin, *Whiskey Rebels*, pp. 263-64. See also Homer Cummings and Carl McFarland, *Federal Justice*, pp. 44-45.
[75] "The insurrection in the western counties of this state . . . may be considered as the first ripe fruit of the Democratic Societies. . . . I hope and trust this will work their own curse." (Letter to Burgess Ball, Sept. 25, 1794. *Writings* (Ford,

The success of the expedition was, to Washington, a demonstration of national strength and unity. This feeling was expressed not
only in his message to Congress but more especially in his private
correspondence. In a letter to Edmund Pendleton he expressed
regret at the expense involved but continued:

I trust no money could have been more advantageously expended,
both as it respects the internal peace and welfare of this country, and
the impression it will make on others. The spirit with which the militia
turned out in support of the Constitution and the laws of our country, at
the same time that it does them immortal honor, is the most conclusive
refutation, that could have been made to the assertions of Lord Sheffield,
that, without the protection of Great Britain, we should be unable to
govern ourselves, and would soon be involved in confusion. They will
see, that republicanism is not the phantom of a deluded imagination. On
the contrary, that, under no form of government, will laws be better
supported, liberty and property better secured, or happiness be more
effectually dispensed to mankind.[76]

The record of the Whiskey Insurrection gives abundant evidence
of Washington's scrupulous regard for the law. Few exceptions
stand out. One, a minor item, was General Lee's recruitment of
troops for the winter period without congressional authorization.
This was obviously done in a quiet manner and on a small scale,
else it would have been unnecessary to complete the recruitment
from the militia of the western counties. Another was the unauthorized oath of allegiance upon which General Lee insisted. Of much
greater importance was the questionable, and in some instances
brutal, round-up of suspects on "the dreadful night." However, in
view of Washington's specific instructions regarding the protection
of the rights of citizens, it is impossible to place the blame for this
regrettable incident on the shoulders of the President. At no time
was there any suggestion of martial law. The President made quite
clear his wish that the military arm was to support, not to supplant,
the civil arm. For an attorney and a judge to accompany the army

---

ed.), Vol. XII, p. 464.) Letters of similar tone were written to General Henry Lee
and Major General Daniel Morgan. (The same, pp. 453, 469.) For a refutation
of this view, see William Miller, "The Democratic Societies and the Whiskey Insurrection," *The Pennsylvania Magazine of History and Biography*, Vol. LXII,
July 1938, pp. 324-29.
[76] *Writings* (Ford, ed.), Vol. XIII, pp. 33-34.

was certainly a novel procedure, but one which is not unreasonable in view of their duties. They did not try offenders and pronounce sentence; their function was to effect legal arrests and to serve process on persons suspected of evading the law.

Whether or not troops were necessary has always been a debatable question. Upon the information reaching Washington concerning the state of affairs in the western counties, even William Findley did not "conclude that it was improper in the President to order the army to advance into the country."[77] From the standpoint of actual violence, however, it is an interesting, though misleading, fact that the militia killed twice as many men on their way to the disturbed area as were killed in the most outstanding instance of opposition to federal officials. Certainly there was no necessity for such a large number of troops. But, as Washington explained to the western delegates, he hoped to effect a double victory by the use of the army. This was the first instance of violent opposition to the law. Everywhere anxious eyes were turned to see whether the new government's power was adequate to meet this challenge to its authority. If an insurrection existed, and if troops were to be sent, a sufficient force to guarantee complete success was necessary. The President also felt that such a demonstration of national power would not only quiet the symptoms of discontent which had appeared in other parts of the country but would convince foreign governments that this nation was capable of defending itself.[78]

There can be little doubt that Washington set up an excellent series of guideposts for later presidents faced with internal disturbances to follow. His patience over a considerable period of law violation, his attempts at conciliation and peaceful settlement, his efforts to enlist the co-operation of state officials, and his especial concern for the protection of the civil rights of the citizenry—all contribute to make Washington's role in the Whiskey Insurrection one deserving of particularly high commendation.

[77] *History of the Insurrection*, p. 310.
[78] The same, pp. 180 ff.

CHAPTER II

FROM WASHINGTON TO JACKSON

Five years after the collapse of the insurrection in the western counties of Pennsylvania, the eastern part of the state furnished the stage for a second demonstration of national power. Once more the trouble arose over the problem of taxation; once more the president called on the military to proceed against citizens of the United States.

ADAMS AND THE FRIES REBELLION[1]

The need for a greatly increased revenue resulted from the nation's preparations for a foreign war. Relations with France had grown steadily worse, and after the XYZ disclosures in the spring of 1798, war seemed inevitable. A glance at the statutes passed during the period from the latter part of April through July shows approximately 25 separate acts relating to an enlargement of our military and naval establishment.[2] To finance these increases the president was authorized to borrow five million dollars, and an additional two million dollars was to be raised by a direct tax, the latter a means contemplated for some years but never before used.[3] To establish a basis for the levying of such a tax, an act was passed

[1] Although commonly called the Fries Rebellion, actually the word rebellion is a misnomer. The incident at most was an insurrection. Frederick L. Schuman's discussion of "Insurrection" is helpful at this point: "It is loosely used along with revolution and rebellion to refer to an armed resistance to government. In general an uprising directed toward a radical modification of the existing political or social order throughout the whole territory of a state is referred to as a revolution, while the word rebellion is more frequently confined to efforts on the part of a portion of a state to throw off the authority of the remainder. Insurrection usually refers to movements smaller in scope and purpose than those described by the other terms.

"... the term insurrection should be limited to the initial stages of movements of opposition to the government which take the form of violence as distinguished from non-violent non-cooperation or passive resistance.

"... an insurrection may be thought of as an incipient rebellion or revolution still localized and limited to securing modifications of governmental policy . . ." *Encyclopedia of the Social Sciences*, Vol. VIII, p. 116.

[2] 1 Stat. L. 553-612.

[3] See *American State Papers, Finance*, Vol. I, pp. 276, 409, 414, 492, 579, 588.

July 9, 1798, providing for the "valuation of Lands and Dwelling Houses, and the enumeration of Slaves within the United States."[4] This was followed five days later by an act apportioning the amount to be raised by each state and the rates to be levied.[5] The tax was graduated from 2 mills on valuations between $100 and $500 to 10 mills on valuations in excess of $30,000. A flat tax of 50 cents was to be levied on each slave.

Opposition to property assessment. The most formidable opposition to the new law came from Bucks, Montgomery, and Northampton Counties in eastern Pennsylvania. In Milford Township, Bucks County, the local assessors were afraid to begin their task, and it was not until the first week in March 1789 that the officials came into the district determined to make the assessments.

In Quakerstown their coming provoked a sizable demonstration against the law; the assessors were captured but later released without harm. The law's loudest critic in this area was an auctioneer by the name of John Fries. He had commanded a company of militia both in the Revolution and in the Whiskey Insurrection. Now, however, his powers of persuasion were being used to frustrate the execution of the national will.[6]

In Northampton County also, public opinion was so hostile that it was deemed inadvisable to proceed with the assessments. Jacob Eyerly, the assessment commissioner of the district, and William Henry, judge of Northampton County, attempted on more than one occasion to explain the law to groups of people gathered to discuss the measure. Their efforts, however, proved unsuccessful, and they finally appealed to the federal authority. Warrants accordingly were issued by District Judge Richard Peters, to be served by the United States Marshal, Colonel Samuel Nichols.

In company with Commissioner Eyerly and Colonel Stephen Balliot, Collector of the Revenue, the Marshal set about his duties. No opposition was encountered until the party reached the home of Henry Shankweiller of Millerstown, where a group of some 50 men had gathered, armed chiefly with clubs, "prepared to prevent

---

[4] 1 Stat. L. 580.
[5] The same, p. 596.
[6] W. W. H. Davis, *The Fries Rebellion.* A general, though not too accurate, account of the insurrection.

the execution of the law." The officers suffered verbal rather than physical assault and, although no violence occurred, Nichols wrote that "it is my opinion that if one single blow had been struck, the whole of the rascals would have fallen on, and we three should have been killed."[7]

Those against whom the warrants had been issued were to meet with Nichols in Bethlehem on March 7, and accompany him to Philadelphia "there to enter into recognizance to appear at the next circuit court to answer." As the result of threats that the prisoners, if such they may be called, were to be rescued, the Marshal called together a *posse comitatus* of about 14 men "who attended unarmed."[8] The threat was not an idle one. On the afternoon of the seventh a group of at least 100 men,[9] many of them armed, some in uniform, came to demand the release of the prisoners. In command of the rescuers was John Fries. The arrests had been made in Northampton County, but the indignation was so great at Milford that a rescue party under Fries was sent to Bethlehem at the same time that a party with similar intentions was being organized at Northampton. The two groups ultimately joined forces and surrounded the public inn where the Marshal, the *posse comitatus*, and approximately 18 prisoners were gathered. After several parleys the Marshal was finally convinced that the only way to avert bloodshed was to surrender the prisoners.[10] This completely satisfied the rescuers, and in a short time they dispersed. In his report to the Secretary of State the Marshal observed,

I am well satisfied, in my own mind, that the laws of the United States cannot be executed by the officers of the Government throughout the county of Northampton, without Military aid; the people are determined to resist; they calculate largely on their strength in this State, and the aid they will have from the neighboring states, and particularly that of Virginia.[11]

---

[7] Report of Nichols to Secretary of State, Mar. 11, 1789, *American State Papers, Miscellaneous*, Vol. I, p. 185.

[8] The same.

[9] Nichols reports at least 100. Davis says that Fries's group alone had 140, not counting the Northampton contingent.

[10] Neither the report of the Marshal nor the statements of witnesses both for and against Fries during the trials indicate that there was any actual violence during the rescue.

[11] *American State Papers, Miscellaneous*, Vol. I, p. 186.

The warrants had been issued by Judge Peters on February 20. On March 11 he sent documents in evidence of the opposition to Colonel Timothy Pickering, Secretary of State, including a deposition from Eyerly and Balliot.

Use of armed force by the government. The very next day President Adams issued a proclamation in which he stated his decision that it was necessary to call forth military force.[12] On March 20, James McHenry, Secretary of War, wrote to Governor Mifflin, who was completing his third term in the gubernatorial chair, requesting that the militia of five eastern counties be called out and be prepared to march within eight days.[13] Brigadier General William McPherson was placed in command, with instructions to use not only the militia but 5½ companies of the regular army, two of which were to come from New York, with a smaller number from New Jersey. The President, incidentally, was acting without congressional authorization in making use of the regular troops in an insurrection, as no such provision was made until 1807.[14] In addition to the militia and the regular army, McPherson was instructed to utilize two volunteer companies of cavalry from Philadelphia,[15] members of the new provisional army established by Congress the preceding year.[16]

In view of President Adams' determined efforts to avoid foreign war it is, at first glance, difficult to believe that he would permit such a display of force, especially since resistance to the law had been of such a mild and bloodless nature. Perhaps the answer is to be found in one paragraph of the instructions to Brigadier General McPherson, where the observation is made that this insurrection against the government had taken place

at a time when its sovereignty and liberties are threatened by a powerful, implacable, and insidious nation, who have been accustomed to divide

---

[12] The same, p. 187. Although he relied on the evidence submitted by the district judge, the President alone was responsible for the decision to use force. The act of Feb. 28, 1795 had eliminated the provision which required the notification to the president by an associate justice or a district judge. (See 1 Stat. L. 264, 424.)

[13] *Annals of Congress,* 6 Cong., p. 1302.

[14] 2 Stat. L. 443.

[15] *Annals of Congress,* 6 Cong., p. 1302. Eight troops of New Jersey Cavalry were ordered by the President to be in readiness to march. (See *Claypoole's American Daily Advertiser,* Mar. 27, 1799, p. 3.)

[16] 1 Stat. L. 558.

and conquer other nations. It is not doubted, therefore, but that they [the troops] will exhibit a useful example upon this service of military promptitude, spirit, vigilance, discipline, and obedience of orders.[17]

The President may have felt also that this display of force would direct the attention of the people from the warmongers, who were intent upon a struggle with France.[18]

The main body of the Philadelphia troops did not leave until April 4. In Montgomery County, General McPherson gave an address in which he explained the house tax, how small was its burden, the elimination of the especially disagreeable parts of the statute,[19] and, lastly, gave warning against lending assistance to the violators of the law.[20]

There was no resistance whatever to the troops. Four companies

---

[17] *American State Papers, Miscellaneous,* Vol. I, p. 189.

[18] That the policy of Adams did not meet with universal approval is indicated by the following editorial from the Philadelphia *Aurora General Advertiser* (Apr. 5, 1799, p. 2):

A FEW HUMBLE QUESTIONS

To the Erect, Manly and High-Toned *Five Headed Directory of America.* Either the late movements in Northampton have been serious and alarming, or not? If alarming why has our first Magistrate deserted his post in the hour of danger, and separated himself four hundred miles from a scene which should be the centre of his attention and assiduity? [Adams had gone to Quincy, Massachusetts, with his sick wife.] If not alarming what means all this bustle and expense in sending to Northampton the blues, the greens, the regulars and irregulars of every color and discription? If you admit, *Gentlemen Directors,* the first part of the dilemma, you throw a charge of neglect of duty on the President, which would render him amenable to a deserved impeachment; if you admit the second, it is a sentence of condemnation on yourselves, as it will be clear, that your bustle is the *noise of party,* your movements the *activity of mischief,* and the unnecessary expense incurred the object of *your pocket's* patriotism.

[19] The law as originally passed provided that the assessment lists for dwelling houses should contain "the number and dimensions of their windows" (1 Stat. L. 586). This phrase led to widespread misunderstanding, as many were afraid that it "was intended as the groundwork of a window tax." (See "Report of Ways and Means Committee," *American State Papers, Finance,* Vol. I, p. 601.) The act was amended Feb. 28, 1799, and the phrase in question was repealed. This apparently caused further confusion in the minds of numerous individuals who now contended that the whole act had been repealed. (See Davis, *The Fries Rebellion,* p. 15.) It is a matter of speculation whether any resistance would have occurred had the purpose and provisions of the law been explained during the first six months after its passage.

[20] The address was printed in German, since a large portion of the inhabitants of this area were Germans. They were also strongly Republican and, as a consequence, opposed to the administration.

of cavalry were sent out after Fries, who, far from leading a force against the army, was peacefully engaged in his occupation as an auctioneer or "vendue crier" at the time of the cavalry's approach. He attempted to escape but was captured and taken to Philadelphia.

The army remained in the area for about three weeks, making arrests as it went from town to town.[21] During this period, apparently, the inhabitants were terrorized, partly from a natural fear of armed forces, and partly from the illegal acts of certain troops.[22] Brigadier General McPherson had been instructed to prevent "by the most pointed orders, any insults to the inhabitants, or unnecessary rigor towards the prisoners taken,"[23] but he was unable to maintain a sufficiently strict control over the heterogeneous forces under his command. It is related, however, that the only casualty of the insurrection was a bull, shot while investigating the contents of a forage wagon.[24]

Trial of Fries. The aftermath of the struggle created as much, if not more, excitement than did the insurrection itself. Fries was indicted, tried, and convicted of high treason in the United States Circuit Court at Philadelphia in May 1799.

President Adams was in Quincy, Massachusetts at the time of the trial. The day after the jury reached its decision, Pickering reported the result of the trial, expressing a "calm and solid satisfaction that an opportunity is now presented, in executing the just sentence of the law, to crush that spirit, which if not overthrown and destroyed, may proceed in its career, and overturn the government."[25]

The Secretary of the Treasury, Oliver Wolcott, wrote in a similar vein. The President seized upon Wolcott's comment that William Lewis, Fries's counsel, had contended all along that the offense did not amount to treason.[26] Charles Lee, the Attorney Gen-

[21] "Detachments were sent out in pursuit of insurgents, and arrests were made at all hours of the day and night." Charles Henry Jones, *Memoirs of William Rodman*, p. 19.

[22] See Davis, *The Fries Rebellion*, pp. 102-14; McMaster, *History of the People of the United States*, Vol. II, pp. 438-39.

[23] *American State Papers, Miscellaneous*, Vol. I, p. 184.

[24] Davis, *The Fries Rebellion*, p. 111.

[25] *The Works of John Adams* (Charles Francis Adams, ed.), Vol. VIII, p. 650.

[26] The same.

eral, was asked by Adams to ascertain the reasons advanced by Lewis.[27]

The President did not share in his party's delight at the result of the trial for, as he wrote Pickering, "The issue of this investigation has opened a train of very serious contemplation to me, which will require the closest attention of my best understanding, and will prove a severe trial to my heart."[28] He asked Wolcott for information concerning Fries's status as a native or foreigner, his financial position, and his character. "It highly concerns the people of the United States, and especially the federal government," he wrote, "that in the whole progress and ultimate conclusion of this affair, neither humanity be unnecessarily afflicted, nor public justice essentially violated, nor the public safety endangered."[29] Any action by the President was postponed when a motion for a new trial was granted on the ground that one of the jurymen was disqualified because he had previously expressed the opinion that Fries and others connected with the case should be hanged.[30]

During the summer Fries and several of the other prisoners sent petitions to the President praying for pardon. Uncertain as to the proper course of action, Adams requested an opinion from the members of his Cabinet. They were unanimously opposed to granting a pardon to any one, at least until the trials were concluded, and they advised against giving any answer to the petitioners.[31]

It was almost a year from the time Fries was first convicted until his second trial began. This time Associate Justice Samuel Chase presided, assisted by Judge Peters.[32] Because of a ruling by Justice Chase, Fries's counsel withdrew, and he was left without any one to assist him.[33] Once more the verdict was guilty of treason; "a crime," according to Justice Chase, "considered in the most civilized

[27] The same, p. 648.
[28] The same, p. 649.
[29] The same, p. 650.
[30] Lee to Adams, the same, p. 653.
[31] *The Works of John Adams*, Vol. IX, pp. 20-23.
[32] Associate Justice James Iridell presided at the first trial.
[33] Chase had debarred "the prisoner from his constitutional privilege of addressing the jury (through his counsel) on the law as well as on the fact." The justice was accused of having conducted himself "in a manner highly arbitrary, oppressive and unjust." (*Report of the Trial of the Honorable Samuel Chase, Associate Justice of the Supreme Court of the United States*, p. 9.) This was the basis for the first of seven articles on which Chase was impeached by the House of Representatives.

countries in the world, as the greatest any man can commit."[34]

Pardon by the President. Again President Adams hesitated. At the second trial two other prisoners had been prosecuted with Fries, and the President disliked to give an order for the execution of all three. He addressed a memorandum to the heads of the departments, in which he asked some very pertinent questions. The following are illustrative:

2. Is the execution of one or more so indispensably demanded by public justice and by the security of the public peace, that mercy cannot be extended to all three, or any two, or one?

4. Is it clear beyond all reasonable doubt that the crime of which they stand convicted, amounts to a levying of war against the United States, or, in other words, to treason?

8. Is there no great danger in establishing such a construction of treason, as may be applied to every sudden, ignorant, inconsiderate heat, among a part of the people, wrought up by political disputes, and personal or party animosities?

10. Is not the tranquility in the western counties, since the insurrection there, and the subsequent submission to law, a precedent in favor of clemency?[35]

Because of Cabinet changes, there were but three heads of departments who replied to the President. Although divided as to the necessity of executing all three of the prisoners, Lee, Stoddert, and Wolcott were agreed that it would "be more just and more wise that all should suffer the sentence of the law, than that all should be pardoned."[36] The President, however, was of a different mind. On May 21, 1800, taking on himself the "responsibility of one more appeal to the humane and generous natures of the American people," he ordered prepared a pardon for the three convicted of treason, and a proclamation of general pardon for those who had opposed the law in the offending counties.[37]

Chase contended, in defense, that the new trial was not on the correctness of the court's decision on the question of law. The new trial was granted, he said, because one juror had declared himself unfavorable to the prisoner and, therefore, there was no point in again taking up the legal discussion of what constituted treason. He was acquitted by a vote of 16 guilty to 18 not guilty. See Judge Chase's answer, Francis Wharton, *State Trials of the United States*, pp. 643-45.

[34] *The Two Trials of John Fries*, p. 200.
[35] *The Works of John Adams*, Vol. IX, p. 57.
[36] The same, p. 59.
[37] The same, p. 60. For the proclamation, see Richardson, *Messages and Papers of the Presidents*, Vol. I, p. 303.

The Federalist party leaders were infuriated by the President's action. Hamilton wrote that "it was impossible to create a greater error," and Pickering condemned Adams for not seeking information from "those qualified to give it impartially—the judges of the court; especially when the presiding judge was Samuel Chase, an old Congressional friend."[38] The suppression of those who objected to the house tax by a resort to the military arm, and, on top of that, the unfortunate incidents surrounding the two trials of John Fries, left a feeling of bitterness in the minds of many people which the President's pardon was unable to erase.

Years later Adams wrote that his action, even though contrary to the wishes of his Cabinet, was one that he recollected "with infinite satisfaction, and which will console me in my last hour."[39] Still later he wrote:

What good, what example, would have been exhibited to the nation by the execution of three or four obscure, miserable Germans, as ignorant of our language as they were of our laws, and the nature and definition of treason. Pitiful puppets danced upon the wires of jugglers behind the scenes or underground. . . . The verdict of a jury, and the judgment of the court, would, to be sure, have justified me in the opinion of the nation, and in the judgment of the world, if I had signed the warrant for their execution; but neither, nor both, could have satisfied my conscience, nor tranquillized my feelings. . . . My judgment was clear, that their crime did not amount to treason. They had been guilty of high handed riot and rescue, attended with circumstances hot, rash, violent, and dangerous, but all these did not amount to treason.[40]

At first glance Adams' action in pardoning the convicted prisoners seems merely to be following the precedent established by Washington. Actually there is little comparison. A pardon was granted by Washington because of the character of the parties, both offenders of little consequence, "two poor wretches, . . . one little short of an idiot, the other, a miserable fellow in the hindmost train of a rebellion."[41] *Washington did not grant the pardon, as did Adams, because he disagreed with the court's decision as to what constituted treason.* This is not to condemn the action of President Adams. He thought the "officers of the law had been injudicious in indicting

[38] Wharton, *State Trials of the United States*, pp. 643-45.
[39] *The Works of John Adams*, Vol. IX, p. 270.
[40] The same, Vol. X, p. 153.
[41] Statement of Hamilton; see Wharton, *State Trials of the United States*, p. 643.

them for any crime higher than riot, aggravated by rescue." To his mind, war had not been levied against the United States.[42]

If Adams had conducted an investigation of the incidents which led to the calling of the troops with the same zeal he displayed in determining that Fries should be pardoned, there probably would have been no troops used. In great contrast to Washington's policy, Adams ordered out the troops immediately upon receipt of the news of the rescue of the prisoners and of the Marshal's report that military aid was necessary to enforce the law. He made no effort, as had his predecessor, to consult with the state officials. Nor did he attempt to persuade the inhabitants, other than by force, to obey the law.

Some years later, in recounting the accomplishments of his administration, Adams wrote:

> I . . . suppressed an insurrection in Pennsylvania, and effectually humbled and punished the insurgents; not by assembling an army of militia from three or four States, and marching in all the pride, pomp, and circumstance of war, at an expense of millions, but silently, without noise, and at a trifling expense.[43]

This statement, so disparaging to Washington's record in the Whiskey Insurrection, is rather unfair. The expedition to the west, under Washington, cost over a million dollars, whereas the eastern uprising was suppressed at less than one-tenth as much.[44] But in the first case opposition to the law was much greater; it was spread over a larger area ten times the distance from the seat of government, and among a people who had little contact with the law. It would seem that Washington's error in overestimating the number of troops needed was proportionately no greater than Adams'. President Adams' determined and successful effort to free the persons whose punishment, he felt, was not commensurate with their crime, mitigates to some degree the censure due him for his use of the troops. It was unfortunate, however, that he did not first attempt to enforce the law by less hasty and less terrifying methods.

[42] *The Works of John Adams*, Vol. X, p. 153.
[43] The same.
[44] Hamilton said that both insurrections cost the government $1\frac{1}{2}$ million dollars. (See Wharton, *State Trials of the United States*, p. 643.) Chase stated that the Fries uprising had cost $80,000. *The Two Trials of John Fries*, p. 202.

THE EMBARGO TROUBLES

In great contrast to the success attending the employment of the armed forces in the rather isolated instances of resistance which the first two presidents faced was the failure of the third president to compel obedience to an exceedingly unpopular federal statute.[45] In August 1808, after eight months of effort to enforce the embargo laws, President Jefferson expressed his perplexity by the statement, "I did not expect a crop of so sudden and rank growth of fraud and open opposition by force could have grown up in the United States."[46]

No American ship was safe on the seas. In their struggles against each other, Great Britain and France, through Orders in Council and Napoleonic Decrees, showed complete disregard for the rights of neutrals. Jefferson hoped, by means of the embargo, to force both countries to cease their depredations upon our commerce and to give a decent consideration to our rights. "It is," he wrote, "the last card we have to play, short of war."[47]

His plan of peaceable coercion was, apparently, having very little effect abroad, but there was no doubt as to its effect at home. Violations of the law were frequent, particularly in the area adjacent to the Canadian border. The trade of New York and the New England states was especially hard hit by the "land embargo," a supplementary act passed in March 1808, which prohibited the exportation of goods by land or inland waters.[48]

The problem of enforcement. As a result of the ever-increasing restrictions on trade, smuggling became very profitable. No sooner was the law passed than the collector of the Vermont District informed the President that the execution of the law would be impossible without the aid of military force.[49] To meet this challenge,

---

[45] The efforts of the presidents to halt conspiracies aimed at seizing territory beyond the nation's borders (the Burr Conspiracy, the Patriot War, the Fenian Invasion of Canada, and others) have been considered as not falling within the scope of this study.

[46] To Gallatin, *The Writings of Thomas Jefferson* (H. A. Washington, ed.), Vol. V, p. 336. The statements of Jefferson which follow were taken from this edition.

[47] To Levi Lincoln, the same, p. 265.

[48] 2 Stat. L. 473.

[49] See *Records of the Governor and Council of the State of Vermont*, Vol. V, p. 472.

Jefferson and his aides drew up an extremely complicated plan of enforcement. It required the co-operation of the Secretaries of the Treasury, War, and State Departments, the marshal, the collector, and finally, the Governor of Vermont. First, the Secretary of the Treasury was to instruct the collector, whose troubles centered around Lake Champlain, to "arm and equip what vessels he can and may think necessary," and to engage volunteers to assist him in enforcing the law. Secondly, in the event resistance was too great for the collector, the Secretary of State was to request the marshal to raise a posse. Lastly, the Secretary of War was to instruct the Governor that if the posse proved inadequate, the Governor should issue a proclamation furnished by the President, and then call on the militia for further assistance.[50]

Three weeks after the plan was formulated, Governor Israel Smith made use of its final provision. A small detachment of militia was ordered out, and Jefferson's proclamation was issued ordering all persons who were combining for the purpose "of forming insurrections . . . to disperse and retire peaceably to their respective abodes."[51] The publication of this document was a blunder, since it had little effect other than to provoke greater discord. In a town meeting in June 1898, the inhabitants of St. Albans drew up a memorial addressed to the President in which they declared there was

no cause for such proclamation. . . . If individuals . . . have attempted to evade the embargo restrictions, and have actually accomplished their purpose, this could never furnish a just cause for proclaiming to the world that insurrection and rebellion were chargeable on the good people of this district; and with confidence your memorialists declare their belief, that nothing more than this had taken place.[52]

Jefferson realized the truth of this protest and, although violations of the law increased, both in quantity and in the degree of violence, he refused to issue further proclamations.

[50] Jefferson to Gallatin, *The Writings of Thomas Jefferson*, Vol. V, pp. 271-72.
[51] *Annals of Congress*, 10 Cong. 2 sess., p. 580. Although the President's proclamation was signed Apr. 19, it was not published in Vermont until May 9. It is to be noted that the proclamation was given to the Governor to be issued *at his discretion*. This was a departure from the previous practice.
[52] *Records of the Governor and Council of the State of Vermont*, Vol. V, p. 474.

Regular troops were used to supplement and in some cases replace the militia. This action was in accordance with the statute of March 3, 1807, which authorized the use of the land and naval forces to suppress insurrections or to cause the laws to be executed.[53] Part of the naval force was already in use, the President having early made the suggestion that the new gunboats assist in enforcing the embargo.[54]

In New York the President followed a different plan. Governor Tompkins had informed Jefferson of the opposition to the embargo laws. Instead of the customary procedure, that is, of issuing a proclamation and calling out the militia, Jefferson shifted the entire responsibility to the Governor. Because of the unfavorable reception of his first proclamation, and perhaps for political reasons (it was less than three months before a presidential election), Jefferson decided to say nothing. He informed the Governor that *since by the laws of New York* "an insurrection can be acted on without a previous proclamation, I should conceive it perfectly correct" to do so. "Should *you* think proper" to act, Jefferson wrote, "I will undertake that the necessary detachments of militia called out in support of the laws, shall be considered as in the service of the United States, and at their expense."[55] Of course the Governor could have called out the militia in his own right, but in that event the state would have been responsible for the financial burden. Jefferson's proposal was novel in that, though the troops were being called into the service of the United States, the President was delegating the determination of the exigency to the Governor. The War Department officials, in the absence of their chief, indicated their opinion that the President's action was irregular by suspending the accounts submitted for the New York militia.[56] Consequently, it was necessary for Jefferson to write General Dearborn, Secretary of War, to request that measures be taken for the "pay, subsistence, and whatever else is requisite," for the militia ordered out by Governor Tompkins.[57]

[53] 2 Stat. L. 443.
[54] *The Writings of Thomas Jefferson*, Vol. V, pp. 244, 316.
[55] The same, p. 343. Italics added.
[56] *The Writings of Albert Gallatin* (Henry Adams, ed.), Vol. I, p. 409.
[57] *The Writings of Thomas Jefferson*, Vol. V, p. 355.

The President's power over the militia had been greatly enlarged by the act of March 30, 1808. Congress authorized him to call the militia into service any time that he judged the "exigencies of the United States require it."[58] There was, however, no authorization to delegate to any one the determination of the exigency.

Such a delegation of power, however, was in accordance with Jefferson's policy during this period. Although desperately anxious that the illicit traffic should be stopped, the President, whenever possible, left the decision as to the proper measure to be taken to others, chief of whom was Albert Gallatin, Secretary of the Treasury. The Secretaries of the War and Navy were, on Gallatin's application, to "yield the aid of their departments without waiting the delay of consulting me."[59] Whether it was a question concerning the use of the regular troops, the militia, or the gunboats, the President instructed Gallatin to act directly.

In New York, as in Vermont, the militia was replaced, where possible, by the regular troops. The President said the members of the militia were to be relieved, as the task of preventing resistance to the law was "irksome to them, expensive, troublesome, and less efficacious."[60] Another reason, which he did not mention, was that the troops, even the regulars, were too often in sympathy with those opposing the law.[61]

Repeal of the embargo. As the year 1808 wore on, attempts at evasion became more frequent.[62] It was impossible for a limited number of troops to patrol such a large area. To Gallatin, Jefferson confided:

This embargo law is certainly the most embarrassing one we have ever had to execute. . . . I am satisfied with you that if orders and decrees are

---

[58] 2 Stat. L. 478. This act was of questionable legality since the Constitution specifies only that the militia may be called out "to execute the laws of the Union, suppress insurrections and repel invasions." The law was to be in effect for a two-year period. Subsequent legislation did not contain such a broad grant.

[59] *The Writings of Thomas Jefferson*, Vol. V, p. 308. See also pp. 291, 316, 336.

[60] The same, p. 359.

[61] See statement of Collector of Revenue as quoted in the *History of the State of New York* (Alexander C. Flick, ed.), Vol. V, p. 199.

[62] For instance of violations, see John Bach McMaster, *A History of the People of the United States from the Revolution to the Civil War*, Vol. III, pp. 304-07; Sears, *Jefferson and the Embargo*, pp. 167-68.

not repealed, and a continuance of the embargo is preferred to war, . . . Congress must legalize all *means* which may be necessary to obtain its *end*.[63]

In his annual message to Congress, November 8, 1808, the President asked for greater authority. In January 1809, less than two months before he was to go out of office, Congress granted his request by passing the enforcement act. This measure, in addition to further strengthening the embargo, legalized the same type of procedure which he had used in New York. The President was authorized to delegate the power of calling out troops, and Congress made it clear that the whole military establishment, the Army and Navy as well as the militia, was to be used if necessary to enforce the embargo laws.[64] In accordance with the power thus granted, Jefferson wrote a circular letter to the governors asking that at each port of entry an officer of the militia be appointed who would be charged with the duty of assembling and employing the militia upon the call of the collector of the district.

The enforcement act, plus the President's letter, produced such a storm of protest that in less than a month Congress executed an abrupt reversal in policy, substituting for the embargo a bill providing for nonintercourse with Great Britain and France. Jefferson wrote that ". . . a sudden and unaccountable revolution of opinion took place the last week, chiefly among the New England and New York members, and in a kind of panic they voted the 4th of March for removing the embargo. . . ."[65]

The judicial system was of little help to the administration. In September 1808, Gallatin wrote from New York, "I find it difficult to have the necessary prosecutions instituted in the northern parts of this state."[66] In Vermont, one man was executed for murder and three were convicted of manslaughter as a result of the killing

---

[63] *The Writings of Thomas Jefferson*, Vol. V, p. 336.

[64] 2 Stat. L. 506.

[65] To Thomas Mann Randolph, Feb. 7, 1809 (*The Writings of Thomas Jefferson*, Vol. V, p. 424). In discussing the action of Congress, Von Holst remarks: "From among themselves they were destined to hear a voice, recalling to their memory the principle which is the kernel of the idea of the republican state, viz; that it is the spirit and duty of republican governments to make laws agreeable to the people, and not endeavor to accommodate the people to the laws." *The Constitutional and Political History of the United States*, Vol. I, p. 215.

[66] To Jefferson, *The Writings of Albert Gallatin*, Vol. I, p. 417.

of three of the militia who were members of a party seeking to capture the *Black Snake,* a notorious smuggling vessel.[67]

Only one case reached the circuit court. Frederick Hoxie opposed the embargo law by resisting the collector of the District of Vermont. For this offense he was indicted and tried for treason, in levying war against the United States. In company with a group of 60 armed men, Hoxie made away with a raft of timber which had previously been seized by the collector while being taken to Canada. The United States troops who were aiding the collector were temporarily away from the raft at the time Hoxie and the others took possession. Shots were exchanged between the raiding party and the soldiers, but no one was injured. The raft was taken into Canada, where the raiders were paid $800 for their work. Had the enterprise failed, they would have received nothing.

Justice Brockholst Livingston, in charging the jury which subsequently acquitted Hoxie, pointed out that "the opposition to the law was feeble, transitory, free from traitorous intention, and conducted for the purpose of private gain. This was not a levying of war." To constitute treason "the object must be of a public and general character."[68] In making this distinction the justice avoided any conflict with the decisions arising out of the Whiskey Insurrection and the Fries Rebellion.

Jefferson, apparently, made no statement about the case. In spite of his hasty proclamation early in the period of disturbance he also believed, or was forced through circumstances to acquiesce in the belief, that the numerous incidents of law violation did not amount to treason.[69]

It is difficult to appraise the President's embargo enforcement policies. Whatever his actions, they were directed toward bringing about the success of the larger issue, the preservation of peace with foreign powers. It is likewise difficult to compare his handling of

[67] For an interesting account of this incident, see the *Vermont Historical Gazetteer,* 1871, Vol. II, pp. 342-47.
[68] *United States* v. *Hoxie,* 26 Federal Cases 397.
[69] ". . . opposition . . . has in one quarter amounted almost to rebellion and treason." Jefferson to Mr. Letue, Nov. 8, 1808, *The Writings of Thomas Jefferson,* Vol. V, p. 384.

the opposition to the embargo laws with the means employed by Washington and Adams to suppress opposition to troublesome revenue measures. In this instance there was no one area upon which attention could be centered, and there was no one individual or group with whom negotiations could be conducted or whose coercion would eliminate annoyance. Jefferson's actions, at times, were somewhat beyond the letter of the law but, harassed as he was from so many quarters and resisted most of all in an area where his popularity was never great, he maintained an evenness of temper and an aloofness from petty recrimination creditable to one in his high office.

CHAPTER III

JACKSON AND TARIFF NULLIFICATION

In 1832-33, for the third time in our history, the revenue laws presented a grave enforcement problem. In contrast with the troubles experienced by Washington and Adams in the western and eastern parts of Pennsylvania, President Andrew Jackson faced the task of enforcing the tariff of 1832 though opposed by the government of a state. In the Whiskey Insurrection the governor and the legislature gave Washington active support. In the Fries incident Governor Mifflin complied at once with Adams' requisition for troops. Jackson faced a warlike governor and a hostile legislature, both of whom were determined that the federal tariff law should not operate within the bounds of South Carolina.

PROTEST AGAINST A TARIFF FOR PROTECTION

According to the southern point of view,[1] a protective tariff, rather than one for revenue only, had been established in 1816 simply as a temporary measure. In this the South had acquiesced and for a good reason. Because of the embargo, the Nonintercourse Act, and the War of 1812, the United States was cut off from its normal supply of manufactured goods from abroad. As a result, considerable capital was invested in manufacturing and many people turned their attention to supplying articles formerly purchased in Europe. At the end of the war these new business establishments were threatened by the prospect of a *"sudden influx"* of foreign products. To guard against such a catastrophe, protective duties were levied in 1816 with the understanding that the rates were to be gradually reduced.

"In violation of the principles of justice and of good faith,"[2] the

---

[1] See *Message from the President of the United States Transmitting Copies of the Proclamation and Proceedings in Relation to South Carolina*, S. Doc. 30, 22 Cong. 2 sess., pp. 20-21.

[2] The same, p. 21.

tariff was increased by the acts of 1820, 1824, and 1828, until by the tariff of 1832 protection had become a settled policy. In addition, the laws were "so framed as to give a direct pecuniary interest to a sectional majority."[3] Under the pretext of aiding the government, acts were passed "for the purpose of securing to the American manufacturers a monopoly in our own markets, to the great and manifest prejudice of those who furnish the agricultural productions which are exchanged in foreign markets for the very articles which it is the avowed object of these laws to exclude."[4] Furthermore, the money thus raised at the expense of the South was expended "almost exclusively" in the North. Finally, the argument ran, the tariff was unconstitutional since it amounted to a regulation of domestic industry by the national government, a subject belonging exclusively to the states.

Protests against the protection system had been sent to Congress by individual districts in South Carolina as early as 1820. In 1825 the legislature declared the law unconstitutional, and even stronger resolutions of disfavor were sent to Congress in 1828 and again in 1830.[5] At this time, however, there was no hint of any forceful resistance. Robert Y. Hayne counseled against doing anything to produce excitement among the people of the state. "We have nothing to gain from violence or shocking even the prejudices of the people at home or abroad," he declared.[6]

ORDINANCE OF NULLIFICATION

After the passage of the tariff of 1832 the character of the opposition changed. Duties imposed for revenue had been reduced, but the protecting duties remained substantially as before. This acted as a further aggravation, since it seemed to the people of South Carolina that an even greater injustice was being done them.

In October 1832, the legislature called for a state convention

---

[3] The same.

[4] The same, p. 22.

[5] The same, p. 30. For the origin of the conflict see David F. Houston, *A Critical Study of Nullification in South Carolina*, pp. 1-64; Chauncey S. Boucher, *The Nullification Controversy in South Carolina*, pp. 1-88.

[6] Letter to James H. Hammond, Mar. 29, 1830, "Letters on the Nullification Movement in South Carolina 1830-1834," *American Historical Review*, Vol. VII (1901), p. 738.

to consider the subject. Delegates were elected, and the convention assembled November 19. A selected group, "The Committee of Twenty-One," reported that *the time has come* when the State must either adopt a *decisive course of action*, or we must at once *abandon the contest* . . . it is now a question of *liberty* or *slavery.*"[7] On November 24 the Committee issued the famous Ordinance of Nullification.[8] This document declared the tariff acts of 1828 and 1832 to be null and void, and not binding upon the state, nor upon its officers and citizens. No cases involving the validity of the Ordinance or of legislative acts passed to give it effect were to be allowed to go before the Supreme Court. The Ordinance and the laws supplementing it were to go into effect February 1, 1833. If Congress passed any act to employ force or otherwise adopted a policy of coercion,

the people of this State will thenceforth hold themselves absolved from all further obligation to maintain or preserve their political connexion with the people of the other States, and will forthwith proceed to organize a separate Government, and do all other acts and things which sovereign and independent States may of right to do.[9]

In an address to the people of South Carolina the delegates advanced the novel doctrine that nullification would preserve rather than destroy the Union. There was little danger, they felt, that force would be used against them, but there was no better way of avoiding hostile measures than "to evince a readiness to meet danger, come from what quarter it will."[10]

The retiring governor, James Hamilton, sent a warlike message to the state legislature in which he recommended that the executive be authorized to accept 2,000 volunteers for the defense of Charleston, to order the removal of the United States troops from the citadel there, and to accept 10,000 volunteers from other parts of South Carolina to be called the "State Guard."[11] The legislature empowered the Governor, when he deemed it necessary, to order into service the whole military force of the state and to purchase

[7] S. Doc. 30, 22 Cong. 2 sess., p. 34.
[8] The same, pp. 36-39.
[9] The same, p. 38.
[10] The same, p. 49.
[11] The same, pp. 59-67.

10,000 rifles.[12] The Test Oath Act was passed, requiring all civil and military officers to swear to "obey, execute and enforce the ordinance to nullify certain acts of the Congress of the United States . . . and all such act or acts of the Legislature as may be passed in pursuance thereof. . . ."[13] To carry the Nullification Ordinance into effect, persons whose goods were seized by the collector of revenue were authorized to recover possession by means of an act of replevin. The sheriff was ordered, if the writ of replevin could not be executed, to seize goods of the collector equal to double the value of the goods being held for the payment of duties.[14] All in all, the provisions of the act were such as to make the enforcement of the tariff laws an impossible task.[15]

JACKSON'S DETERMINATION TO "PRESERVE THE UNION"

In the meantime Jackson was not idle. In early September he had received word that the Nullifiers were attempting to win to their side the commanding naval officer in Charleston. In reporting this news to Levi Woodbury, Secretary of the Navy, Jackson wrote, "While I will not admit the probability of things in the South coming to a desperate issue, yet it behoves [sic] us to be ready for any emergency."[16] He also suggested that arrangements be made for substituting another body of troops for those in Charleston. The Nullifiers, he said, hoped "by the treachery of our officers to get possession of our Forts, and thereby prevent a blockade. *This must be guarded against and prevented.*"[17] The change of troops was to

[12] The same, pp. 74-76.
[13] The same, pp. 76-78. Edward McCrady, a member of the Union Party, was elected a Lieutenant of the Militia in Charleston. His commission was not granted because of his refusal to take the oath of allegiance. He appealed and the case went to the state Circuit Court of Appeals, where the section of the Militia Act which related to the oath was declared unconstitutional. The decision was very unpopular and a constitutional amendment was passed requiring the oath. Largely as a result of this case the Court was abolished at the next session of the legislature. "Letters on the Nullification Movement in South Carolina," *American Historical Review*, Vol. VII (1901), p. 116.
[14] S. Doc. 30, 22 Cong. 2 sess., pp. 70-73.
[15] For a summary of the various provisions see Boucher, *The Nullification Controversy in South Carolina*, pp. 219-23.
[16] *Correspondence of Andrew Jackson* (John Spencer Bassett, ed.), Vol. IV, p. 474.
[17] The same.

be made quietly "without a hint of the cause until it is effected, and as the common rotine [sic] of the army."[18]

Jackson relied to a considerable degree on the information furnished by his versatile friend Joel R. Poinsett, the leader of the Union Party in Charleston. Poinsett suggested that two or three hundred muskets be placed in the Citadel for the protection of the members of his party. He pointed out that if, as most people believed, no measures were to be taken against the Nullifiers, there was nothing to do but sit back and witness the triumph of Calhoun.[19]

Jackson had no intention of letting the Nullifiers triumph. As Channing points out, "it is rather singular that the South Carolina leaders should not have realised what Jackson's real feelings on the matter were; but most of them had no conception of the strength of his affection for the Union, or realized the length to which he would go to the performance of what he looked upon as his duty."[20]

Even before the convention, Jackson issued instructions for the officers of the forts in the harbor at Charleston commanding them to guard "with vestal vigilance" against any surprise attack.[21] To determine, if possible, the sympathies of the revenue, postal, and other governmental officials, Jackson sent George Breathitt, brother of Kentucky's governor, to Charleston. Breathitt, ostensibly, was a Post Office agent, but "as a stranger having curiosity to examine your capacity for defense and facilities for commerce," he was also to observe the degree of vulnerability of the forts in the harbor.[22]

In October, Poinsett had asked that two or three hundred muskets be stored in the Citadel. A month later he asked for one hundred United States rifles, a quantity of hand grenades, small rockets, and bayonets. He requested also that some of the repair work on the small vessels of war might be done in the Charleston harbor. Not only would the presence of the ships have a good effect, he thought, but the repair job would allay some of the discontent among those who felt that part of the revenue raised in that vicinity should be

[18] To Andrew Donelson, the same, p. 476.
[19] The same, p. 481.
[20] Edward Channing, *History of the United States*, Vol. V, p. 423.
[21] To Lewis Cass, *Correspondence of Andrew Jackson,* Vol. IV, p. 483.
[22] To Poinsett, the same, p. 485.

spent there also.[23] However, before this letter reached Jackson, the President had already ordered two armed ships to proceed to the Charleston harbor. In contrast to Poinsett's modest request, the President ordered 5,000 stand of muskets to be placed at his friend's disposal.[24] In early December four companies of artillery and several cannon were sent from Fort Monroe, Virginia, to be stationed at Fort Moultrie. Major General Winfield Scott was sent to take command.[25] "In forty days," Jackson wrote a few days later, "I can have within the limits of So. Carolina fifty thousand men, and in forty days more another fifty thousand. . . . The Union will be preserved."[26]

All of these things of course were done quietly. The Nullification Ordinance had been adopted after the President had prepared his annual message to Congress. Apparently he made no change, treating nullification, as he had written Van Buren on November 18, "as a mere buble [sic]."[27] He promised the members of Congress, however, that he would promptly notify them in the event the laws proved inadequate.[28]

The first public indication of Jackson's reaction to the proceedings in South Carolina was the proclamation of December 10.[29] In contrast to the practice of Washington, which had been followed, in turn, by Adams and Jefferson, Jackson's proclamation was of great length, approximating 9,000 words. The Nullification Ordinance had stated certain objections to the laws, and these criticisms Jackson took up one by one. He discussed the questions of sovereignty and of secession, and the place of the states in the Union. An

---

[23] The same, p. 488.
[24] To Poinsett, the same, p. 493.
[25] "Orders Given to Land and Naval Forces at Charleston," *Debates in Congress*, Vol. IX, Pt. II, App., p. 199.
[26] To Poinsett, *Correspondence of Andrew Jackson*, Vol. IV, p. 498.
[27] The same, Vol. IV, p. 489.
[28] For the message to Congress, see James D. Richardson, *A Compilation of the Messages and Papers of the Presidents*, Vol. II, p. 599.
[29] 11 Stat. L. 771. The proclamation was put in final form by Edward Livingston, Secretary of State. (See *Correspondence of Andrew Jackson*, Vol. IV, p. 494.) James O'Hanlon, a leader of the Unionists, wrote Jackson that when the President's proclamation was read to his group, they were much heartened and one man cried out, "What have we to fear, we are right and God and Old Hickory are with us." The same, p. 503.

effort was made to appease the southern interests by admitting that there were inequalities in the law and by implying that they would be removed. He emphasized his determination "to execute the laws —to preserve the Union by all constitutional means—to arrest, if possible by moderate but firm measures, the necessity of a recourse to force."

The proclamation has been called the "ablest and most impressive state paper of the period."[30] However, a young lieutenant in the militia of South Carolina held a less respectful opinion. To the newly elected governor, Robert Y. Hayne, the lieutenant wrote: ". . . based as it is upon the notoriously false assumption that South Carolina intends to resist the laws [and] Congress with the bayonet, the spirit of it to every intelligent mind, is as ridiculous, as its arguments are absurd."[31] Then, strangely enough, he offered his services to raise a corps of volunteers.

Governor Hayne was, indeed, actively leading the effort to make ready a volunteer force. At the same time that he issued a counter-proclamation calling on the people to "protect the liberties of the state,"[32] he was attempting to raise a volunteer corps of 10,000 men plus the necessary arms. Books of instructions on manoeuvers and tactics were distributed. In addition to the volunteers, the Governor wanted a body of "Mounted Minute Men," ready to act on short notice. Although individual units of the troops were to undergo training, Hayne made it clear that the volunteers would not be called into service "until an emergency shall arise which may render this necessary."[33]

Neither Jackson nor Hayne wanted the troops under his command to be the first to provoke bloodshed. Each was doing a certain amount of bluffing. Jackson was not sure of the extent of his powers and as a consequence his actions in the latter part of 1832 were much more mild than his words.[34] He could order troops from

[30] Frederick A. Ogg, *The Reign of Andrew Jackson*, p. 175.
[31] "Letters on the Nullification Movement in South Carolina," *American Historical Review*, Vol. VI, p. 751. The officer was James H. Hammond, later governor.
[32] S. Doc. 30, 22 Cong. 2 sess., p. 111.
[33] "Letters on the Nullification Movement in South Carolina," *American Historical Review*, Vol. VI, p. 759.
[34] Notice his especially belligerent letter to Van Buren, Dec. 15, 1832. "I am

Fort Monroe to proceed to Fort Moultrie, but was there any authorization for their use if the necessity had arisen? As Governor Hayne pointed out in his proclamation, neither the act of 1795 nor that of 1807 was applicable, since they related

entirely to combinations of individuals acting of themselves without any lawful authority. The constituted authorities acting under the laws of the State, and its citizens yielding obedience to its commands, cannot possibly be considered as a mere mob forming combinations against the authority and laws of the Union, to be dispersed by an Executive proclamation.[35]

The President must have entertained similar thoughts, for when Major General Scott was ordered to take command at Charleston he was instructed only to defend the government posts. Even if a crisis arose and the civil authorities were unable to execute the laws, Scott was not authorized to do anything. Instead, in such an event, "the President shall determine the course to be taken and the measures to be adopted."[36]

Jackson was equally cautious about giving the followers of Poinsett any military status. In early December he wrote,

. . . should the civil power with your aid as a *posse comitatus* prove not strong enough to carry into effect the laws of the Union, you have a right to call upon the Government for aid and the Executive will yield

now waiting for the information from the assembly of South Carolina, of their having passed their laws for raising an army to resist the execution of the laws, which will be a levying of war, when I will make a communication to congress, laying before that body, the *ordinance of rebellion*, and the *acts of treason*, ask for the power to call upon volunteers to serve as the posse comitatus of the civil authority, to open our courts which they have shut, direct process to be issued against the leaders, direct them to be prosecuted for treason, have them arrested wheresoever to be found, delivered over to the authority of the law, to be prosecuted, convicted, and punished. If the assembly authorizes twelve thousand men, to resist the law, I will order thirty thousand to execute the law." (*Correspondence of Andrew Jackson*, Vol. IV, p. 500.) Here Jackson states that the passage of a law for raising an army would constitute a levying of war. Van Buren cautioned the President to be sure that such an act was treason before sending any communication to Congress. (The same, p. 507.) In his message of Jan. 16, 1833, Jackson altered the position he had taken in the letter to Van Buren. A distinction was made between an authorization of the use of military force by the legislature, which South Carolina had done, and their actual embodiment as a law-resisting force, which had not been done.
   [35] S. Doc. 30, 22 Cong. 2 sess., p. 108.
   [36] "Orders to Land and Naval Forces at Charleston," *Debates in Congress*, Vol. IX, Pt. II, App., p. 199.

it as far as he has been invested with the power by the constitution and the laws made in pursuance thereof.[37]

A week later Jackson emphasized the position of Poinsett's men. He wrote that the arms had been deposited "subject to your requisition, to aid the civil authority in the due execution of the law, whenever called on as the *posse comitatus.*"[38] The members of the Union Party, many of whom were enrolled in Poinsett's volunteer army, were disinclined to take a stand against the state government merely on the strength of a summons from the federal marshal. They preferred to be called out by the President as members of the militia.[39]

Even though there was some question in Jackson's mind concerning the extent of his power, he would undoubtedly have acted had South Carolina offered open resistance. The President asked Secretary Cass for a report "stating with precision" the equipment that was ready for the field. He wanted three divisions of artillery prepared to move from New York.[40] Arrangements were made to call on the governors of the states for 35,000 men.[41] A second proclamation was to be issued "the moment the nullies authorise an army to be raised and enter upon it."[42] Although various units of volunteers were being trained in South Carolina, there was no grand assemblage. Jackson, consequently, delayed, and in fact never did issue a further proclamation.

However, the President was not hesitant about asking Congress for greater authority. In his message of January 16 he recommended that legislation be enacted similar to the powers granted Jefferson during the embargo troubles.[43] He also suggested that the act of 1795, which was still in force, be modified to suit the existing crisis. He was anxious that Congress take action before February 1, the date the Nullification Ordinance was to take effect. Subsequent

---

[37] *Correspondence of Andrew Jackson*, Vol. IV, p. 493. This statement is much more vague than it at first appears.

[38] The same, p. 498.

[39] Poinsett to Jackson, *Correspondence of Andrew Jackson*, Vol. V, p. 6.

[40] *Correspondence of Andrew Jackson*, Vol. IV, p. 502.

[41] Marquis James, *Andrew Jackson, Portrait of a President*, p. 321.

[42] To Van Buren, Dec. 25, 1832, *Correspondence of Andrew Jackson*, Vol. IV, p. 502; also Vol. V, p. 11.

[43] See p. 35. For Jackson's message, see S. Doc. 30, 22 Cong. 2 sess., pp. 1-19.

events, however, made unnecessary the speedy passage of the measure.

The support promised by several states added greatly to the President's confidence.[44] To Van Buren he boasted that from Virginia alone he could march 40,000 men in 40 days; that "from good old democratic Pennsylvania I have a tender of upwards of 50,000, and from the borders of So.C., in No. C., I have a tender of one entire Reggt."[45] He wrote an encouraging letter to Poinsett stating that if necessary he could march 200,000 men in 40 days. "I repeat to the union men again, fear not, *the union will be preserved.*"[46]

ORDINANCE OF NULLIFICATION REVOKED

Five days after the President's special message to Congress, South Carolina made a surprise move. At an informal meeting in Charleston, presided over by officials of the state and of the convention, it was decided to suspend the Ordinance of Nullification.[47] Several reasons have been advanced for this action. First of all, the response to the appeal to other states made by the convention had been singularly disappointing. Then, too, there was the feeling that Congress would shortly relieve the worst features of the tariff. Finally, and most important, Jackson's firm stand made a collision inevitable. To avoid bloodshed, somebody had to give in. The citizens of Charleston, although still affirming their right of secession, wisely decided to reduce greatly the prospect of such a collision by a suspension of the Ordinance.

To Poinsett, however, troop movements in the interior indicated that danger was not yet past. The members of the Union Party sensibly decided to refrain from any action until authorized by the

[44] Governor William Carrol of Tennessee wrote that he could march 10,000 men at a moment's notice. The Governor was not worried about making use of the equipment in the state arsenals. "I shall not stop to inquire whether the State has passed a law or not authorizing me to use the arms." *Correspondence of Andrew Jackson,* Vol. VI, p. 513.

[45] The same, Vol. V, p. 4.

[46] The same, p. 11.

[47] For an account of this meeting see David F. Houston, *A Critical Study of Nullification in South Carolina,* pp. 122-23. Houston points out that "this was practically the nullification, by general consent, of a fundamental statute emanating from the sovereignty of the State."

federal government.[48] To have pursued any other course would have been suicidal. Poinsett asked for a force of 1,000 regulars to be stationed in the city as a nucleus around which the Union men could rally.[49] Jackson replied that to do so would exceed his constitutional power but that he would send a protective force as soon as he was notified of any actual assemblage of an armed force.[50]

In the meantime Congress was working on two measures of considerable importance to South Carolina. The compromise tariff proposed by Clay was rushed through with relatively little debate and passed both houses February 26.[51] The "Force Bill," or the "Bloody Bill," embodied Jackson's recommendations for enforcement of the revenue laws. Wilkins, of Pennsylvania, chairman of the Senate Judiciary Committee, pointed out that the only novel feature of the bill authorized the President under particular circumstances to remove the Custom House.[52]

Calhoun argued that the bill was unconstitutional since the resistance of a state was looked upon, not as that of a body having sovereign or political rights, but merely "as the lawless acts of so many individuals."[53] As it related to the use of force, the law simply authorized the President to employ the means already in effect by the acts of 1795 and 1807. There was no enlarged military power whatever. There was, however, an added restriction on the President. He was to call on the military when "officially informed, by the authorities of any state, or by a judge of any circuit or district court of the United States in the state,"[54] that the laws were obstructed in a manner too great to be overcome by the ordinary methods of procedure. Both the tariff act and the "Force Bill" were signed by the President on March 2.

[48] For the plans of the Union forces, see J. Fred Rippy, *Joel R. Poinsett, Versatile American*, p. 154.
[49] Jan. 30, 1844, *Correspondence of Andrew Jackson*, Vol. V, p. 13.
[50] Feb. 7, 1833, the same, p. 15.
[51] The bill was introduced in the House of Representatives in the afternoon of February 25. That evening the question was put and carried on engrossing the bill for a third reading. For comment on this extraordinary procedure see Thomas H. Benton, *Thirty Years' View*, pp. 309-12; see also *Register of Debates*, Vol. IX, Pt. II, pp. 1772-80.
[52] The same, Pt. I, p. 184.
[53] The same, p. 536.
[54] 4 Stat. L. 634. This, it will be noted, is very similar to the act of 1792.

The authorities in South Carolina waited until Congress had acted before reassembling the Convention. The delegates met for a second time on March 11. A report was made stating that as a result of the efforts of South Carolina, a "beneficial modification" of the tariff of 1832 had been effected, "beyond what existing circumstances would have authorized us to expect."[55] The Ordinance of Nullification, consequently, was rescinded. On the last day of the Convention a report of the "Force Bill" was read, reminding the delegates that though the state had triumphed the contest was not ended until "this act shall cease to disgrace the statute books."[56] An ordinance was adopted declaring the "Force Bill" null and void. For many months popular interest was sustained throughout the state in the activities of the various groups of militia. The struggle over the test oath and the contest between the Unionists and Nullifiers made impossible any great degree of harmony. But from a national point of view, nullification, temporarily at least, was a dead issue.

In view of the tense excitement during the controversy, it is remarkable that no act of violence occurred. Had Jackson been less cautious in stating the circumstances necessary for federal intervention, it is very probable that a clash might have been precipitated between Poinsett's volunteers and the militia of South Carolina. Fortunately, both President Jackson and Governor Hayne were determined to let the opposition make the first untoward move.

Jackson's treatment of nullification has been called "the critical act" of his presidency.[57] From the moment his proclamation was issued until the Nullification Ordinance was revoked, the President's actions were entirely within the law. Throughout the period of disturbance his mind was centered on preserving the Union. His policies, however, were far from being those of an autocrat. In his proclamation, in the orders to General Scott, in his correspondence with Poinsett, and in his signing of a compromise tariff, he displayed a remarkable degree of solicitude for the people of his

---

[55] *State Papers on Nullification*, p. 348.
[56] The same, p. 372.
[57] F. N. Thorpe, *The Principles of American Statesmanship*, p. 12.

native state. He was determined that the laws should be upheld, but he did not insist upon a one-sided victory.[58]

[58] When race riots threatened, Jackson had no qualms about sending troops immediately. In 1831, several requests for aid by municipal officials were answered in the affirmative. In one rather famous case, when the mayor of Norfolk reported a slave insurrection in Southampton County, Virginia, the officer in command of Fort Monroe, on his own initiative dispatched a detachment of troops to the trouble zone. The request was received at 3 A.M., August 24, and two hours later the troops were on their way. They traveled 60 miles in 24 hours. Jackson was quick to express his satisfaction at the "promptitude" of the commanding officer. (Frederick T. Wilson, *Federal Aid in Domestic Disturbances*, S. Doc. 263, 67 Cong. 2 sess., p. 224.) Early in September, the Secretary of War directed that troops be sent to Washington to guard the Greenleaf Point Arsenal. (Adjutant General's Office, *Letters Sent, No. 9*, 1830-1832.) Troops were sent to Wilmington, Del., at the request of the municipal authorities (the same), to Newburn, N.C., and, apparently at the request of the state authorities, to Baton Rogue, La. (*Annual Report of Major Alex Macomb for 1831*, H. Doc. 2, 22 Cong. 1 sess.).

CHAPTER IV

EARLY STATE REQUESTS FOR ASSISTANCE

In 1795 Congress authorized the president to suppress an insurrection within a state providing the state made proper application for assistance.[1] For almost half a century the law was unused. Two incidents of a political nature, one in Pennsylvania in 1838, the other in Rhode Island in 1842, focused the nation's attention upon this long dormant though highly important delegation of power.

THE BUCKSHOT WAR

The Pennsylvania election of 1838 was a bitter contest between the Democrats and the Anti-Masonic—Whig coalition. A contest arose over control of the House, where the returns showed 48 Democrats, 44 Whigs, and 8 seats in dispute because of a double set of returns. On December 4, the Secretary of the Commonwealth, Thomas H. Burrowes, who was also state chairman of the Anti-Masons, sent to the House the election returns as certified by the Whig minority instead of those certified by the Democratic majority of the election board in Philadelphia County. Both groups claimed to have a majority and both then proceeded to organize the House, each electing a Speaker.

Although the Whigs retained control of the Senate, there was a contest over the Philadelphia County seats. Angry citizens in the galleries, many of whom were not residents of the city, threatened violence to the Whig leaders. The scene has been described as "one of fearful confusion, disorder, and terror."[2] Speaker Penrose could no longer retain control and, with Burrowes and Thaddeus Stevens, escaped through a window.[3]

---

[1] 1 Stat. L. 424. The clause referred to was first incorporated in the act of 1792, 1 Stat. L. 264.

[2] William H. Egle, "The Buckshot War," *The Pennsylvania Magazine of History and Biography*, Vol. XXIII (1899), p. 146.

[3] "They were pursued only by their own guilty consciences." (Statement of Congressman Beatty, *Congressional Globe*, 25 Cong. 3 sess., p. 39.) Stevens was

Governor Joseph Ritner, an Anti-Mason who had been defeated for re-election, thereupon issued a proclamation stating that because of the "lawless, infuriated, armed mob from the counties of Philadelphia, Lancaster, Adams, and other places" which had assembled in the city, it was necessary for the military forces of the state to hold themselves in readiness for a call to the capital.[4]

The next day the Governor ordered Major General Robert Patterson of Philadelphia to muster his militia command and proceed to Harrisburg. In addition he requested aid of Captain E. V. Sumner, in charge of the federal troops at Carlisle Barracks. Sumner refused on the ground that it would be improper for him to interpose his command between two contending political factions.[5]

On December 7, Ritner appealed to President Van Buren for help. His plea was based on the constitutional provision that the United States shall protect the states against domestic violence.[6] Lest the President might feel that it would be improper to intervene unless upon application of the legislature, the Governor pointed out that neither branch could "with freedom and safety, meet for the transaction of business."[7]

The President replied through his Secretary of War Joel R. Poinsett, whose experiences in South Carolina six years previously now stood him in good stead. Poinsett stated that since the President's duty was discretionary, it behooved him to exercise the utmost care before complying with any requisition. The commotion threatening the peace of Pennsylvania, he wrote, did not arise from any opposition to the laws but from a political contest between different

a member of the House, and one of the leaders in attempting to retain Anti-Masonic—Whig control. For many years his enemies reminded him of this inglorious leap for safety. At the time of Mississippi's secession from the Union, Congressman Lamar said of the incident: "I almost tremble for the South when I recollect that the opposing forces will be led by the distinguished hero of the Buckshot War. However gloomy the catastrophe, his saltatory accomplishments will enable him to leap out of any difficulties in which he may be involved. I understand that he gave in a peaceable way a practical illustration of peaceable secession." Alphonse B. Miller, *Thaddeus Stevens*, p. 55.

[4] *Correspondence—Governor of Pennsylvania*, H. Doc. 28, 25 Cong. 3 sess., pp. 7-8.
[5] The same, p. 5.
[6] Art. IV, sec. 4.
[7] H. Doc. 28, 25 Cong. 3 sess., p. 6.

members of the government. Any interference by the federal authority "would be attended with the most dangerous consequences to our republican institutions." In the opinion of the President, interference was justified only when the application for aid was clearly within the meaning of the law and where "the domestic violence . . . is of such a character that the State authorities, civil and military, after having been called upon, have proved inadequate to suppress it." Information received after the Governor's request, Poinsett continued, was to the effect that the legislature was able to transact business. Until a requisition came from the legislature, or until it was fully determined that they were not able to meet, and until it was demonstrated also that the authorities in Pennsylvania were incapable of quelling the disturbance, the President believed it unwise to lend federal assistance.[8]

This letter angered Governor Ritner, who condemned the Secretary of War for relying on other than official sources for his information.[9] Apparently neither Van Buren nor Poinsett wished to prolong the argument. The reply of the Secretary of War to the Governor's denunciation was a simple note expressing the regret of the President that the reasons given for denying the requisition were unsatisfactory.[10]

Meanwhile, Major General Patterson arrived in Harrisburg with about 900 militia. Before leaving Philadelphia his men had been supplied with 12,000 musketball and buckshot cartridges and other ordnance stores from the United States arsenal at Frankford. The commanding officer of the arsenal had complied with the Governor's requisition, and for this unauthorized act he was reprimanded by the War Department.[11] General Patterson acted with considerable independence. He made clear to the Governor that the troops were not to be used for political purposes.[12] Since there was no disorder in the city, Patterson's command was ordered to return less than a week after arriving in Harrisburg.

[8] The same, p. 6.
[9] The same, p. 10.
[10] The same, p. 11.
[11] The same, pp. 14-16.
[12] See Egle, *The Pennsylvania Magazine of History and Biography,* Vol. XXIII, pp. 151-53.

The dispute in the legislature was subsequently decided in favor of the Democrats when a number of the Whig members took seats in the House organized by their opponents. The Senate saw the futility of further refusal to recognize the Democratic House, and on December 27 the Governor was notified that both houses were organized. The "Buckshot War," the "last kick of Anti Masonry," was over.

THE DORR REBELLION

Of much greater importance was the Dorr Rebellion. The act of 1795 was again invoked. But John Tyler, following the precedent established by Van Buren, was also careful to have the issue clearly defined before exercising the power delegated by Congress.

Difficulty arose over the making of a new constitution for the state of Rhode Island. The fundamental law of the state, even in 1840, was the charter granted by Charles II in 1663. The General Assembly was an almost omnipotent body. It controlled the governor and the judiciary and, to the great discontent of a large portion of the population, refused to enlarge the suffrage qualifications as the surrounding states had done. No revision in the suffrage law had been made since 1798, when it was established that to vote one must have property valued at $134 or which would bring a rental of $7.00 a year.[13] This restriction was so great that, even excluding aliens, probably not one-half of the men over 21 were voters.[14] A second major objection to the continuance of the charter was over the problem of representation. Although provision was made for an elective assembly, the charter fixed the number of representatives allotted each town. Newport was to have six; Providence, Portsmouth, and Warwick, four each; all other towns were to have but two.[15] By 1840 the industrial growth of the area created a great disproportion between the representation accorded the four towns mentioned in the charter and that of other cities in the state. For example, Providence, with 23,000 inhabitants,

---

[13] The eldest son of such a property owner was also allowed to vote.

[14] Arthur M. Mowry, *The Dorr War*, pp. 75-76. This is an excellent, scholarly account of the rebellion.

[15] Charter granted by King Charles II. To be found in *Interference of the Executive in the Affairs of Rhode Island*, H. Rept. 546, 28 Cong. 1 sess., p. 638. This document is also known as Burke's Report.

retained its four representatives, while 16 towns whose total population was less than that of Providence sent 32 representatives to the General Assembly.[16]

Efforts to extend the franchise. Scattered attempts were made by the non-freemen or non-voters to enlarge the franchise, but they were handicapped by lack of proper organization. However, in 1840, several suffrage associations were formed, and a considerable degree of interest was manifest in the doings of the suffragists. "Worth makes the man, but sand and gravel makes the voter," and "Virtue, Patriotism, and Intelligence versus $134 worth of dirt," were slogans in popular use.[17]

The agitation of the suffragists was sufficiently effective to cause the General Assembly to provide for a constitutional convention. This convention, to be held in November 1841, was known as the "Landholders'" or "Freemen's" convention. Fearing the result of the action that might be taken by the "landocracy," however, the suffragists issued a call for a "People's" convention, to be held in October of the same year.

At both conventions the constitutions drawn up provided for certain extensions of the suffrage. The People's constitution was submitted to a vote on December 27, 1841. All citizens over 21 who were residents of the state were permitted to vote. In the election, which of course was not authorized by the existing government, a majority of the votes cast were in favor of adopting the constitution.[18]

In the election authorized by the General Assembly, many of the suffragists were entitled to vote because of a clause giving all those who would vote under the enlarged suffrage provisions of the Freemen's constitution the right also to vote for its adoption. Their

[16] Mowry, *The Dorr War*, p. 78. There were other objections to the charter, though of less importance. One of these was the insufficient check on the power of the General Assembly. Mowry quotes a remark alleged to have been made during the course of a debate in the legislature. "Mr. Speaker, the member from ——————— is very much mistaken when he supposes that this General Assembly can do anything that is unconstitutional. Sir, I conceive that this body has the same power over the non-freeholders of this state that the Almighty has over the Universe" (p. 80).

[17] The same, p. 63.

[18] Mowry shows there is considerable doubt as to whether the constitution was actually accepted by a majority of the people. The same, pp. 114-18.

vote was large enough to cause the defeat of the Freemen's constitution. This action has been called an error of great moment, since,
had the Freemen's constitution been adopted, the suffragists would
have been in position to greatly influence if not to exercise complete
control of the government.[19] There would, consequently, have been
no occasion for the Dorr Rebellion.

Two sets of state officials. The General Assembly passed a law
providing severe punishment both for persons serving as election
officials and for persons taking office under the People's constitution.
Notwithstanding this action, preparations went ahead for the election to be held April 18. The ticket underwent numerous changes,
since many candidates who feared the penalties proposed by the
General Assembly refused to run. However, a list of candidates
was finally completed shortly before the date set for the election.
Thomas Wilson Dorr, a former member of the legislature and a
leader in the suffrage movement, was elected governor. On April
20, at the regular election, Samuel Ward King was again chosen
governor.

Requests for federal aid to prevent violence. The fear of violence
had prompted King, two weeks before the first election, to appeal
to President Tyler for assistance. A commission of "three of our
most distinguished citizens" was appointed to confer with the President.[20] The Governor also sent two letters to Tyler. One was merely
a formal request for protection. The other was a statement of his
reasons for requesting federal intervention and a plan for avoiding
violence. King suggested that the President issue a proclamation
and send to Rhode Island a military officer whose presence would
"convince the deluded that, in a contest with the government of this
State, they would be involved in a contest with the Government of
the United States, which could only eventuate in their destruction."
The Governor then presented a new interpretation of the authority
of the United States by saying that "the Government of the United
States has the power to *prevent*, as well as to defend us from
violence."[21]

[19] The same, p. 126.
[20] The Commissioners were John Whipple, John Brown Francis, and Elisha R.
Potter. For the letter announcing their appointment, see *United States Troops in
Rhode Island*, H. Doc. 225, 28 Cong. 1 sess., p. 9.
[21] The same, pp. 9-10.

President Tyler was unwilling to accept this point of view. He declared that "no power is vested in the Executive of the United States to anticipate insurrectionary movements." He assured the Governor, however, that when an insurrection against the government of Rhode Island actually existed and when a requisition was made, he would furnish protection to the state. Tyler stated that instead of entering into the controversy, it was the duty of the Executive "to respect the requisitions of that government which has been recognized as the existing government of the State through all times past, until I shall be advised in regular manner, that it has been altered and abolished, and another substituted in its place, by legal and peaceable proceedings, adopted and pursued by the authorities and people of the State."[22] This letter, needless to say, caused numbers of people who were wavering between the two groups to support the "Charter government.[23]

Although the President openly refused any measure of protection to Governor King, the army, nevertheless, swung quietly into action. The commanding officer of the newly constructed Fort Adams was instructed to see that no depot of arms or ammunition belonging to the United States should fall into the hands of "improper persons."[24] The garrison at Fort Adams was more than doubled and other troops, "with tents for detached service," were held in readiness at Fort Columbus, New York.[25] Major General Scott desired that some "discreet, intelligent citizen" be selected to obtain the "fullest intelligence possible" about the probability of disorder, and to send daily reports of his findings.[26]

The legislature declares a state of insurrection. On May 3, the officials elected according to the provisions of the People's con-

[22] The same, p. 11.
[23] Mowry, *The Dorr War*, p. 144.
[24] Assistant Adjutant General Freeman to Major Payne, Apr. 11, 1842, H. Doc. 225, 28 Cong. 1 sess., p. 55.
[25] The same, Apr. 26, 1842, p. 56.
[26] A more direct indication of the side which the national government would support in the event of disorder was given on May 5, the day after Governor King took office. The Governor, together with a number of other officials, including the Secretary of State, the Attorney General, and the judges of the Supreme Court, were invited by Major Payne to inspect Fort Adams. The guests were given a 15-gun salute, a review of the troops was held, and "a fine collation was served." They "expressed their gratification in the highest terms at the discipline and appearance of the men." *Niles National Register*, Vol. LXII (1842), p. 265.

stitution were inaugurated. The legislature was in session but two days, and then adjourned leaving Dorr the full responsibility. On the fourth of May the Charter government officials took office. The legislature passed a resolution declaring the existence of an insurrection and calling for the interposition of federal authority. Once more a delegation was sent to President Tyler.[27] He now had before him the resolutions of two legislatures, Dorr having sent those of the People's legislature announcing the setting up of a new government.

The President made no answer to Dorr. To King, Tyler replied that later information than the Governor's dispatches indicated that the danger was "hourly diminishing." He again assured King of assistance when resistance should become so great that "the *civil posse* shall be unable to overcome" it. In a private letter to the Governor, Tyler suggested that all difficulties would cease if a general amnesty were issued, and a call made for a new convention based upon more liberal principles. The President emphasized that this suggestion was made as a result of reliable advice which had come to him and not from any off-hand judgment of his own.[28] He re-emphasized the desire to avoid the use of force in the statement that "a government never loses anything by mildness and forbearance to its citizens."[29]

Dorr's government, meanwhile, was in a state of collapse. Some of the officials were arrested; others resigned. Dorr himself went to New York City, where he was considerably encouraged by promises of support.[30] He returned to Rhode Island on May 16, and issued a proclamation calling on the military to hold themselves in readiness, and declaring that the state would become the "battleground of American freedom" if the national forces set foot on Rhode Island soil.[31] Some old revolutionary field pieces were secured, and during the night of May 17, Dorr with over 200

---

[27] The delegation of the Charter government consisted of Richard D. Randolph, Speaker of the House, and Elisha R. Potter, a member of the state senate.
[28] The President did not indicate the source of his information. It may have been from the investigator selected at the behest of Major General Scott.
[29] H. Doc. 225, 28 Cong. 1 sess., p. 28.
[30] He went first to Washington, but apparently received little encouragement.
[31] H. Doc. 225, 28 Cong. 1 sess., pp. 31-32.

followers attempted to seize the well-guarded arsenal at Providence.[32] Fortunately the cannon were in such poor condition that Dorr's order to fire could not be carried out. His men began to desert and the next morning he also fled.[33]

Appeal for federal troops subject to state requisition. Apparently the opposition had disintegrated, but the Governor was greatly disturbed by rumors of an attacking force composed of Dorr's sympathizers in surrounding states. Once more he wrote President Tyler, this time expressing confidence that any uprising wholly within the state could be suppressed but asking for a body of troops to be stationed at Fort Adams sufficient to deter an invasion.[34] King made the rather bold suggestion that the federal troops be subject to his requisition.

The President, however, maintained the position he had originally taken; no intervention unless absolutely necessary. His disapproval of the Governor's suggestion to place the troops at the disposal of the state is indicated briefly but clearly in the statement that "should the necessity of the case require the interposition of the authority of the United States, it will be rendered in the manner prescribed by the laws."[35] No additional troops were transferred to Fort Adams, although Colonel Bankhead at Newport, Rhode Island, and Brigadier General Eustis at Boston were instructed by the Secretary of War to select carefully some responsible persons who would determine the extent of Dorr's military preparations.[36] Daniel Webster, Secretary of State, was also requested by Tyler to select a friend who would investigate the state of affairs in Rhode Island. Seven-eighths of the people, according to Webster's friend, reporting as of June 3, were of the opinion that "deserted by his followers at home, and disgraced in the estimation of those who sympathized with him abroad, Mr. Dorr has it not in his power to do any further serious mischief. . . . Governor King

---

[32] Both the militia and the citizenry had responded with great alacrity to the call of Governor King.

[33] See Mowry, *The Dorr War,* pp. 181-97. Governor King offered a reward of $1,000 for Dorr's capture. See *Niles National Register,* Vol. LXII (1842), p. 225.

[34] H. Doc. 225, 28 Cong. 1 sess., pp. 32-33.

[35] The same, p. 34.

[36] The same, pp. 34-36.

and his Council alone, of all the intelligent persons with whom I have consulted, fear an irruption upon them of an armed force."[37] In three weeks' time, events proved the President's informers to have been grossly in error, and Governor King and the one-eighth minority to have been correct.[38]

The Chepachet affair. On June 22 Colonel Bankhead wrote the Secretary of War about the sudden activity at Woonsocket and Chepachet, villages north of Providence. Cannon were being moved to Chepachet, powder had been stolen, and armed men in considerable numbers were moving about.[39] The next day four men who had been seized as spies by the insurgents aroused the capital city by their account of the military preparations in the two towns.

For the fourth time, Governor King called on the President for federal assistance.[40] To give added strength to his appeal, a letter from the mayor of Providence was sent, together with the sworn statements of the four men who had observed the activities in Woonsocket and Chepachet.

For the fourth time Tyler refused aid. On this occasion he relied on the technicality that the Rhode Island legislature was the proper authority to make application, since it was then in session. The President contended that King had misapprehended the meaning of his letter of May 7.[41] The confusion, apparently, arose over Tyler's statement that "if an exigency of lawless violence shall actually arise, the Executive Government of the United States, on the application of your excellency, under the authority of the resolutions of the legislature already transmitted, will stand ready to succor the authorities of the State in their efforts to maintain a due respect for the laws."[42] The Governor placed great emphasis on the clause "under the authority of the resolutions of the legislature already transmitted," and sent his request to the President without any further action on the part of the legislature. Tyler evidently be-

---

[37] The same, pp. 37-38.
[38] Colonel Bankhead also believed there would be no further disturbance. See his letter to the Secretary of War, the same, p. 39.
[39] The same.
[40] The same, p. 40.
[41] The same, p. 41.
[42] The same, p. 27.

lieved that since the legislature which met in May had adjourned, a new requisition was necessary. The United States Senators from Rhode Island explained to the President that, though the legislature was meeting by adjournment, it was "in law regarded as the May session of the General Assembly and can be regarded in no other light than if it had been a continuous session of that body, held from day to day by usual adjournments."[43] This argument had no effect on Tyler. His policy of refusing aid had worked so well on three preceding occasions that he may have used this means as a subterfuge to effect further delay.

The President was finally stirred to action by Bankhead's report of June 27. The Colonel indicated that a conflict was unavoidable between the 2,000 men assembled at Providence, under the Governor, and the force at Chepachet "estimated at from 800 to 1,000 men armed with muskets, about 1,500 without arms and 10 or 12 cannon mounted."[44] Bankhead recommended a force of 300 regular troops.

In spite of this alarming report, and notwithstanding the entreaties of United States Senators Simmons and Sprague, who wanted an immediate compliance with the Governor's requisition, Tyler's caution was unabated. He prepared a proclamation and delivered it to the Secretary of War with instructions to proceed to Rhode Island.[45] "In the event of a requisition being made on the President in conformity with the laws of the United States," the Secretary was to publish the proclamation and, if necessary, call on the governors of Massachusetts and Connecticut for a sufficient number of militia to terminate the insurrection. The regular troops near Providence were to be used *to defend* the city.

It seems scarcely possible for the President to have moved with greater deliberation. Every point in his letter of instructions called for delay. He could have issued the proclamation at once, or he could have instructed the commanding officer at Fort Adams to move against the insurgents. Instead, Tyler insisted on another requisition from the state, even before the publication of the procla-

---

[43] The same, p. 47.
[44] The same, p. 46.
[45] For the proclamation and the letter of instruction, see the same, pp. 36-37.

mation. The regular troops were to be used for defense purposes only. No federal movement against the insurgents was to be made until a force was gathered through the time-consuming procedure of calling for troops from other states.

In the meantime there was great activity in Rhode Island. On June 25, Dorr, with a small group of men from New York, arrived in Chepachet where 200 or more armed men had gathered and were already constructing defense works on Acote's Hill. A call was issued for other members of the People's militia to join them.[46]

Governor King was determined, with or without federal aid, to maintain the authority of the "Charter" government. Militia in large numbers responded to his orders and by Sunday, June 26, a force of perhaps 2,500 men had collected in Providence.[47] The city was placed under martial law and carefully guarded by the militia.

But again Dorr's men had gathered to disperse without firing a shot. Convinced, finally, that the majority of the people did not approve of the use of force, Dorr dismissed his followers and once more left the state.

Even before Tyler issued his instructions to Secretary of War Spencer, Dorr had dismissed the troops at Chepachet. Consequently, there was no need for the Secretary to publish the President's proclamation, or to call upon the militia of other states. No sooner did Spencer arrive in Providence than he was asked to review the troops of the Charter government. He expressed his pleasure at the appearance of the soldiers, and congratulated the people of Rhode Island on the "signal success" with which their "sacrifices" had been attended.[48]

The insurrection was over. Martial law, however, continued for more than a month throughout the entire state. Many arrests were arbitrarily made, homes were broken into, and prisoners were mistreated.[49] In a case arising out of this period of martial law, the

[46] Mowry, *The Dorr War*, p. 210.
[47] About 4,100 members of the militia saw some service during the insurrection. Their pay at $1.00 per day totaled approximately $23,000. See *Niles National Register*, Vol. LXIII (1842), p. 67.
[48] The same, Vol. LXII (1842), p. 307. This unauthorized action was later a cause of embarrassment to the President.
[49] "The Newport Mercury, a moderate paper, states that the whole number of prisoners taken and examined under martial law" was 184. (*Niles National Reg-*

Supreme Court declined to enter the controversy as to which government should be recognized. This was declared to be a political, not a judicial, question. By implication, the Court upheld the act of 1795 in which Congress delegated to the president the power to protect the states against domestic violence.[50]

Dorr remained out of the state for over a year. The requisition for his arrest issued by Governor King was not honored in either New Hampshire or Connecticut. Dorr, however, returned voluntarily the latter part of October 1843. He was tried before a jury and the supreme court of the state and found guilty of treason against the state.[51] He was sentenced to life imprisonment. The *Providence Journal* pointed out that this punishment was provided by law and that any leniency would necessarily come from the state legislature.[52] A year later, in June 1845, through the aid of the Democratic party the legislature pardoned Dorr. Shortly afterward the Whigs got control but in 1851, the Democrats having regained power, the legislature passed a resolution restoring Dorr's civil and political rights. Three years later the General Assembly passed a law annulling the judgment against him.[53] Most of the other prisoners had been discharged in 1844 as a result of a resolution of general amnesty passed by the legislature. The only requirement was an oath to support the constitution of the state and of the United States.[54]

Meanwhile, and an important contributing factor to Dorr's loss of support, plans for a new constitution were being perfected. The General Assembly had adopted a report calling for a constitutional convention before the incident at Chepachet. A constitution was drawn up in September and approved by the people two months

---

ister, Vol. LXII (1842), p. 386.) Mowry estimates the number to be almost twice that. See *The Dorr War*, p. 227.

[50] *Luther* v. *Borden*, 7 Howard 1. For the statement of the Court concerning the presidency see the same, pp. 43-45.

[51] "Wherever allegiance is due, there treason may be committed. Allegiance is due to a State, and treason may be committed against a State of this Union." Charge to the jury by Chief Justice Durfee, "Report of the Trial of Thomas W. Dorr," H. Rept. 546, 28 Cong. 1 sess., p. 993.

[52] See *Niles National Register*, Vol. LXVI (1844), p. 277.

[53] Mowry, *The Dorr War*, pp. 255-58.

[54] *Niles National Register*, Vol. LXVI (1844), p. 304.

later. Both the apportionment clause and the suffrage clause were greatly liberalized, the latter completely eliminating any property qualification for those male citizens over 21 who had lived in the state two years and had paid a tax amounting to $1.00 for the support of the schools.[55] The new constitution went into effect May 2, 1843.

Criticism of the President's policy. In spite of the four-fold refusal of the President to answer the requisitions of Governor King, Tyler was subjected to a tremendous amount of criticism from the followers of Dorr, and from members of the Democratic party who hoped thereby to hasten the President's downfall. In February 1844, a minority of the Rhode Island legislature petitioned the House of Representatives to conduct an inquiry into the "interference of the Executive in the affairs of Rhode Island."[56] A resolution in favor of such an inquiry was passed by a close vote and the President was requested to lay before Congress the documents in evidence of the part played by all federal officials in the insurrection.[57]

The petitioners from Rhode Island placed the chief responsibility for the overthrow of the "peoples constitution and government" on President Tyler.[58] The wording of his first letter to Governor King,[59] they argued, "conveyed the threat of federal intervention. By increasing the number of troops at Newport, and by other demonstrations within striking distance, he gave all the advantages of actual military co-operation and invasion to the old charter party."[60] The President denied that there was any movement of troops other than to strengthen the garrison at Fort Adams. If this statement were correct, the petitioners answered, why were the troops at Fort Columbus ordered to be "held in readiness, with tents, for detached service"? Objection was made also to the system of "military espionage" established by the order of Major General Scott.[61]

[55] Constitution of the State of Rhode Island, Art. II, sec. 2. H. Rept. 581, 28 Cong. 1 sess., pp. 129-42.

[56] H. Rept. 546, 28 Cong. 1 sess., p. 1.

[57] See *Congressional Globe*, 28 Cong. 1 sess., pp. 428, 436.

[58] H. Rept. 546, 28 Cong. 1 sess., p. 3.

[59] See p. 57.

[60] H. Rept. 546, 28 Cong. 1 sess., p.2.

[61] See p. 57. For arguments against the action of Tyler, see H. Rept. 546, 28 Cong. 1 sess., pp. 1-4, 52-63.

There was no equivocation in Tyler's able defense of his recognition of the Charter government. "I . . . resist the idea," he wrote, "that it falls within the Executive competency to decide, in controversies of the nature of that which existed in Rhode Island, on which side is the majority of the people, or as to the extent of the rights of a mere numerical majority." He pointed out that Rhode Island had "conducted all her domestic affairs" under the "Charter" government, and that it was his duty to deal with that government.[62]

Undoubtedly there was some degree of truth in the Dorrite contention that Tyler's promise of federal assistance caused numbers of people to ally themselves with the "Charter" government.[63] It was certainly unfair, however, to place the chief blame for the failure of the Dorr government on the President, who on four separate occasions refused the importunities for aid of the recognized governor of a state.[64]

The President's chief policy had been "to bring the dispute to a termination without the interposition of the military power of the United States."[65] In this he had succeeded. It was an opportunity to put into actual practice the principles he had enunciated ten years earlier. He had vigorously opposed Jackson's threat of force in South Carolina, declaring that it was "idle to talk of preserving a republic for any length of time with an uncontrolled power over the military, exercised at pleasure by the President."[66] His action in Rhode Island was exactly in accordance with his statement in the Senate December 6, 1832, that "when he was called on for military force he should be disposed to inquire whether every other means had been exhausted before resort was had to the sword."[67] A decade

[62] The same, pp. 652-55.
[63] The Court recognized this in the case previously cited. Tyler's interference, they held, even though by merely "announcing his determination," was as effectual as if he had assembled the militia and should be just as "authoritative." *Luther v. Borden*, 7 Howard 1.
[64] In 1844, Webster, who had been Tyler's Secretary of State at the time of the insurrection, wrote as follows to the President: "Your conduct of that affair will appear hereafter . . . one of the most fortunate incidents in your administration, for your own reputation." Lyon G. Tyler, *The Letters and Times of the Tylers,* Vol. II, p. 199.
[65] H. Rept. 546, 28 Cong. 1 sess., pp. 652-55.
[66] To Governor Floyd of Virginia, Jan. 16, 1833. Oliver P. Chitwood, *John Tyler, Champion of the Old South,* p. 113.
[67] *Register of Debates,* 22 Cong. 2 sess., p. 21.

later the President demonstrated his earlier belief that "we can never be too tardy in commencing the work of blood."[68]

THE SAN FRANCISCO VIGILANCE COMMITTEE OF 1856

The extraordinary caution exercised by the makers of the Constitution in the wording of Article IV, section 4, operated to the advantage of President Franklin Pierce just as it had previously aided Presidents Van Buren and Tyler to avoid interference with the affairs of a state. The paragraph subjected to so many interpretations reads: "The United States shall guarantee to every State in this Union a Republican Form of Government, and shall protect each of them against Invasion; and on Application of the Legislature or of the Executive (when the Legislature cannot be convened) against domestic Violence." Each president demanded that the state's legislature participate in the call for federal assistance. Pierce placed great emphasis on the parenthetical phrase "when the Legislature cannot be convened."

Formation of the Committee. In 1856 local officials in San Francisco County, unable or unwilling to enforce the law to the satisfaction of a large portion of the people, were pushed into the background by an illegal, though highly effective, governing agency, the San Francisco Committee of Vigilance. California had been a member of the Union for only seven years. Political organization had proceeded with rapidity, but organization alone was insufficient to maintain a stable society. It is unnecessary here to discuss the many influences promoting instability. Suffice it to say that there was great need for a more effective system of control over the social order.[69]

Disorder was especially rampant in the city of San Francisco. To combat an increasing criminal element, the Vigilance Committee of 1851 had been organized. The work of the Committee was so effective that for a time a feeling of security existed. In 1854-55, however, a new era of lawlessness was experienced. Political corruption was at its worst. Through such devices as the "double improved

---

[68] The same, p. 375.
[69] See Mary F. Williams, *History of the San Francisco Committee of Vigilance of 1851*, Chap. VII.

back action ballot box" every election was controlled.[70] The affairs of the city were consequently in the hands of the worst element, and it was useless to expect a criminal housecleaning without a political housecleaning as well. An added cause for despair was a severe depression in business. The decline in mining production, over-speculation in property, the failures of merchant and financial houses, all contributed to create a "frenzy of insecurity and uncertainty, full of terrors and almost without hope."[71]

A crisis was reached when on May 14, 1856, James King of William was murdered. A relentless enemy of evil, King had for some months published a small newspaper openly attacking political and financial corruption in the city. His murder was the climax of a long series of ruthless, gangsterlike incidents. Public opinion was quickly crystallized, and within three days a reorganized Vigilance Committee had an enlisted force of over 3,000 men willing to do its bidding.[72] While Governor J. Neely Johnson looked on, the Vigilantes marched to the jail and demanded the murderer, James Casey. The sheriff's force was so greatly outnumbered that there was no alternative. Some days later Casey was tried, found guilty, and hanged.

Action by the Governor. At first the Governor was not hostile to the Vigilantes, who continued to mete out their own brand of justice.[73] The enemies of the Committee, however, persuaded him to take action, and on June 3 he declared San Francisco County in a state of insurrection. All persons subject to military duty were ordered to report to Major General William T. Sherman, who was in charge of the second division of the state militia.[74] The Governor then asked Major General John E. Wool, who was commanding

[70] Theodore H. Hittell, *History of California,* Vol. III, p. 461. The box was constructed with false bottom and sides so that ballots could be hidden in advance. Also see W. O. Ayres, "Personal Recollections of the Vigilance Committee," *Overland Monthly,* Vol. VIII, Second Series, August 1886, p. 172.

[71] Hittell, *History of California,* Vol. III, p. 462.

[72] For an exciting first-hand account of the period immediately after the attack on King, see Ayres, *Overland Monthly,* Vol. VIII, pp. 165-71. See also Hubert Howe Bancroft, *Popular Tribunals,* Vol. II, pp. 23-243.

[73] See statement of William T. Coleman, chairman of the committee, in "San Francisco Vigilance Committee," *Century Magazine,* November 1891, p. 140.

[74] *Vigilance Committee in California,* S. Ex. Doc. 101, 34 Cong. 1 sess., p. 6.

the Pacific Division of the United States Army, to furnish arms and other munitions of war.[75] Wool replied that he had no authority to grant the request, and suggested that the application be sent to the President.[76] Captain David G. Farragut, in charge of the Mare Island Navy Yard, also declined to make any commitments.[77] Two representatives were appointed by the Governor to proceed to Washington as speedily as possible. Each of them was specifically instructed to ask, not only for arms and ammunition, but also for the aid of the military and naval forces of the United States.[78] In his letter to the President, however, Johnson asked only for arms and ammunition. This omission, though perhaps not a decisive factor, was an error on the part of the Governor.

Pierce turned to Attorney General Caleb Cushing for an opinion on the legal questions involved. Cushing ruled that there was no legal justification for federal intervention. He pointed out that Johnson's call was irregular since it was "made by the governor of the State, not by its legislature, and made by him without any allegation that the legislature could not be convened." When an insurrection occurs within a state, Cushing continued, the President is authorized, upon proper application, to call forth the militia of other states or the forces of the United States.[79] But Johnson did not "in terms" make such a request. He asked only for arms and ammunition. The Attorney General, relying on the decisions of the Supreme Court,[80] emphasized the fact that "it is the function of the President of the United States, indubitably, to decide, in his discretion, what facts constitute the case of insurrection contemplated by the statutes and by the Constitution." He refused to state any opinion on the question whether, when the fact of insurrection was known, the president could grant assistance in the event of an

[75] The same, p. 5.
[76] *Vigilance Committee in San Francisco*, S. Ex. Doc. 43, 34 Cong. 3 sess., p. 6. There was a bitter controversy between Wool on the one hand, and Sherman and Johnson on the other, as to the answer which the federal officer had given when he was asked for arms and ammunition. The same, pp. 2-7, 12-15, 22-29. See also "Sherman and the San Francisco Vigilantes," *Century Magazine*, December 1891, pp. 302-06.
[77] *Century Magazine*, December 1891, p. 302.
[78] S. Ex. Doc. 101, 34 Cong. 1 sess., pp. 6, 7.
[79] 1 Stat. L. 424; 2 Stat. L. 443.
[80] *Martin* v. *Mott*, 12 Wheaton 19; *Luther* v. *Borden*, 7 Howard 1.

incorrect application. Intervention by the president in cases of *"doubtful* legal condition," Cushing held, should be reserved "for circumstances of the utmost emergency." No "superlative exigency" existed in the present case since there had been no actual "shock of arms between the insurgents and the State." His final argument against intervention was that since the Governor had made no effort to call together the legislature, although the city had been subject to Vigilante rule for more than a month, it was apparent that the whole constitutional power of the state had not yet been exerted.[81]

The report of the Attorney General and a letter from W. L. Marcy, Secretary of State, were sent to Johnson on July 19. The President was convinced, Marcy wrote, that the conclusions reached by the Attorney General constituted "insuperable obstacles" to any action on the part of the federal government.[82]

Arrest of Justice Terry. Meanwhile, on June 21, a justice of the California Supreme Court, David S. Terry, had become involved with the Vigilantes. Six cases of muskets being shipped to the regular officials were seized by the Vigilantes and an effort was made to arrest James Maloney, who had been in charge of the shipment. Maloney, Terry, and a number of others were on their way to one of the militia armories when they were overtaken. In the struggle which ensued, Terry very seriously stabbed a Committeeman named Hopkins. Notwithstanding his position as a justice of the Supreme Court, the Vigilantes arrested Terry and held him for trial. Fortunately, Hopkins recovered and, although Terry was found guilty of resisting by violence the officers of the Committee, he was released. For over six weeks he had been in the hands of the Committee.

Every effort was made to get the federal military and naval officials to rescue Terry from the hands of the Vigilantes. According to Farragut, the arrest of Terry had caused a division of public opinion which up to that time had been largely with the Vigilantes.[83] The release of the justice, therefore, caused a feeling of relief

[81] S. Ex. Doc. 101, 34 Cong. 1 sess., pp. 8-13.
[82] The same, pp. 7-8.
[83] The same, p. 16.

throughout the city. Tension was further eased when the men who had seized the shipment of arms were found not guilty of the charge of piracy. The problem of how to maintain the authority of the United States District Court during and after the piracy trial was a matter of considerable concern to the United States Marshal.[84] He could get no help from General Wool, who refused to take any action without specific instructions from Washington. The Marshal's worries were over, however, with the announcement of the verdict of not guilty.

Precautionary measurers taken by federal government. In spite of Pierce's early action in declining to assist Governor Johnson, the President kept in touch, as best he could, with events in San Francisco. Early in August, the Secretary of the Navy, J. C. Dobbin, instructed William Mervine, Commander of the Pacific Squadron, to station "two or three national" vessels at San Francisco.

> The President considers it wise under the circumstances to be prepared for emergencies. The present object is the protection of the public property and the officers of the federal government. . . . However much the President may be shocked at the apparently rebellious attitude of the people towards the government of their State, however strong may be his conviction that it is a case of "domestic insurrection," yet he has no authority of his own mere volition to order the interposition of the army and navy, and cannot exercise that power except in strict accordance with the Constitution and until certain forms pointed out by statute have been fully complied with by the authorities of that State.[85]

In like manner the Secretary of War, Jefferson Davis, instructed General Wool to concentrate a sufficient body of troops near the city to protect the "property and officers of the United States against lawless violence or revolutionary aggression."[86] Fortunately, there was no need for military action. The work of the Vigilantes was ended. The organization was formally disbanded, and with the election in November came the beginnings of an "era of good

---

[84] See McDuffie to Wool, the same, p. 10.
[85] The same, pp. 13-15.
[86] S. Ex. Doc. 43, 34 Cong. 3 sess., p. 9. Early in June, at the request of the Collector of Customs, Wool had furnished a guard for the protection of the United States mint. (The same.)

government characterized by public order, decency, and economy, which had not before been experienced."[87]

By his action in declining to grant the request of Governor Johnson, President Pierce allowed the Vigilante movement to run its course. Even though the Governor's requisition had been properly made, it is highly probable that the decision made by Pierce would not have been changed. A presidential election was in the offing, and to have been in the act of putting down an insurrection at such a time would have jeopardized the party's chances at the polls. Furthermore, California was a long way from the seat of government, and the conflicting reports the President received undoubtedly made him doubly careful to refrain from any hasty decision to assist the Governor. Then, too, the ease with which the Committee raised a force of 3,000 men in a three-day period demonstrated that a vast majority of the people of San Francisco were behind the Vigilante movement. To have taken control of the city would have necessitated a considerable force, for it is highly unlikely that San Francisco, as it was in 1856, would have submitted meekly to domination by either state or federal forces. It is probable also that any large force of United States troops would have been resented by the people of the entire state, since a seven-year period of membership in the Union was not sufficient to closely bind California to the national government. Finally, and perhaps of greatest moment, the government was not prepared to furnish any immedite assistance. In June, when Governor Johnson asked for troops, there were less than 50 available men at San Francisco.[88] Most of the 2,500 officers and men in the Department of the Pacific were in active service against the Indians.[89] With such an inadequate force at hand, President Pierce had no other choice than to refrain from intervention.

[87] Hittell, *History of California*, Vol. III, p. 640.
[88] S. Ex. Doc. 43, 34 Cong. 3 sess., p. 9.
[89] *Report of the Secretary of War*, S. Ex. Doc. 5, Pt. II, 34 Cong. 3 sess., pp. 246-47. See also pp. 149-202.

CHAPTER V

THE GREAT RIOTS OF 1877[1]

Less than five months after President Hayes took office, the country was embroiled in a fierce internal conflict. Local, and even state, authorities were helpless to stem the impulsive and imprudent outbursts of violence. In a period of eight days during July 1877, no fewer than nine governors called on the President to assist in maintaining the peace. Singularly enough, in view of the domestic uprisings in preceding years, the wrath of the people was not directed against the government of the nation or of any state. For the first time in history the country was in the throes of a great industrial strike.

RAPID SPREAD OF THE RAILROAD STRIKE

The business depression following the panic of 1873 had been particularly hard on the railroads. With revenues already lowered, the railroads added to their financial difficulties by starting a destructive war of rate reductions. The average rate per ton-mile in 1876 was .92 of a cent, only 42 per cent of the rate in 1868.[2] To compensate as much as possible for this loss of income the railroads, by various expedients, had reduced the sums paid to their employees. The resistance point was reached when a 10 per cent wage reduction was put into effect in the summer of 1877.[3]

[1] There was constant turmoil in the southern states during the first decade after the Civil War. Military government prevailed for a large part of the time. Since conditions during the period of reconstruction, however, were so inextricably linked with the war, the disorders prior to the administration of President Hayes have been viewed as not coming within the scope of this study.

[2] From a report of the Division of Internal Commerce of the Treasury Department, published in the *National Republican*, Washington, D.C., July 28, 1877, p. 2.

[3] For example, on the Baltimore and Ohio the pay of firemen ranged from $1.50 to $1.75 per day. This was reduced to $1.35 and $1.58. No compensation was given for the time lost while waiting to make a return run. (Joseph A. Dacus, *Annals of the Great Strikes*, p. 27.) It was suggested that the New York Central could have met the demands of its workers by a reduction of the dividend rate,

West Virginia. Disorder first broke out at Martinsburg, West Virginia, when the railroad workers went on strike and with the assistance of numerous sympathizers seized control of and blocked the Baltimore and Ohio Railroad. Because of the action of the West Virginia legislature two years before in prohibiting the enrollment of the militia, the small volunteer force at the state's disposal was entirely inadequate. On July 18, Governor Henry M. Mathews addressed a formal request to President Hayes. He pointed out that the legislature was not then in session and could not be convened in time to deal with the emergency. The President requested a complete statement of facts as to the strength of the insurgents and the reasons for the state's inability to cope with the disorder. Mathews explained the action of the legislature and stated that of four companies of volunteers, two were at Martinsburg and in sympathy with the rioters; one was 38 miles from the railroad; and only one, a group of 40 men, could be relied on for effective resistance. There were, he asserted, some 800 rioters.[4]

Hayes, acting through his Secretary of War George W. McCrary, thereupon ordered troops from the Washington Arsenal and from Fort McHenry to proceed to Martinsburg. They were instructed to take no action until after the publication of the President's proclamation.[5]

One day after the Governor's call, a force of approximately 260 troops was in Martinsburg.[6] The proclamation was circulated and an additional notice was given out by the commanding officer warning against efforts to impede the forces of the United States.[7] There

which had been maintained at 8 per cent through the depression. (In reply see the *Commercial and Financial Chronicle*, Aug. 11, 1877, p. 126.) However, of the total number of railroads in the country, less than one-quarter were operating at a profit. (See statement taken from Poor's Manual of Railroads in the *National Republican*, Aug. 1, 1877, p. 2.) For a criticism of the peremptory manner in which the wage reduction was effected, see James Ford Rhodes, *History of the United States from Hayes to McKinley*, pp. 18-19.

[4] For the correspondence relating to this incident see Frederick T. Wilson, *Federal Aid in Domestic Disturbances*, S. Doc. 263, 67 Cong. 2 sess., pp. 269-71.

[5] For the proclamation see 20 Stat. L. 803-04.

[6] See "Distribution of United States Troops Employed in Connection with Recent Labor Strikes" in *Report of the Secretary of War*, H. Ex. Doc. 1, 45 Cong. 2 sess., Pt. 2, pp. 92-98.

[7] S. Doc. 263, 67 Cong. 2 sess., p. 271.

was no violence, and on July 22 most of the soldiers were moved to Cumberland, Maryland.

Maryland. Governor John Lee Carroll of Maryland had been asked by the railway officials and others to send a detachment of militia to Cumberland. He ordered out the Fifth Regiment from Baltimore, but before they could be assembled an uprising of such serious proportions occurred in Baltimore itself that the order was countermanded and a general militia call was issued. In a clash between the militia and the great crowds of strike sympathizers, ten persons were killed and many others injured. Governor Carroll then issued a formal call for federal forces. The President issued a second proclamation and directed that all available troops be sent to Baltimore.[8] The commandant at Fort McHenry was ordered to report with the soldiers at his disposal to Governor Carroll. Marines in the Washington Navy Yard were dispatched to Baltimore, but this command was shortly revoked because of the danger of an outbreak in the capital city. Troops at Fort Monroe and sailors and marines from Norfolk were moved to Washington. Two war vessels were also stationed at the Navy Yard.[9] Major General W. S. Hancock, who was in command of the military district of the Atlantic, arrived in Baltimore July 22 to take command of the federal troop movements. The presence of the troops there and at Cumberland was sufficient to maintain order, and General Hancock moved on to Philadelphia.

Pennsylvania. Pennsylvania was in an uproar. A particularly destructive riot in Pittsburgh had caused a considerable loss in life and a loss of millions of dollars worth of property. Governor John Hartranft had left, July 16, on a trip to the west, leaving the state, he said, at a time "when the peace of the Commonwealth seemed assured."[10] Three days later a strike on the Pennsylvania Railroad stopped the movement of all freight trains. The Adjutant General of the state, at the request of the sheriff of Allegheny County,

[8] 20 Stat. L. 804. For the call of the Governor and the various military dispatches, see S. Doc. 263, 67 Cong. 2 sess., pp. 271-73.

[9] Some of the marines later went to Baltimore. For the precautionary measures in Washington, see Dacus, *Annals of the Great Strikes*, p. 97. See also *Report of the Secretary of the Navy*, H. Ex. Doc. 1, 45 Cong. 2 sess., Pt. I, pp. 40-41.

[10] "Papers of the Governors," *Pennsylvania Archives*, 4th series, Vol. IX, p. 585.

called out the militia in the vicinity of Pittsburgh. Later, in response
to a second appeal, a detachment of 650 militia from Philadelphia
was sent to the city. In a clash with the crowd shortly after their
arrival, 16 persons were killed.[11] Instead of bringing order to the
city, the militia brought upon themselves the fury of the towns-
people. The Philadelphia troops took refuge in the Pennsylvania
Railroad roundhouse, where they were subjected to continuous
firing from armed members of the rioters. The roundhouse was
set on fire and the militia was compelled to flee from the city. Six-
teen soldiers and 50 rioters were reported to have been killed.[12]
Saturday night and Sunday, July 21 and 22, the railroad properties
were burned, including over 125 locomotives, more than 2,000
freight cars, the depot, and other properties.[13] With the militia
forced out of the city it was impossible for the local police to stop
the pillaging which accompanied the brief reign of terror.

President Hayes felt that he could do nothing without a requisition from the Governor.[14] However, to protect the arsenal, a force
of about 50 men was moved from Columbus, arriving in Pittsburgh
on July 23. By this time the rioters had spent their energies and a
local citizens' committee had taken charge. On the twenty-third
also, the President received the first of a series of telegrams from
Governor Hartranft. Pittsburgh was not mentioned. Instead, the
call was for "troops to assist in quelling mobs within the borders of
the State of Pennsylvania." The Governor suggested that Hayes

---

[11] Dacus, *Annals of the Great Strikes*, p. 119.

[12] Letter of Adjutant General J. W. Latta to Governor Hartranft, July 22,
1877. "Papers of the Governors," *Pennsylvania Archives*, 4th series, Vol. IX,
p. 621.

[13] S. Doc. 263, 67 Cong. 2 sess., p. 167. See also James Dabney McCabe, *The
History of the Great Riots*, pp. 76-124.

[14] A call to the President, in the name of the Governor, was sent by James W.
Latta, Adjutant General, and Matthew S. Quay, Secretary of the Commonwealth.
Latta sent a message to Hartranft on the twenty-second stating that the Pennsylvania cabinet was meeting that day and that the subject of an appeal to the President was to be considered. The Governor was asked to send specific directions.
Apparently none came, for Latta, writing the next day, states that he and Quay
had, in Hartranft's name, appealed to Hayes. The papers in S. Doc. 263, 67
Cong. 2 sess., and in the Hayes Memorial Library at Fremont, Ohio, give no
indication that the President acted on any other message than that of the Governor
himself. For the letters of Latta to Hartranft see "Papers of the Governors,"
Pennsylvania Archives, 4th series, Vol. IX, p. 585.

"order troops from adjoining States, and prepare to call volunteers authorized by Congress."[15] Hartranft's first call was sent from Wyoming Territory at midnight of July 22. At ten o'clock the next day, from Ogallalla, Nebraska, a second message was sent calling upon Hayes to save the country from "anarchy and revolution." Apparently someone advised Hartranft that his application was too informal, for at twelve o'clock he dispatched a third telegram from North Bend, Nebraska, in which he asked that his requisition be amended "by adding the words domestic insurrection exists in Pennsylvania which the State authorities are unable to suppress and the legislature is not in session and cannot be convened in time." Since he had received no word from the President, Hartranft sent a fourth telegram, this time from Lamville, Iowa, asking for an answer to his requisition and stating that he would arrive at Beaver, Pennsylvania, on the twenty-fourth.[16]

Even before President Hayes had received the Governor's formal request, he had, in response to a message from the mayor of Philadelphia, ordered troops to that city to protect federal property. Soldiers of numerous posts in New England who were on their way to the strike area were instructed to halt at Philadelphia.

No sooner did the President receive Governor Hartranft's message than he issued a third proclamation, this time, of course, applying to Pennsylvania.[17] General Hancock was given full authority to move the troops within his division, an order which raised an interesting question of federal-state jurisdiction. In both West Virginia and Maryland the soldiers had acted under the orders of the governors.[18] Hancock, not quite sure of his position, sent a telegram to the Secretary of War advancing the doctrine that when a state calls for aid, the civil authority admits its inability to maintain control and should, therefore, allow the federal government to assume complete command. Under such circumstances the President would exercise full authority. The state would occupy a subordinate position until order was restored.

[15] S. Doc. 263, 67 Cong. 2 sess., p. 167.
[16] These messages are to be found in the *Hayes Papers* at the Hayes Memorial Library, Fremont, Ohio.
[17] 20 Stat. L. 805.
[18] S. Doc. 263, 67 Cong. 2 sess., items 102, 103, 114, 115, 123.

Before his message could be considered, Hancock received word that the federal troops were to act under the orders of Governor Hartranft. Sometime later the General received a second message. His telegram had been considered and the President had accepted his view of the federal government's position. Hancock was instructed to take command of both federal and state forces. This message was received after Hancock, acting on the strength of the first telegram, had placed the troops under the Governor's control. They were allowed to remain there pending a demonstration of "absolute failure to accomplish successful results."[19]

No further outbreaks had occurred in Pittsburgh, but no agreement had been reached between the authorities of the Pennsylvania Railroad and the strikers. Freight traffic was still blocked and the Governor had been informed that further rioting might occur unless coal and provisions reached the city.[20] On July 26 Hartranft, in command of the federal and state forces, left Philadelphia for Pittsburgh. No trouble was experienced during the two weeks the troops were there. The work of the regulars in Pennsylvania was not over, however, as striking railroaders and anthracite coal miners seemed to make necessary the presence of troops at Easton, Reading, Wilkes-Barre, Harrisburg, Mauch Chunk, and Scranton.[21]

Ohio. Although the strike extended across many parts of Ohio, there was no formal call from the state for federal assistance. Instead, Governor Young telegraphed the President on July 24, asking for arms from the arsenal in Columbus. This request was granted.[22] On August 2, Lieutenant E. S. Otis, who was passing through Toledo on his way to Indiana, was asked by the authorities to remain in the city. He was informed by General Hancock that since Governor Young had made no request for troops it would be improper to lend any assistance unless "legally summoned as a part of a posse comitatus."[23]

---

[19] The same, items 125, 127, 131.
[20] "Papers of the Governors," *Pennsylvania Archives*, 4th series, Vol. IX, p. 501.
[21] *New York Times*, July 25, 1877, p. 2. During July and August a total of 2,185 officers and enlisted men of the regular army saw service in Pennsylvania. War Department Archives, *Adjutant General's Office*, 45615-1896.
[22] S. Doc. 263, 67 Cong. 2 sess., p. 170.
[23] The same, p. 282.

Indiana. A peculiar situation existed in Indiana. On July 21 railroad workers in Fort Wayne refused to go on duty. To protect a large government arsenal located in Indianapolis, a small detachment of federal troops was ordered to move to the arsenal from the headquarters in St. Louis. Judge W. Q. Gresham, of the federal district court, telegraphed the President July 25 that the local authorities were unable to resist or subdue the mob, which had become the "supreme authority in the State."[24] On July 26, Governor James D. Williams asked the President to authorize the commandant at the arsenal to aid the state government. On the ground that this call was incorrectly made, Williams was informed that the federal troops could be used only to protect property of the United States and to enforce the processes of the federal courts.[25] This last point was of considerable importance, since a part of the railroad network in Indiana had been placed in receivership by Judge Gresham. Over such roads the maintenance of order was in the hands of United States marshals. Additional troops were sent to Indiana but they were responsible, not to the Governor, as in the previous cases, but to the federal authorities.

It is difficult to determine the degree to which political considerations influenced the President's reply to Governor Williams. The Governor was a Democrat and, when a member of Congress, had opposed the use of troops to assist the government of a state. However, as an editorial in the *New York Times* pointed out, his failure to use the correct formula in calling for troops may have been due to a "confusion of terror rather than willful disregard of the Constitution."[26] The formal request which the President demanded, and which the Governors of West Virginia, Kentucky, and Pennsylvania had given, stated:

1. Disorder existed.
2. The state authorities were incapable of preserving the peace.

---

[24] The same, pp. 280-81. Judge Gresham had asked for troops at an earlier date only to hear from Attorney General Charles Devens that the troops at the disposal of the Secretary of War were so few that it would be impossible to furnish them at once. See Matilda Gresham, *Life of Walter Quintin Gresham*, Vol. I, p. 384.

[25] S. Doc. 263, 67 Cong. 2 sess., p. 281.

[26] July 28, 1877, p. 4.

3. The legislature was not in session.

4. The legislature could not be convened in time to meet the emergency.

5. The appeal to the President was to protect the state against domestic violence.

None of these criteria appeared in the message of Governor Williams. He simply stated that "in view of the threatened domestic violence growing out of the railroad strike, I request that authority be at once given to the Commandant of the Arsenal to render me all the aid possible in preserving the public peace.[27] It was highly embarrassing to Indiana's governor to have his request refused.[28] At the same time the President did not quibble over the matter of giving protection to the state. The presence of the troops was all that was needed, and for this he provided by sending in detachments of regulars from seven southern states.[29] Those arrested for interfering with trains in the hands of receivers were held for contempt of court. A number so held were sentenced to jail for periods of from thirty days to six months.[30]

Illinois. The strike reached Chicago on July 23. Fearful of an outbreak, Governor S. M. Cullom inquired of the Secretary of War whether any troops would soon be in the city. He was informed that a part of the Twenty-Second Infantry en route from Dakota would arrive within a very short time. A minor outbreak on the morning of the twenty-fifth and the increasing signs of further conflict caused the Governor to issue a formal call to President Hayes. Cullom's request was promptly granted. Colonel R. C. Drum, the commanding officer, was instructed to use the troops to suppress riots, under the orders of Governor Cullom.[31] The Governor, in turn, asked Drum to report to the mayor of Chicago. Several people were killed and many others wounded in a clash with the police during the morning of July 26, and the mayor sent an urgent request for assistance to Colonel Drum. However, no sooner had the Colonel

[27] S. Doc. 263, 67 Cong. 2 sess., p. 281.
[28] The *New York Times* spoke of the "stupid or dishonest Governor's request for troops," July 28, 1877, p. 5.
[29] H. Ex. Doc. 1, 45 Cong. 2 sess., Pt. 2, pp. 92-98.
[30] Gresham, *Life of Walter Quintin Gresham*, Vol. I, p. 407.
[31] S. Doc. 263, 67 Cong. 2 sess., p. 283.

placed the troops at the disposal of the state, in accordance with his first instructions, than word came that President Hayes wanted the troops used only to protect government property and to enforce the orders of the federal courts. Should an emergency arise he was to telegraph to Washington for further orders "unless circumstances make it impossible."[32] The reason for this sudden about-face, apparently, was that Hayes did not wish to issue a proclamation, and to place the troops at the Governor's disposal without such a proclamation would, he thought, be improper.[33] By July 30 some 650 regulars had reached Chicago. Although there were no further outbreaks, most of the troops remained in the city until the middle of August.[34]

In the southern part of Illinois at East St. Louis, and across the river in St. Louis, federal troops were used to protect the railroads which were under receivers appointed by the United States courts. This proved to be a very effective way of handling the strikers and their sympathizers. The presence of the troops, whose activities were limited to the protection of government property and the enforcement of court processes, had a salutary effect upon the whole body of strikers in that area. Within a few days the dispute was settled and without any appreciable damage.

Other states. The governors of Michigan, Wisconsin, and California also made requests of President Hayes, but with varying success. Fortunately, a critical situation did not develop in any of these states. Michigan's governor wanted the troops at Fort Wayne, near Detroit, made subject to his orders. This request was refused. Governor Ludington of Wisconsin wanted to know if the "three hundred old soldiers" at the Soldiers' Home in Milwaukee could be used as "a part of the national force, or as a part of the State militia." It was a week before his telegram was acknowledged, and in the meantime the danger had disappeared. In California, where

[32] The same, p. 284.
[33] See telegram to Lieutenant General Phil Sheridan, the same. See also George Frederick Howes, "President Hayes' Notes of Four Cabinet Meetings," *The American Historical Review*, Vol. XXXVII (1932), p. 289.
[34] From 20 to 35 people were killed during the rioting on July 25 and 26. An account of the disturbance in Chicago may be found in an unpublished thesis of Howard Barton Myers, *The Policing of Labor Disputes in Chicago: A Case Study*, pp. 108-59 (University of Chicago).

disturbances took the form of anti-Chinese demonstrations, Governor Irvin asked that the United States vessels at Mare Island take a position close to the city of San Francisco and the sailors be made subject to his call. He also requested arms and ammunition. Concerning his proposal to secure arms, the Governor was referred to the commanding officer of the area, who was given full discretion.[35] The Navy, however, was ordered to co-operate with the Governor.

Altogether there were disorders in 14 states.[36] In view of the lack of a strong national labor organization, it seems inconceivable that, within little more than a week after the strike at Martinsburg, the country should have experienced such widespread strife. The rapidity of the movement caught municipal and state governments unexpectedly. They were in too many instances totally unprepared to handle the hugh crowds of strike sympathizers and those of the lawless element who were quick to take advantage of the labor warfare.

THE POLICY OF HAYES

President Hayes became the target of all those who felt that their lives or their property were in danger. Railroad executives and other business interests, state and local government officials, even the strikers themselves, entreated the President to bring order out of the threatened or actual chaos.[37] Hayes did not take this added responsibility lightly.

Beginning on Saturday, July 21, the President held daily meetings with the Cabinet until the crisis was past. At their meeting Sunday, July 22, it was decided that when the President was agreed the state authorities could no longer cope with the strikers, he had the right to declare martial law.[38] The military forces of the United States would then occupy the districts where lawlessness prevailed. Fearful of creating a bad feeling between the states, the members of the Cabinet were of the opinion that the use of national forces would be preferable to calling the militia into the service of the federal

[35] S. Doc. 263, 67 Cong. 2 sess., pp. 287-88. See Howes, *The American Historical Review*, Vol. XXXVII, p. 289.

[36] Thomas A. Scott, "The Recent Strikes," *North American Review*, Vol. CXXV (1877), p. 357.

[37] *Hayes Papers* at Hayes Memorial Library, Fremont, Ohio.

[38] *New York Times*, July 23, 1877, p. 1.

government. They also discussed the necessity of calling the Congress into special session as that body had adjourned without making any appropriation for the army.[39] From early afternoon until midnight of what Hayes described as that "awful Sunday," the President kept in communication with the commanders who were moving troops.[40] That was the day when Pittsburgh was given over to the control of the mob, when the militia were driven from the city and the railroad properties were consumed in flames. Philadelphia was calling for protection; and the Secretary of the Treasury, John Sherman, was demanding a large federal force in Washington to guard the treasury and other government properties. On Monday morning the Cabinet met again. Notwithstanding the rapid spread of the strike, it was decided that events did not as yet warrant any such extreme measure as martial law.[41] At the Tuesday meeting, it was decided to furnish arms and ammunition from the government arsenals to bodies of citizens who were organized under local officers.[42] At the meeting on Wednesday, Secretary Evarts raised the question whether the government should not put the rioters in the position of levying war against the United States. Apparently this suggestion was favorably received. Hayes advised that a proclamation be prepared announcing the government's new stand. However, the decision as to its issuance was postponed. The proclamation, if prepared, was never published.[43]

Basis for federal action. Hayes made no effort to take control from the local authorities on the ground that the strike interfered with the exercise of a federal function, the handling of the mail. The strikers were careful in many instances to allow the mail cars to go through, but there were enough incidents to the contrary to have

---

[39] The Democratic House had refused to pass the army appropriation bill except on condition that certain limitations be placed on the use of the troops. On the ground that the House provisions interfered with the President's power as commander-in-chief, the Senate insisted on striking out the House amendments; hence, no appropriation. David Dudley Field, "The Army Bill," *Albany Law Journal*, Vol. XVI (1877), p. 198.

[40] *Diary and Letters of Rutherford Birchard Hayes* (Charles Richard Williams, ed.), Vol. III, p. 440.

[41] *New York Times*, July 24, 1877, p. 5.

[42] This was done in Ohio and Missouri.

[43] Howes, *The American Historical Review*, Vol. XXXVII, p. 188.

given a justifiable basis for action by the national government.[44] As early as July 22, the mail was stopped near Buffalo. At the same time, in Pittsburgh, mail was neither received nor sent but, instead, was stored in a warehouse until an opportunity arose for its transmission.[45] Service, in fact, was so interrupted that Postmaster General Key secured permission of the Superintendent of the Canadian Postal Service to send through mail, for points west of Toledo, on the Great Western Railway in charge of Canadian agents.[46]

Nor, although much advocated, was the interruption of interstate commerce used as a basis for federal action.[47] Troop movements took place for three reasons only: first, upon receipt of a formal call from an embarrassed state; second, to protect federal property; third, to enforce the mandates of the United States courts. The President expected the states to act first. A newspaperman who called at his home on Sunday evening, July 22, reported that Hayes thought vigorous measures should be used, but that the federal government would do nothing more than respond to calls made by the states.[48]

Strength of federal forces. As a matter of fact the states had to accept the responsibility. The federal government, regardless of what it might have wanted to do, was handicapped by lack of an adequate force. According to the Secretary of War, when the disturbance occurred in Pennsylvania, "there could not be found within that great state, so many as fifty Federal soldiers."[49] Congress had reduced the army to 25,000 men, and although the 3,300 soldiers in the Atlantic Division were supplemented by troops from other areas, Indian hostilities and Mexican border troubles made

[44] The interruption of the mail was not intended as an act of hostility toward the federal government. At Terre Haute, Ind., the United States Marshal, General Ben Spooner, reported that he felt it was his duty to move the mail train. With the assistance of 50 federal soldiers, he succeeded. However, this road was in the possession of a receiver. No effort was made to move trains belonging to railroads not under the jurisdiction of the United States courts. See Gresham, *Life of Walter Quintin Gresham*, Vol. I, pp. 399, 400.

[45] *New York Times*, July 23, 1877, p. 5.

[46] The same, p. 2.

[47] As early as 1866 Congress had passed legislation relating to the interstate transportation of goods by railway. See 14 Stat. L. 66.

[48] *National Republican*, July 23, 1877, p. 4.

[49] H. Ex. Doc. 1, 45 Cong. 2 sess., Pt. 2, p. iv.

inexpedient the transfer of the major portion of the regulars to strike duty.

With the small number of troops available, the army established a splendid record.[50] Their presence seemed to inspire confidence in the people and with but one exception there was no indication that the regulars had an irritating effect upon the rioters.[51] The record of the army was due, in part, to the President's desire for restraint in the use of the troops. Although confused by questions of command, both in relation to the army's position when aiding a state and when assisting federal marshals, Hayes was fixed in his determination to avoid unnecessary bloodshed.[52]

Charge of Communist influence. The newspapers were quick to place the blame for the disorders upon the Communists and their sympathizers. The President, on the other hand, was reported as denying that the outbreaks were "any evidence of the prevalence of a spirit of Communism, since their attacks had not been primarily directed against property in general, but merely against that of the railroads with which the strikers had had difficulties."[53]

The larger issue. Hayes was painfully aware of the fact that the mere restoration of order did little to settle the quarrel between employer and employee. He stated the issue in his diary for August 5: "The strikes have been put down by force; but now for the

[50] When, in the Cabinet meeting of July 26, Sherman reported that Hancock had found 3,000 troops east of the Mississippi, Secretary Evarts replied, "Well as the rioters kill none of them, that may be enough." Howes, *The American Historical Review*, Vol. XXXVII, p. 289.

[51] The troops were fired on at Johnstown while they were en route to Pittsburgh. The Secretary of War pointed out that the resistance "may have been in ignorance of the fact that it was made against the national troops." H. Ex. Doc. 1, 45 Cong. 2 sess., Pt. 2, p. xiii.

[52] See, for example, the command of Secretary of War McCrary to General Hancock, July 27, 1877. ". . . It is not deemed expedient at the present time to employ the military in making arrests of strikers, but process issued to assist in recovering possession of property may be enforced with the aid of the military if necessary. Bloodshed is to be avoided if possible and before other means are employed a demand should be made upon the insurgents to disperse and desist from resisting the process of the United States. . . ." *Hayes Papers.*

[53] *National Republican*, July 23, 1877, p. 4. In Pittsburgh, according to a *New York Times* editorial (July 24, p. 4), the rioters showed rare discrimination in not damaging private property. Such was "their tenderness for non-combatants that they actually carried a citizen's pile of lumber from the roundhouse which they had set on fire."

real remedy. Can't something [be] done by education of the strikers, by judicious control of the capitalists, by wise general policy to end or diminish the evil?"[54]

Appraisal of the President's course. The careful restraint of the President, added to the "specific accomplishment of exact orders" which characterized the troop movements, made a very favorable impression upon the country. The *New York Times* said that "the President and his advisers have exhibited from the very earliest manifestations of violence a degree of firmness and vigor beyond all praise."[55] The *National Republican* said that the President's handling of the strike "has caused the General Government to be everywhere recognized as a grand and beneficent power for good within its legitimate sphere."[56] All was not praise, however. Thomas A. Scott, president of the Pennsylvania Railroad, whose company had suffered severe losses in Pittsburgh, thought the strike had ably demonstrated the weakness of the governmental structure. He pointed out the long time interval that elapsed before effective aid was forthcoming. If the local governments were unable to handle the strikers, an appeal was sent to the state. If the state was unsuccessful, an appeal was then sent to the President. He thought it strange also that the only railroads which procured direct attention were those in receivership.[57]

It was true that the President's only positive employment of troops was to enforce the court processes. Even this procedure was not used until late in the strike period, and after he had observed the success attending the movements of the regular troops. It is, of course, impossible to say what the result would have been had not the President waited for an appeal from the states. A considerable force dispatched promptly to Pittsburgh might have prevented the events of that "awful Sunday," and, in addition, have prevented the spread of the strike. A statute passed in the reconstruction period could have been interpreted to authorize

---

[54] *Hayes Diary*, Vol. III, p. 440.
[55] Editorial of July 26.
[56] Editorial of July 28.
[57] "The Recent Strikes," *North American Review*, Vol. CXXV (1877), pp. 351-62.

such a procedure, regardless of a request from the state officials.[58] But there was no such force. It must be remembered, too, that Pennsylvania was using its own militia and was, apparently, able to care for itself. Had Hayes ordered the small number of troops available into the Pittsburgh inferno, they almost certainly would have been swallowed up. This, in turn, would have jeopardized the government's prestige throughout the entire country. Instead, the cautious and deliberate policy which Hayes pursued strengthened, rather than weakened, the position of the government. All in all, it is difficult to challenge the statement by a Washington writer that the President exercised "prudence and care" in his performance of "delicate and responsible duties."[59]

[58] Revised Statutes, 5299.
[59] *National Republican*, editorial, July 28, 1877, p. 2.

CHAPTER VI
THE COMMONWEAL AND THE PULLMAN STRIKE

The customary method of demonstrating the unimportance of Coxey's famous army of the unemployed is to point out that, upon reaching Washington, the 300 hungry survivors of the long trek were ignominiously arrested for walking on the grass. What is not mentioned is the fact that the President, the Attorney General, federal judges, United States marshals with hundreds of their deputies, and several hundred of the regular troops were endeavoring to maintain order and, to a considerable degree, control the movements of the Commonwealers who were moving toward Washington from remote parts of the country. Actually, the importance of the Commonweal has been greatly underestimated. The measures taken by the Cleveland administration to handle the minor disorders growing out of the efforts of Coxey's followers to reach the national capital in the spring of 1894 established precedents which were immediately drawn upon to suppress the much-publicized Pullman strike.

COXEY'S MARCH ON WASHINGTON

The Commonweal movement was the product of the business depression of 1893. The J. S. Coxey Good Roads Association of the United States had proposed a $500,000,000 issue of fiat money to be expended in highway improvement.[1] To focus the attention of Congress, and of the country at large, on the plight of those suffering from the depression, Coxey planned a march of the unemployed to Washington. The original army starting from Massillon,

[1] For the text of the bill and a contemporary account of the movement see Henry Vincent, *The Story of the Commonweal*, pp. 51-52. Coxey also proposed a non-interest-bearing bond bill. Any governmental unit wishing to make public improvements could deposit with the Secretary of the Treasury a 25-year bond, in an amount not to exceed one-half of the assessed value of its property. Treasury notes would then be issued to the unit. The same, pp. 52-53.

Ohio,[2] gave the Cleveland administration little cause for worry.[3] Conditions were such, however, that Coxey's idea quickly spread, and other armies were organized. Many hundreds of men started from remote points in the west. The long distance to Washington made some form of train travel indispensable. Where transportation was not given, it was taken. Hence arose the necessity for governmental action.

Federal intervention usually resulted from the fact that many of the western railroads were in the hands of receivers appointed by the United States courts. A district court would issue an order to the federal marshal to protect the receivers and to prevent the railway property from being molested. Injunctions were often issued, and any interference by the Coxeyites with the railroads would subject them to contempt proceedings. Numerous deputy marshals were necessary to execute the orders of the courts. In a period of two months so many deputies were required to maintain the peace in the 14 states and two territories where disturbances occured that Attorney General Richard Olney was compelled to ask for a deficiency appropriation of $125,000.[4]

With little regard for the orders of the courts or the efforts of the deputies, the Army of the Commonweal was determined to make its way eastward. Trains were seized on at least nine separate occasions in the states of Oregon, California, Wyoming, and Montana, and in Utah Territory.[5] The most famous incident occurred in Montana, where the Coxeyite contingent, commanded by a General Hogan, "took a loan on the rolling stock" of the Northern

[2] "When Coxey and Brown on Easter Sunday began their famous march from Massillon to Washington there were only about a hundred industrial soldiers in line behind the Army of the Commonweal, but this small force was escorted by no fewer than 43 special correspondents with four Western Union telegraphic operators and two line men. Never in the annals of insurrection has so small a company of soldiers been accompanied by such a phalanx of recording angels." (W. T. Stead, " 'Coxeyism,' A Character Sketch," *Review of Reviews*, Vol. X, 1894, p. 52.) Stead spoke of "Coxey and his tatterdemalion followers" as the "peripatetic advisers of social misery."

[3] Secret Service operatives kept a close watch on Coxey and his subordinates. For the reports of the operatives, see *The Papers of Grover Cleveland*, Mss., Library of Congress.

[4] *Fees and Expenses of U. S. Marshals*, S. Ex. Doc. 120, 53 Cong. 2 sess., p. 2.

[5] The same, pp. 2-20.

Pacific at Butte. In an effort to stop the Hogan forces, part of a bluff on the Crow reservation was dynamited. Not to be deterred by this maneuver, the General ordered his men to seize the tool car of the Montana division, which, as it happened, was in a railroad yard a short distance away. With picks and shovels the men cleared the rocks and dirt from the track. At Billings they were overtaken by a force of 100 deputy marshals. Outnumbered by more than six to one, the deputies got the worst of the general free-for-all which followed their attempts to arrest the members of the Commonweal. The eastward progress of this branch of the Coxeyites was suddenly terminated, however, when at midnight on April 25 the sleeping Hogan forces were surrounded by 250 soldiers of the regular army from Fort Keogh. They made no effort to resist and were taken to Helena.[6]

The marshals' appeals for aid were handled largely by Attorney General Olney. In this instance, however, he called the attention of the President to the activities of Hogan and his men. In addition to the requests for aid sent to Olney by the district judge, the United states attorney, and the marshal, Governor G. E. Rickarts telegraphed Cleveland asking that "Federal troops be ordered to overtake them."[7] That seemed the only solution. The court's injunction against meddling with railway property had been disregarded; the deputies had been overpowered in their efforts to arrest the marauders; the state's militia, according to the Governor, was of no value; and only the federal forces remained. After a conference with Major General John M. Schofield, Cleveland instructed the army to take action.[8]

General Schofield did his utmost to keep the army free from the charge of unduly harassing the members of the Commonweal. For example, James J. Hill proposed to Daniel S. Lamont, Secretary of War, that since the military authorities had exclusive control of

---

[6] Since there was no place to quarter such a large body of prisoners and their guards, the marshal was temporarily obliged to pay $25 a day for the use of a race track. (The same, p. 6.) Hogan received a 6-month jail sentence. Three other leaders received a 60-day sentence. War Department Archives, *Adjutant General's Office, 6370*, 1894.

[7] *The Washington Post*, Apr. 26, 1893, p. 1.

[8] The same.

Indian reservations it would be an easy matter to keep the trains from carrying "bodies of men other than regular passengers" beyond the boundaries of the reservations. Schofield replied to this suggestion in a memorandum to the Secretary, May 18, 1894:

[The members of the Commonweal] have the same right as others to the use of public highways, even though those public highways cross a military or Indian reservation. . . . It seems at least probable that many of the "Commonwealers" are only actuated by the laudable desire to get out of a country where they are no longer able to obtain subsistence. Would it not be better to let them go quietly, slowly and laboriously make their way whither they wish to go, while the necessary precautions are taken to prevent their seizing trains, destroying property, or otherwise violating the law.[9]

Schofield had previously given instructions that "no action of the troops shall tend to aggravate the difficulty or prevent an amicable adjustment between the contending parties." In a telegram to Brigadier General Merritt, the Chief of Staff stated that the policy of the administration was "to prevent, so far as may lawfully be done, the drift of unemployed and lawless persons toward the East; but no law is known which would justify the arrest of such a movement so long as the parties commit no crime, and only exercise the rights of citizens to go and come as they please."

Schofield was also quite insistent that the army officers understand the true legal position of the troops. He pointed out that the function of the army was not to assist the United States marshals, especially in arresting particular persons, but that the troops were to "act as the military power of the United States to do as required by law and under the orders of the Commander in Chief of the Army those things which the civil power had been unable to do. Hence the responsibility of the military commander to his military superiors for all his acts."[10]

During April, May, and June 1894, the government received numerous requests to prevent interference with the railroads. The procedures which were employed so successfully against the Commonweal were also used where the interference resulted from

[9] War Department Archives, *Adjutant General's Office, 6370,* 1894.
[10] The same.

strikes. Olney instructed the marshals to enforce the processes of the United States courts.[11] In the event resistance was greater than the marshals could overcome, federal troops were brought into action. One exception to this procedure, however, was later to plague the government. When the marshal for the Southern District of Illinois asked for troops to protect the railroads in receivership against violence from strikers, Olney replied as follows: "Understand State of Illinois is willing to protect property against lawless violence with military force if necessary. Please advise receivers to take proper steps to procure protection of property by civil authorities of the State. If such protection proves inadequate, the governor should be applied to for military assistance."[12] In apparently every other instance the Attorney General authorized the use of deputies or troops to execute the orders of the courts.

Olney's request for a deficiency appropriation to pay the deputies, who had been used chiefly against the Commonweal, was sent to Congress one day before the members of the American Railway Union joined the Pullman strikers. When renewed trouble broke out on the nation's railroads, Olney merely enlarged upon, and strengthened, the pattern which had worked so successfully during the preceding three months.

AMERICAN RAILWAY UNION V. THE PULLMAN COMPANY

The Pullman strike, like the Coxey movement, was a result of the hard times. Wages at the Pullman Palace Car Company had been reduced 25 per cent, although salaries of the officers and managers remained untouched, and although dividends had actually been increased.[13] In order to keep the plant operating, the company had taken contracts at a price less than the cost of labor and materials. In the opinion of the President's investigating commission, which was appointed near the end of the strike and which reported some months later, an undue proportion of this loss was thrown on the

[11] Following is a typical message of the Attorney General: "You are instructed to execute any order of the U. S. Court for the protection of persons and property against lawless violence by employing such number of deputies as may be sufficient for that purpose." S. Ex. Doc. 120, 53 Cong. 2 sess., p. 18.

[12] The same.

[13] A considerable part of the company's revenue came from the rental of Pullman cars.

workers by the reduction in wages.[14] Contending that wages and
rents were unrelated, the company refused to concede any reduction
in the high charges for living quarters.[15] Expression was finally
given to the "chronic discontent" of the employees when, on May
9, a committee representing all the departments went to the management and requested that the old wage level be restored. This
request which, according to the President's commission, was unreasonable, was refused. The company, unfortunately, would make
no concession whatever. On May 10, three members of the committee were laid off. That evening, the men, most of whom were
members of the American Railway Union, voted to strike. The 600
nonunion workers were immediately laid off, and the plant was
closed.

Action of the union. The American Railway Union was a new
organization whose object was to embrace all railway employees in
one brotherhood. Its growth was phenomenal, having secured a
membership of 150,000 in the period following its inception in
June 1893. The Pullman employees had joined the union little
more than a month before the strike occurred. They were considered
eligible for membership on the ground that the company had a
50-mile railway at Pullman with its own engines, shops, and yard,
and because the service was the same character as that of the roads
regularly engaged in transportation.[16] The Strike Commission was
of the opinion that it was very unwise on the part of the union to
construe its constitution so as to "include as eligible members those
who build cars and run them in and out over private switches."[17]
President Cleveland afterwards contended that the employees of
the Pullman Company

could not on any reasonable and consistent theory be regarded as eligible
to membership in an organization devoted to the interests of railway
employees. . . . It created a situation which implicated in a compara-

---

[14] *Report on the Chicago Strike by the United States Strike Commission,* S. Ex.
Doc. 7, 53 Cong. 3 sess., pp. xxi, xxxii, xxxiii.
[15] For a recent discussion of the living conditions in Pullman, see Almont Lindsey, "Paternalism and the Pullman Strike," *The American Historical Review,*
Vol. XLIV (1939), pp. 272-89.
[16] Testimony of George W. Howard in S. Ex. Doc. 7, 53 Cong. 3 sess., p. 15.
[17] S. Ex. Doc. 7, 53 Cong. 3 sess., p. xxvii.

tively insignificant quarrel between the managers of an industrial establishment and their workmen, the large army of the Railway Union.[18]

The error, however, was made, and the Pullman employees were
accepted as members.

In June, delegates from all parts of the country gathered in
Chicago for the convention of the American Railway Union. The
strike was a subject of considerable discussion, and committees were
selected to meet with Pullman officials. The company, however,
spurned all overtures on the part of the union. The convention
thereupon voted that if by June 26 the company remained unwilling
to arbitrate the dispute, the members of the union would no longer
handle Pullman cars. Thus the country's entire railroad system
was affected by the strike of 2,500 Pullman employees.

General Managers' Association as representative of employers.
The railroads also were organized and were determined to prevent
the union from carrying the boycott of Pullman cars into effect.
Some years before, the 24 lines centering in Chicago had formed an
extra-legal, it not illegal,[19] General Managers' Association. At a
meeting with an officer of the Pullman Company on June 22, the
association resolved to "act unitedly" in resisting the boycott.[20] The
Strike Commission reported that the General Managers' Association
established a strike headquarters, made provision for hiring men in
place of those who were discharged, and set up a press information
service. Later, the association kept constantly in touch with the civil
and military officials as to the most efficacious use of the armed
forces. It was responsible for "all the leadership, direction, and
concentration of power, resources, and influence" of the railroads.[21]

Olney recommends strong measures against strikers in Chicago.
The efforts of the union to cut out all Pullman cars from the trains
and the counter-movements of the railroads resulted very quickly
in a greatly impaired mail and transportation service. Reports of this
came to Attorney General Olney on the second day after the boycott
went into effect. His reply to a telegram from the United States

---

[18] Grover Cleveland, *The Government in the Chicago Strike of 1894*, pp. 5-6.
[19] S. Ex. Doc. 7, 53 Cong. 3 sess., p. xxxi.
[20] The same, p. xlii.
[21] The same, p. xliii.

attorney in San Francisco was later sent to the federal attorneys in many cities. It follows:

See that the passage of regular trains carrying United States mails in the usual and ordinary way, as contemplated by the act of Congress and directed by the Postmaster-General, is not obstructed. Procure warrants or any other available process from United States courts against any and all persons engaged in such obstruction, and direct marshal to execute the same by such number of deputies or such posse as may be necessary.[22]

The same message was sent to Thomas E. Milchrist, the United States attorney in Chicago. Accounts of the Pullman strike have failed to point out that the government's first act in Chicago was a definite alliance with the railway interests. Before any interference whatever with the trains carrying mail, Milchrist, on June 29, attended a meeting of the General Managers' Association and informed them of Olney's message. The next day he attended a conference of the various railroad lawyers and called their attention to the pertinent laws and cases. Milchrist wrote the Attorney General that "at these conferences the gentlemen referred to expressed their gratification with the resolute position assumed by you as shown by your telegram to me of the 28th instant, as well as with my willingness to aid in the repression of lawlessness and to suggest the means of so doing."[23]

Certainly the General Managers' Association should have been grateful to have the federal government as an ally. The action of Milchrist, taken apparently without Olney's knowledge, was merely the first step. The Attorney General was also to be of great help to the railroad interests. Desirous of the most expert legal assistance, Olney asked Edwin Walker, an able railroad attorney, to act with Milchrist in the government's behalf.[24] The determination of the Attorney General to curb the strike at its place of origin is seen in a letter to Walker on the day of his appointment. "It has seemed

[22] *Appendix to the Annual Report of the Attorney General for the Year 1896*, H. Doc. 9, 54 Cong. 2 sess., Pt. II, p. 17.

[23] The same, p. 58.

[24] According to Allan Nevins, the appointment of Walker was made at the suggestion of the General Managers' Association. *Grover Cleveland, A Study in Courage*, p. 616.

to me," Olney wrote, "that if the rights of the United States were vigorously asserted in Chicago, the origin and center of the demonstration, the result would be to make it a failure everywhere else and to prevent its spread over the entire country. . . ." He then suggested that the best means of breaking the strike would be "to go into a court of equity and secure restraining orders which shall have the effect of preventing any attempt to commit the offense." Olney ended his letter by giving Walker a hint as to how far the government was prepared to go in breaking the strike. He had authorized the employment of deputies as a matter of course, but "the true way of dealing with the matter," Olney concluded, "is by a force which is overwhelming and prevents any attempt at resistance."[25]

Walker had his own ideas about the procedure for the government to follow. He was in favor of criminal action against those who were delaying the mail. To call a special grand jury and investigate all offenses, he argued, would have a greater restraining effect than to proceed by injunction. To this plan Milchrist was opposed on the ground that since the fine for interfering with the mails was but $100, a conviction would have little effect.[26] Olney approved of Walker's plan, but only as a supplementary measure.[27] He favored, first of all, the plan of proceding under the injunction which Milchrist and the railroad attorneys had drawn up.[28]

The writ of injunction. The writ of injunction was unquestionably a masterpiece. Its scope was all inclusive, its provisions complete in every detail. In addition to enjoining all persons against any interference with the trains or from attempting to control the employees through "threats, intimidation, persuasion, force or violence," the injunction contained one paragraph which completely confounded the members of the American Railway Union. It follows:

And Eugene V. Debs and all other persons are hereby enjoined and restrained from sending out any letters, messages, or communications directing, inciting, encouraging, or instructing any persons whatsoever to interfere with the business or affairs, directly or indirectly, of any of

---

[25] H. Doc. 9, 54 Cong., 2 sess., Pt. II, p. 60.
[26] The same, p. 65.
[27] The same, p. 66.
[28] The same, p. 63.

the railway companies hereinabove named, or from persuading any
of the employees of said railway companies while in the employment of
their respective companies to fail or refuse to perform the duties of their
employment.[29]

An injunction of so sweeping a nature was highly satisfactory
to the railroad interests.[30] From many areas came requests for a
copy of the bill. Indeed, some action was necessary, for, by July 8,
Olney had received word of obstructions to the mails in at least
eleven states.[31]

Olney prepares the way for use of federal troops. To be effective,
Olney's plan of a vigorous assertion of the rights of the United
States at the "origin and center of the demonstration" had to be
carried out at once. Although he believed that the President had
the right to act on his own initiative to prevent interference with
interstate commerce and with the mails, the Attorney General proceeded on the supposition that Cleveland "could not be induced to
move except in support of the judicial tribunals."[32] "The Department of Justice," Olney wrote some years later, "in order to be
prepared for the exigency, *took measures to put itself in the position
which had induced the President to authorize the use of troops as
against the Coxey movement.*"[33]

Olney's telegrams to various United States attorneys, and his
special instructions to Milchrist and Walker, were parts of such
preparation. From Blue Island, outside Chicago, the United States
marshal had telegraphed, July 2, for troops to move the trains
and to handle a crowd of 2,000 rioters. Olney, apparently, took this
message to Cleveland, prepared to hear the President's refusal to
act. In this he was not disappointed. Cleveland, Olney records,
"deemed it best to follow strictly the precedent made in the Coxey
case and not to move until satisfied that he must do so by proof

[29] S. Ex. Doc. 7, 53 Cong. 3 sess., pp. 179-80. The injunction was based on the
Sherman Act of 1890.
[30] The General Managers' Association called the injunction "a gatling gun on
paper." Nevins said that "it was rather an entire battery." *Grover Cleveland, A
Study in Courage*, p. 618.
[31] H. Doc. 9, 54 Cong. 2 sess., Pt. II, pp. 4-213.
[32] "Extracts from Olney's Memorandum," in Henry James, *Richard Olney and
His Public Service*, p. 203.
[33] The same, p. 201. Italics added.

that could not be resisted."[34] If Olney's way of dealing with the strike by an overwhelming force was to be used, evidence must be supplied showing that troops were necessary to uphold the processes of the courts. This the Attorney General proceeded to get. On July 3, he dispatched a suggestive telegram to Edwin Walker:

> . . . Legal situation could not be improved. . . . Understand you think time for use of United States troops has not arrived. If the time does come they will be used promptly and decisively. Rely upon you to advise me when the exigency necessitates use of troops. If practicable have United States attorney and marshal and judges unite in statement of the justifying facts.[35]

A similar telegram was sent to Milchrist.[36] The attorneys saw what Olney wanted and immediately secured a statement from Marshal J. W. Arnold, which they and Judge P. S. Grosscup signed.[37]

During the same morning, July 3, Cleveland talked with Major General Nelson A. Miles, Commanding General, Department of the Missouri. Miles advised against the use of troops, but he had been away from his headquarters in Chicago for some time and his opinion, consequently, carried little weight. Major General Schofield, who had issued orders the preceding day to have the troops at Fort Sheridan prepared to move into the city, had been somewhat irked to learn that Miles was not in Chicago. The departmental commander had come from New York to Washington, but he did not remain long in the capital city for Cleveland agreed with a suggestion made by Schofield that the General return at once to his command.[38]

Miles was already on his way when the telegram arrived signed by the marshal, the judge, and the attorneys. The message had an immediate effect. The President, Olney wrote, was "perfectly content to be able to justify himself on the ground that they [the troops] were employed merely to enforce judicial processes."[39] At 4:00 P.M. General Schofield gave the order for the command at Fort Sheridan

[34] The same, p. 202.
[35] H. Doc. 9, 54 Cong. 2 sess., Pt. II, p. 66.
[36] The same, p. 65.
[37] The same, p. 66.
[38] J. M. Schofield, *Forty-Six Years in the Army*, p. 494.
[39] James, *Richard Olney and His Public Service*, p. 50.

to move into the city.[40] He instructed Colonel Crofton, who was in charge of the troops, to confer with Marshal Arnold and Attorneys Milchrist and Walker. Nothing was said about conferring with the governor of Illinois or the mayor of Chicago. No notification, even, was sent them. They were entirely ignored.[41]

Altgeld protests use of federal troops. Governor John P. Altgeld strongly resented the uninvited entry of federal troops into the state. On July 5, in a sharp protest to Cleveland, the Governor pointed out that during a recent coal strike the militia had twice given satisfactory assistance to the United States marshal for the Southern District of Illinois.[42] If the marshal for the Northern District needed militray aid, continued Altgeld, he would have received it upon receipt of the request. The Governor challenged Cleveland's right to send troops into the state:

> . . . the conditions do not exist here which bring the cause within the Federal statutes, a statute that was passed in 1881 [1861], and was in reality a war measure. This statute authorized the use of Federal troops in a state whenever it shall be impracticable to enforce the laws of the United States within such states by the ordinary judicial proceedings. Such a condition does not exist in Illinois. There have been a few local disturbances, but nothing that seriously interfered with the administration of justice or that could not be easily controlled by the local or State authorities, for the Federal troops can do nothing that the State troops cannot do.[43]

Altgeld was in error in his statement that the statute under which Cleveland acted was a war measure. The law to which the Governor

[40] Schofield, *Forty-Six Years in the Army*, p. 497.

[41] *Biennial Message of John P. Altgeld, Governor of Illinois to the 39th General Assembly*, Jan. 9, 1895, p. 45. The arrival of the troops, according to Superintendent Michael Brennan, was opportune. Calls from the railway companies were frequent, and the 3,000 members of his force were about worn out. For several days they had been on duty almost constantly in an effort to police adequately the 2,100 miles of railroad and the 186 square miles of territory within the city limits. (S. Ex. Doc. 7, 53 Cong. 3 sess., p. 354. See also p. 349.) At this time the mayor had made no effort to relieve the police by calling for the state militia even though Governor Altgeld had previously extended immediate assistance to other localities requesting help. See Harry Barnard, *"Eagle Forgotten," The Life of John Peter Altgeld*, pp. 290-93.

[42] At Olney's direction the marshal had requested aid from the state. See p. 91.

[43] For the correspondence between Cleveland and Altgeld, see Robert McElroy, *Grover Cleveland, The Man and the Statesman*, pp. 151-63.

referred was passed in 1861, but it was largely a revision of the acts of 1795 and 1807.[44] Altgeld's contention that no condition existed making impossible the enforcement of laws by ordinary judicial proceedings may have been true. Cleveland had been informed otherwise and, in the wording of the statute, "the judgment of the President" was the controlling factor.

Cleveland took issue with Altgeld on only one point: his right to send troops into the state. The President's reply follows:

Federal troops were sent to Chicago in strict accordance with the Constitution and laws of the United States, upon the demand of the postoffice department that obstruction of the mails should be removed, and upon the representations of the judicial officers of the United States that the process of the Federal courts could not be executed through the ordinary means, and upon competent proof that conspiracies existed against commerce between the States. To meet these conditions, which were clearly within the province of Federal authority, the presence of troops in the city of Chicago was deemed not only proper, but necessary, and there has been no intention of thereby interfering with the plain duty of the local authorities to preserve the peace of the city.

With federal intervention based on three different grounds, this statement sounded very convincing. Yet it was not sufficient to satisfy Governor Altgeld. He immediately sent a second telegram of protest. Of even greater length than the first message, this one also was a curious compound of truth and error. By this time the situation in Chicago had become such that the President was in no mood for argument. His reply was very brief:

While I am still persuaded that I neither transcended my authority or duty in the emergency that confronts us, it seems to me that in this hour of danger and public distress discussion may well give way to active effort on the part of all authority to restore obedience to law and protect life and property.

This message was sent when Cleveland's "patience was somewhat

---

[44] See the *Congressional Globe*, 37 Cong. 1 sess., July 16, 1861, pp. 145-46. For the acts of 1795 and 1807, see 1 Stat. L. 424 and 2 Stat. L. 443. Altgeld's biographer makes the same mistake when he says that the law of 1861 was enacted "purely as a war measure." See Waldo R. Browne, *Altgeld of Illinois, A Record of His Life and Work*, pp. 165-66.

strained.[45] Whether or not the rebuke was deserved, it effectively took the place of a reply to the Governor's arguments. Cleveland, in fact, never did undertake that task.

State militia called out. There was good reason for the President to be worried. For over a week following the arrival of the regular troops, Cleveland watched with great anxiety as outbursts of violence became frequent. Freight cars were overturned and burned or their contents scattered, switches were torn apart, and railroad buildings and other property destroyed. Traffic on a number of lines was at a standstill. Efforts of the soldiers to move the trains were stubbornly resisted. General Miles kept calling for re-enforcements. The railroad managers had no plans. "We are simply waiting for more troops—that's all we can do," said a stockyards official.[46] Mayor Hopkins, who thus far had made no appeal for the state's militia, now (July 6) asked Altgeld for five regiments.[47] Within a half hour Hopkins received word that the troops had been ordered to the city. They arrived during the night. By this time the armed force was quite large. All told, there were 14,000 men in Chicago engaged, at some time during the strike, in the effort to preserve order. Of this number only 2,000 were federal troops, the remainder being composed of 3,000 policemen, 4,000 members of the militia, and 5,000 deputy marshals.[48]

The President's tardy proclamation. During this period the President was in constant touch with Olney, Schofield, and Secretary of War Lamont. The Secretary, in fact, stayed at the White House.[49] A special wire was provided from there to the headquarters of

[45] Cleveland, *The Government in the Chicago Strike of 1894*, p. 44.

[46] *The Washington News*, July 6, 1894, p. 1.

[47] Edwin Walker wrote Olney concerning the Mayor: "I do not believe he realized how serious the situation was until Friday morning, the 6th instant, when he requested the Governor to call out the State militia. From that date on I have heard no criticism upon the action of the Mayor, and I believe he has done everything in his power to preserve the peace and protect property." H. Doc. 9, 54 Cong. 2 sess., Pt. II, pp. 92-93.

[48] S. Ex. Doc. 7, 53 Cong. 3 sess., p. xix. The deputies proved to be very ineffective. Walker pointed out that many of them were "worse than useless." For the activities of the deputies see Barnard, *"Eagle Forgotten," The Life of John Peter Altgeld*, pp. 312-14. See also *The Policing of Labor Disputes in Chicago: A Case Study*, pp. 250-60. This is a manuscript of Howard Barton Myers, University of Chicago, 1929.

[49] *The Washington News*, July 5, 1894, p. 1.

General Miles.[50] On July 8, Cleveland prepared a proclamation declaring that those who resisted or obstructed the execution of the laws of the United States "cannot be regarded otherwise than as public enemies."[51] The President was in error in so long delaying the issuance of the proclamation. He did so only after being roused by a blast from Governor Pennoyer of Oregon concerning Cleveland's first reply to Altgeld. "When the President asserted that the Federal troops were sent to Chicago in strict accordance with the Constitution and laws of the United States," said Pennoyer, "he probably forgot that by section 5300 of the Revised Statutes, based upon an old common law rule, he is positively required to precede the use of troops by proclamation. It was for a like non-compliance with a like parliamentary requirement that King Charles I of England lost his head."[52] This statute had been completely overlooked.[53] At no time during the Coxeyite troubles had the requirement been followed.[54] Cleveland lost no time in rectifying the oversight.

When General Miles was asked whether the proclamation meant martial law, he replied: "It amounts to the same thing. It means that whoever disobeys it is a public enemy, and as such is to be destroyed."[55] Walker had early made the suggestion that martial law be proclaimed, but Olney thought it impossible until Altgeld invoked federal aid, an action which, he said, would thereby put the "United States in complete control of the situation."[56] This interpretation of the government's position, that is, full control, was the same as that which President Hayes had reached, but which was never put into practice in the railroad strikes of 1877. Nor was it on this occasion. It is highly unlikely that Cleveland considered his proclamation as a declaration of martial law. Such a step would not have been consistent with his first reply to Altgeld that, even

---

[50] The same, July 12, p. 1.

[51] 28 Stat. L. 1249.

[52] *The Washington News*, July 7, 1894, p. 4.

[53] Revised Statute 5300 is as follows: "Whenever, in the judgment of the President, it becomes necessary to use the military forces under this title [Insurrection-containing R. S. 5298 under which Cleveland acted] the President shall forthwith, by proclamation, command the insurgents to disperse and retire peaceably to their respective abodes, within a limited time."

[54] Olney admitted as much. James, *Richard Olney and His Public Service*, p. 205.

[55] *The Washington News*, July 9, 1894, p. 1.

[56] H. Doc. 9, 54 Cong. 2 sess., Pt. II, p. 77.

though federal troops were called out, "there has been no intention of thereby interfering with the plain duty of the local authorities to preserve the peace of the city."

Overlapping lines of authority. One development in the handling of troops was the subject of much confusion and the cause of great irritation to General Schofield. His theory was that "when the civil power ceases to be effective and the President is required to exercise his authority as commander-in-chief of the army, his acts become purely military, untrammeled by any civil authority whatever."[57] The troops, he believed, were not required to heed either the state officials or the federal marshals. With the sanction of the President and the Attorney General, Schofield had issued an order embodying such a principle during the troubles with the Commonweal. Issued May 25, 1894, as General Orders, No. 15, Schofield's instructions were as follows:

Whenever the troops may be lawfully employed, under the orders of the President, to suppress "insurrection in any State against the government thereof," as provided in section 5297 of the Revised Statutes; or to enforce the execution of the laws of the United States "when by reason of unlawful obstructions, combinations or assemblages of persons" it has "become impracticable, in the judgment of the President, to enforce, by the ordinary course of judicial proceeding, the laws of the United States," as provided in section 5298 of the Revised Statutes, the troops are employed as a part of the military power of the United States, and act under the orders of the President, as commander-in-chief, and his military subordinates. They cannot be directed to act under the orders of any civil officer. The commanding officers of the troops so employed are directly responsible to their military superiors. Any unlawful or unauthorized act on their part would not be excusable on the ground of any order or request received by them from a marshal or any other civil officer.[58]

Schofield expected the same procedure to be followed during the time the troops were in Chicago, but for over a week there was confusion concerning the position the federal marshal occupied in the disposition of the soldiers. Finally, however, it was definitely established that troop movements were to be the sole responsibility of the military authorities.

The fact that there were soldiers of two governmental jurisdic-

[57] Schofield, *Forty-Six Years in the Army,* p. 508.
[58] The same, pp. 505-06.

tions under no central command was also a source of worry. In a confidential report to the Adjutant General, General Miles expressed his fears:

There is in a military sense, a condition of affairs which ought not to exist. There are six regiments belonging to the State of Illinois, now on duty in Chicago under the orders of the Mayor of the City. I am not apprised even of their location or any of their movements. I learn indirectly they are in some cases together and in others scattered as police parties. Should any serious outbreak occur, like those that have occurred in other cities, . . . there would be great danger of the armed forces of the United States coming in conflict with those of the city and state.[59]

The General's position was undoubtedly sound. Fortunately, however, his fears were unrealized.

While public attention was chiefly directed toward Chicago, the President was literally besieged with reports of disturbances in other parts of the country. In Sacramento, the federal marshal appealed to the governor of the state for militia to assist him in moving the trains. The soldiers, however, were unreliable and refused to act. Regulars and marines were then brought in and the trains were moved without difficulty. In Oakland, because of the dearth of troops, 370 sailors and marines were taken from their ships, organized as an infantry unit, and used for guard duty at the railroad terminal.[60] In Los Angeles, 300 troops under Colonel William R. Shafter were used to guard the railroad depots and trains. That the workers were not alone at fault was demonstrated by United States Attorney George J. Denis, who successfully adopted a new device for moving the trains. He served an injunction not only on the strikers but also on the managers of the Southern Pacific and Southern California roads. "The purpose of the Government," he said, " is to show that every one on whom the injunction applies shall be served with it. There is nothing to prevent the companies from moving trains, and as the Government has furnished ample protection, it wants to know why the roads do not move."[61]

[59] July 18, 1894. *Adjutant General's Office, 1348*, File 1, No. 10.
[60] *Report of the Secretary of War*, H. Ex. Doc. 1, 53 Cong. 3 sess., Pt. II, p. 114.
[61] *The Washington News*, July 6, 1894, p. 1. See also H. Doc. 9, 54 Cong. 2 sess., Pt. II, pp. 28-40.

Governor W. J. McConnell of Idaho sent a formal appeal to the President for assistance in preventing violence in Shoshone County. The disorder there was caused chiefly by striking miners, who gave little trouble after the arrival of the troops.

Disturbances in other states. Requests for aid came to Washington in such great numbers that it was impossible to keep in close touch with all the troop movements.[62] Finally, General Schofield reported, ". . . it became necessary to confer upon the commanding generals of six departments . . . full authority in executing the orders of the President, to employ the entire military force under their command, according to their own best judgment and the instructions they had received from Headquarters of the Army."[63]

In most of the states where disturbances threatened, the procedure was the same, namely, concerted action by three federal officials, attorney, judge, and marshal. The state authorities were usually in agreement with such action. Altgeld was not alone, however, in his protests. Governor Hogg of Texas telegraphed Cleveland that "the State of Texas is able to control the situation and to enforce the law and protect rights guaranteed by the State and Federal Constitution and she will do it. You are notified that you may not feel called upon by the plea of any alarmist to use United States troops here unless requested by State authority."[64]

In Colorado, troops were called out when a force of 290 deputies proved unable to cope with the strikers.[65] Governor Waite protested against such action. He advanced the same argument as Altgeld, that county and state authorities should have been asked to help before federal troops were brought onto the scene. The action of the marshal in this instance must have been extraordinary, for Waite's message to Cleveland added: ". . . by whose authority does Marshal Israel violate the Constitution as to arrests and usurp your authority to suspend the writ of habeas corpus in Colorado?"[66]

---

[62] On July 9, the President issued a second proclamation, this time applying to "North Dakota, Montana, Idaho, Washington, Wyoming, Colorado, California, and the Territories of Utah and New Mexico." 28 Stat. L. 1250.

[63] H. Ex. Doc. 1, 53 Cong. 3 sess., Pt. II, p. 60.

[64] Quoted from Nevins, *Grover Cleveland, A Study in Courage*, p. 626.

[65] H. Doc. 9, 54 Cong. 2 sess., Pt. II, pp. 42, 44.

[66] *The Washington News*, July 7, 1894, p. 4.

Disorders in Missouri caused the marshal at Kansas City to employ over 650 special deputies.[67] Governor Stone refused to take any action, condemning the government instead for its "impertinent interference." He addressed a protest to Cleveland against the "arbitrary and unnecessary misuse of Federal authority in this State."[68]

The procedure in one other state should be noted. In spite of federal deputies, a mob at Hammond, Indiana, had caused considerable damage to railroad property. On July 8, the federal judge, the marshal, and the district attorney in a joint telegram to Olney asked for troops. They stated further that Governor Matthews was working with them and that he also "asks the cooperation of Federal troops in protecting the mail trains and Federal officers." It is difficult to say whether the Attorney General's reply was merely an exception to his customary response or whether, and this seems more probable, by this time the pressure from dissatisfied governors had caused him to exercise greater caution. Whatever the reason, Olney suggested that the Governor call "upon the President for protection against domestic violence under article 4, section 4, of the Constitution of the United States."[69] This Governor Matthews proceeded to do. Hammond is but 20 miles from Chicago, and the regulars arrived sometime before the state militia, who had also been called. The efforts of the federal forces to move the trains angered the mob, and a clash resulted in which one or more rioters perished. With the arrival of the militia, the regulars withdrew.

Trial of Debs. On July 10, indictments for conspiracy were returned against Debs and other leaders of the American Railway Union, and they were at once placed under arrest. Debs was released on bail but when, a week later, contempt proceedings were instituted, he made no effort to raise the bond of $3,000 and was at once committed to jail. Debs testified later that "the strike was broken up by the Federal courts of the United States, and not by the Army, and not by any other power, but simply and solely by

---

[67] H. Doc. 9, 54 Cong. 2 sess., Pt. II, p. 142.

[68] *The Washington News*, July 7, 1894, p. 4.

[69] For the message quoted above, see Frederick T. Wilson, *Federal Aid in Domestic Disturbances*, S. Doc. 263, 67 Cong. 2 sess., pp. 298-99.

the action of the United States courts in restraining us from discharging our duties as officers and representatives of the employees."[70] Debs had paid little attention to the injunction but chose
instead to keep in touch with the strikers in all parts of the country.
According to Edwin Walker, the strike leader sent an average of
300 telegrams a day down to the eighth of July.[71] This, of course,
was a direct violation of the writ. Debs's statement of the reason for
the strike's failure is deserving of special attention. He did not say
that his arrest and removal from the scene caused the breaking of
the strike. It had largely collapsed before he was placed in jail.
The action of the court in "restraining" the union leaders from
discharging the duties of their offices demoralized the railway employees. To them it seemed evident that they were fighting not only
the railroads but the government of the United States as well.

Olney thought it unaccountable that Debs had not been advised
to try to break the injunction in the courts. The question of its
legality and propriety, he pointed out, could have been raised immediately by a motion for dissolution.[72] However, since, as Nevins
had indicated, Judges Grosscup and Woods, who issued the injunction, had also aided Milchrist in drawing up the application, it is
highly improbable that such a motion would have been favorably
received.[73]

Debs and several other strike leaders were found guilty of contempt and sentenced to jail for terms varying from three to six
months. They appealed to the Supreme Court for a writ of habeas
corpus, but their petition was denied. In an opinion handed down
May 27, 1895, Justice Brewer upheld the power of the executive
branch to prevent obstructions to the mails and to interstate commerce either by means of physical force or through recourse to the
civil courts.[74]

Cost of the strike. Compared with the railroad troubles in the
Hayes administration, the total loss in lives and property over the
entire area was considerably less than the loss in Pittsburgh alone

[70] S. Ex. Doc. 7, 53 Cong. 3 sess., pp. 143-44.
[71] H. Doc. 9, 54 Cong. 2 sess., Pt. II, p. 85.
[72] James, *Richard Olney and His Public Service*, p. 203.
[73] *Grover Cleveland, A Study in Courage*, p. 618.
[74] *In re Debs*, 58 U.S. 564 (1895).

during the great riot of July 1877. The President's Strike Commission reported that "in Chicago and vicinity" twelve persons were shot and fatally wounded. They estimated the loss to the railroads "in property destroyed, hire of United States deputy marshals, and other incidental expenses" to be "at least $685,308."[75] The Chicago fire department estimated the damage in the city at $355,612.[76] Although the property loss throughout the rest of the country is unknown, there is no indication that the total was very high.

Appraisal of Cleveland's course. Whether this loss could have been avoided had the government pursued a more conciliatory course is a matter of speculation. The terms of the injunction were undoubtedly too far-reaching. With this, however, Cleveland had little to do; too little in fact. Every action of the administration was directed toward breaking the strike. There is no evidence that Cleveland or any federal official, either before or during the period of violence, attempted to bring about a settlement of the dispute. There was little sympathy manifested by the government toward the American Railway Union. Many people, in fact, thought it deserved no sympathy. After all there had been deliberate interference with the nation's transportation system in order to win a local struggle.

It would be futile to amass the evidence showing the necessity, or lack of it, for sending federal troops to Chicago. Cleveland was within the law.[77] Even so, his failure to co-operate with the state and local authorities was a blunder. That the protests of Altgeld were not taken lightly was demonstrated when the time came for

[75] S. Ex. Doc. 7, 53 Cong. 3 sess., p. xviii. A number of the marshals in Chicago were hired, directed, and paid by the railroads. (The same, p. 340.) Others in Chicago and those commissioned in the different states were paid by the government. Olney asked for an appropriation of $255,000 to pay them. H. Doc. 9, 54 Cong. 2 sess., Pt. II, p. 224.

[76] *Biennial Message of John P. Altgeld, Governor of Illinois to the 39th General Assembly,* p. 43.

[77] In his excellent book, *"Eagle Forgotten," The Life of John Peter Altgeld,* Harry Barnard states (p. 315) that Cleveland "knew well the accepted procedure for suppressing disorder, that first the local authorities are to act, then the state authorities, and only after both have failed and call for help does the national government enter the picture. Yet he disregarded that procedure ruthlessly, without conducting any investigation of his own." This statement is obviously in error. A national law does not depend upon state enforcement, nor are the orders of a federal court dependent upon state action. The statement is correct when applied to a state's inability to enforce its own law.

the removal of the troops. Both General Miles and Secretary of War Lamont sent telegrams to Mayor Hopkins asking if, in his judgment, the soldiers should remain any longer.[78]

Nevins' conclusion, that the President was unduly influenced by his Attorney General, is inescapable.[79] Cleveland, apparently, took no part in the preliminary struggle, and by the time the matter was brought to his attention the government's course was already charted. The President's only choice was to go ahead. He was willing to go to the extreme of calling out the troops, however, only after he was satisfied that their use was necessary to enforce the processes of the courts. This statement is important and demands further amplification. In his first reply to Altgeld, Cleveland based federal interference on three grounds, namely, to uphold the courts, to prevent obstructions to the mails, and to protect interstate commerce. In his address at Princeton in 1904, on "The Government in the Chicago Strike of 1894,"[80] Cleveland further emphasized the mail and interstate commerce aspects as bases for his decision to use force. Actually, if Olney's account is correct, Cleveland did not use the forces of government directly to prevent hindrance to the mails and to interstate commerce. There was no precedent for such an action and the President was hesitant to exercise the power. Obstructions to the mails and to interstate commerce were restrained by the orders of the courts. Cleveland acted to enforce the court processes.[81] In so doing he was treading upon familiar ground.

[78] S. Ex. Doc. 7, 53 Cong. 3 sess., p. 352.
[79] *Grover Cleveland, A Study in Courage*, p. 627.
[80] Later issued by the Princeton University Press, the address first appeared in the July 1904 issue of *McClure's Magazine*. Altgeld was dead but Debs replied to the President. (See *The Chicago Socialist*, Aug. 27, 1904, pp. 1-2.) While preparing the address, Cleveland wrote to Olney, Jan. 7, 1902, as follows: "My remembrance is a little hazy as to the legal steps, injunctions, and certificates of inability to serve or enforce which preceded *troops*." Allan Nevins, *Letters of Grover Cleveland*, p. 554.
[81] "The fact remains a matter of public notoriety that the troops were called out to aid in the enforcement of equity process." (See Charles C. Allen, "Injunction and Organized Labor," 28 *American Law Review* 850 (1894).) The use of troops on the Northern Pacific Railroad adds further support to the contention that Cleveland's action to prevent obstructions to the mails and to interstate commerce was indirect rather than direct. By act of Congress the Northern Pacific, whose construction was due to federal appropriations, had been designated as a post route and military road subject to the use of the United States for various kinds of government service. It was also in receivership. There was no question here about

Fresh in Cleveland's memory was the easy, yet effective, manner in which the military had protected the railroads while the various Coxeyite contingents were struggling to reach the national capital. On July 3, 1894, the evidence presented to the President caused him to believe that the time had again come when the use of the army was necessary. Perhaps no one was more surprised than he at the great furor caused by his decision.

It is unfair to condemn Cleveland solely on the basis of his part in the handling of the strike at Chicago. The operations of the railroads, as the President pointed out, were affected, to some extent, in 27 states and territories.[82] Disorder, either threatened or real, was a cause for worry in many states. Some action by the government was essential. Had the administration permitted the strike to continue and to grow, it is highly probable that a major disturbance would have resulted, for it is almost inconceivable that the General Managers' Association would have admitted defeat. As it was, every available soldier in the military departments of the west was in action.[83]

Yet it seems very unfortunate that Cleveland was persuaded to proceed with such haste. By so doing he neglected to observe the amenities so essential to the preservation of good relations between the nation and the states. A cause for even greater regret is the fact that, without thorough investigation and without any attempt to reconcile the differences between the railroads and the strikers, the President permitted the legal and physical forces of the federal government to be used in a manner which was of almost exclusive benefit to one of the disputants.

---

the use of troops. For weeks they accompanied the trains. The point is that where Cleveland was sure of his position, he acted in a direct manner. But where there was neither an act of Congress nor any precedent to serve as a guide, he chose to rely on the much-abused procedure for enforcing the orders of the courts.

[82] Cleveland, *The Government in the Chicago Strike of 1894*, p. 3.
[83] *The Washington News*, July 6, 1894, p. 1.

CHAPTER VII

DISTURBANCES IN IDAHO'S COEUR D'ALENE

Within a period of seven years three presidents, Harrison, Cleveland, and McKinley, were called upon by as many worried governors to assist in preserving the peace in Idaho's Coeur d'Alene mining region. Located in the northern part of the state, in Shoshone County, the district was famed for its lead mines, the ore from which yielded a considerable amount of silver.

PRESIDENT HARRISON AND THE DISTURBANCES OF 1892

Quarrels between the mine owners and their employees were frequent. The problems of wages and unionization were twin obstacles of considerable magnitude. Efforts of the union to force an increase in the wage level caused the operators to import workers from other areas. The riot at Homestead, Pennsylvania, on July 5, 1892, was reported to have encouraged the men in the Coeur d'Alene also to resort to violence as a means of combating the mining companies. On July 11, the mill at one mine was blown up. Three nonunion men were killed and a number of others wounded. Other mines were compelled to surrender their property and to dismiss their nonunion workers.[1] The town of Wardner was seized, and further destruction of life and property seemed imminent.

Governor Norman B. Willey thereupon telegraphed to President Harrison requesting that troops from Fort Sherman be dispatched to the disturbed district. The Governor pointed out that he was calling on the 196 members of the National Guard but that such a force was insufficient. Furthermore, he continued, the legislature was not in session and could not be promptly convened. Help was expected from the government also because Fort Sherman was but

---

[1] See testimony of John A. Finch in *Report of the Industrial Commission on the Relations and Conditions of Capital and Labor Employed in the Mining Industry*, Vol. XII, p. 490. Also see letter of Governor Frank Steunenberg in *Coeur d'Alene Labor Troubles*, H. Rept. 1999, 56 Cong. 1 sess., p. 18.

a few miles from Wardner, whereas, due to the geography of the country, the state forces were a long journey distant.

Harrison was in the state of New York and did not receive the message until the following day. He immediately instructed Major General John M. Schofield, who was serving in the dual capacity of Army Chief and Acting Secretary of War, to send an adequate force, "with orders to co-operate with the civil authorities in preserving the peace and protecting life and property."[2] Apparently as an after-thought, "as a measure of precaution, and in the hope that it may tend to allay excitement,"[3] Harrison issued a proclamation commanding those resisting the laws to "disperse and retire peaceably to their respective abodes."[4] This was not sent, however, until July 16, after the rioting had ceased.

In the meantime, on July 13, United States Senator W. B. Heyburn sent his colleague, Fred Dubois, a description of the tense situation existing in the mining area:

We are as helpless as children. It looks as though the soldiers would get there in time to act as funeral escorts to our dead if weather is favorable. . . . We are unable to understand why it should take twenty-four hours to get troops from Sherman to Wardner in time of War when it takes five hours in time of peace. . . .[5]

The troops arrived at Wardner on July 14. Colonel William P. Carlin, who was in command, defended the late arrival of the regulars. The superintendent of the Bunker Hill mine, Carlin reported, fearful of another dynamiting episode, had asked that the coming of the troops be delayed so that the nonunion men could have time to get out of town.[6] As a matter of fact, a second clash had occurred on July 12, when workers who were waiting for a steamboat to take them out of the district were set upon by armed rioters.

[2] The messages of Governor Willey and President Harrison are to be found in Frederick T. Wilson, *Federal Aid in Domestic Disturbances*, S. Doc. 263, 67 Cong. 2 sess., p. 191.
[3] Statement of Secretary of War S. B. Elkins, the same, p. 192.
[4] 27 Stat. L. 1030.
[5] War Department Archives, *Adjutant General's Office*, 34728, 1892.
[6] Senator Heyburn contended that Carlin had been deceived by bogus messages. However, the commanding officer's careful approach to Wardner was "fully approved" by General Schofield. The same.

The Fort Sherman regulars, reinforced by detachments from Fort Spokane, Washington, and Forts Missoula and Keogh, Montana, and the Idaho National Guard, met with no resistance whatsoever.[7] Strange indeed, in view of the fact that federal soldiers had been sent to "support" and "assist" civil authorities was the position of the Idaho troops. They acted "in conjunction with the United States troops and in accordance with the directions" of Colonel Carlin.

All told, over 300 persons were arrested.[8] Army officials refused to honor the application of the federal marshal for troops to act as prison guards without specific authorization from the President. Harrison immediately directed that the aid of the troops "be given to the United States Marshal in guarding the prisoners in his custody, and, if necessary in transit to Boise City, or wherever they may be taken for trial."[9]

Although there was no longer any violence, Governor Willey was very anxious that the troops remain "for a considerable time." To his request, Secretary of War Elkins replied that "the President does not desire that the troops shall remain under your orders longer than absolutely necessary to assist you to restore order. He can not say how long they should remain, but hopes you can, through the militia and civil power, soon relieve the situation, so the troops can be withdrawn."[10] This indefinite answer was very satisfactory to the Governor, who needed the troops to lend weight to his proclamation of martial law. Some of the regulars remained to guard the prisoners until the courts could dispose of the cases, and it was after the middle of November before civil authority was completely restored and the last of the troops removed.[11] Peace was

[7] Letter of Colonel William P. Carlin in *Report of the Secretary of War*, H. Ex. Doc. 1, 52 Cong. 2 sess., Pt. II, pp. 110-11.

[8] Colonel Carlin's enthusiasm in following the rioters led him into a legal indiscretion. With three companies he set out in pursuit of a body of 90 men who were rumored to be near the Montana line. He telegraphed Governor Toole for permission to cross into Montana, then went on without waiting for a reply. Unable to find the rioters, he returned next day to find that the Governor had refused his request. The same, p. 112.

[9] War Department Archives, *Adjutant General's Office, 34728, 1892.*

[10] S. Doc. 263, 67 Cong. 2 sess., p. 298.

[11] War Department Archives, *Adjutant General's Office, 34728, 1892.*

established but, unfortunately, the undercurrent of ill feeling remained.

FEDERAL TROOPS ORDERED TO WARDNER BY PRESIDENT CLEVELAND

The Pullman strike was the signal for a new outbreak. On July 3, 1894, forty masked men shot and killed one John Kneebone, who had been a principal witness for the state in 1892. Some days later a mine superintendent was taken captive. An attempt was made to blow up the power house of the Bunker Hill mine at Wardner. As a result of these incidents, many inhabitants of the district became terror-stricken.[12] Once again the governor, this time W. J. McConnell, called for federal troops.[13] His request was granted by President Cleveland, and an infantry company from Fort Sherman was stationed in Wardner for a period of three weeks.

PRESIDENT McKINLEY AND THE OUTBREAK OF 1899

In the years following 1894 there were isolated instances of violence, but it was not until 1899 that an outbreak occurred which the governor deemed too large for state authorities to handle. In April, an effort was made to unionize completely the Bunker Hill and Sullivan Mining Company at Wardner and to compel the payment of regular union wages. On April 29, a Northern Pacific train was seized and the engineer compelled to carry the miners from several towns to Wardner. Nearly 1,000 men, some 200 of whom were armed and masked, gathered at the Bunker Hill mine. By means of 3,500 pounds of stolen dynamite, the $250,000 concentrator, one of the world's largest, was blown to bits.[14] Two men were killed in the hail of bullets which signalled the success of the project of destruction.[15] After this demonstration, the men boarded the train,

[12] Letter of Governor Steunenberg to Elihu Root, Secretary of War, H. Rept. 1999, 56 Cong. 1 sess., pp. 18-19.
[13] S. Doc. 263, 67 Cong. 2 sess., p. 199.
[14] The company claimed the mill was worth $250,000. However, by the sworn statement of the management, the mill had been placed on the tax duplicate of the county at a valuation of $51,000. See remarks of Representative John J. Lentze in *Congressional Record*, 56 Cong. 1 sess., App., p. 464.
[15] See "Review of Evidence," *Report of the Industrial Commission*, Vol. XII, pp. xvi-xvii. Also see H. Rept. 1999, 56 Cong. 1 sess., pp. 6-7.

later to be denominated the "Dynamite Express," and without further incident returned from whence they came.

Declaration of martial law by Governor. Without consulting the local authorities, in whom he had no confidence, Governor Frank Steunenberg immediately appealed to President McKinley. The members of the Idaho National Guard, Steunenberg said, were in the Philippines, and a force of 5,000 troops was essential to maintain the peace.[16] The Governor's appeal was acted upon immediately. Brigadier General H. C. Merriam, commanding the Department of the Colorado, was instructed to confer with the Governor and to call upon "such troops as may be most convenient without regard to departmental lines."[17] Merriam thereupon instructed detachments from seven different army posts, a total of over 500 men, to proceed to the Coeur d'Alene region. As he was not sure whether Governor Steunenberg intended to proclaim martial law, Merriam decided to take matters into his own hands. On May 2, he sent the following cipher telegram to Adjutant General H. C. Corbin:

Troops concentrating at Wardner and Mullan will control outlets from mining camps. If not disapproved, I will direct to scrutinize travel outward and detain suspected passengers. This is martial law, but no other course likely to secure rioters.[18]

His message was submitted to McKinley and approved.[19] This situation, of course, was somewhat irregular. Here was a limited form of martial law being established by the United States although it was preceded by no announcement either from the President or from the commanding officer. On May 3, however, Steunenberg declared martial law. That General Merriam was not sure of his position is evidenced by his statement that the Governor's telegram announcing the declaration "was received with great satisfaction, for it seemed to me preferable in every way that the executive of the state should establish martial law, if it were to be applied within his State."[20]

[16] H. Rept. 1999, 56 Cong. 1 sess., p. 7.
[17] Letter of Adjutant General H. C. Corbin, the same, p. 8.
[18] "Report of the Major General Commanding the Army," in *Report of War Department*, H. Doc. 2, 56 Cong. 1 sess., Pt. I, p. 30; War Department Archives, *Adjutant General's Office*, 231071, 1899.
[19] H. Doc. 2, 56 Cong. 1 sess., Pt. I, p. 30.
[20] The same.

On May 4, Merriam was asked whether the situation was such as to require a presidential proclamation. He replied that there was no sign of any organized resistance.[21] Since there was no disturbance, McKinley thought a proclamation unnecessary and, as a consequence, did not issue one at all.

Order concerning re-employment. Shortly after martial law was declared, State Auditor Bartlett Sinclair, the Governor's representative, issued an order forbidding all operators to employ any miner who did not have a permit from the state authorities. A copy of the order was submitted to General Merriam, who suggested an additional clause requiring the applicant for a permit to deny his participation in the riot of April 29 and to renounce membership "in any society which has incited, encouraged, or approved of said riots or other violations of public law." At the bottom of the order, under the signature of Sinclair, appeared the statement "examined and approved," followed by the signature of General Merriam.[22]

Labor organizations at once sent letters of protest to McKinley. At first, apparently, he gave little thought to the subject, and answers to the letters were handled through the regular channels in a rather desultory fashion. Protests continued to come, however, and by May 26 the President's frame of mind had changed entirely. On that day his Acting Secretary, George B. Cortelyou, sent word to Secretary of War Alger that "it is the President's understanding that no orders whatever have been issued by General Merriam as to who shall work or not work, and that he has only been supporting the State authority in preserving the peace. The President desires to know whether his information on this point is correct." That evening at eleven o'clock the following message from Adjutant General Corbin was sent to Merriam directly from the White House:

It is charged . . . that owners of mines in the Coeur d'Alene district are denied the right of employing any man unless he first makes affadavit that he is a non-union miner, and the army sent to aid the State authorities to preserve peace and protect property is being used to enforce the alleged order. The statement must be the result of some misunderstanding

---

[21] The same, p. 31.
[22] The same, pp. 34-36.

which should be promptly corrected. The President wishes a statement of facts at once.[23]

Merriam denied the charge, and the incident was closed with Alger's admonition that "the army must have nothing whatever to do with enforcing rules for the government of miners or miners' unions."[24] In the minds of the labor leaders, this message absolved the administration, although not General Merriam, from what was considered a gross restriction on their right of contract.[25]

Arrest and imprisonment of rioters. From the moment of their arrival the troops were busily engaged assisting the state authorities in their efforts to effect a complete roundup of all persons suspected of participating in the dynamiting and murder at the Bunker Hill mill. Within three days 350 arrests were made, usually without warrant. All told, over 700 persons were arrested, but some were released very quickly.[26] Of the 528 for whom statistical records were made, 396 proved to be foreign born and of these over half were aliens.[27]

Upon their arrest the miners were placed in a warehouse. It was very soon filled to capacity, and about 200 were quartered in box cars where "an abundance of hay" was furnished, as in the warehouse, to make their stay more comfortable.[28] At the end of three weeks, during which Merriam wrote the Governor that all the prisoners "are very uncomfortable and with unsanitary conditions which will soon become intolerable," a new prison was made ready. By the middle of June there were still 330 prisoners. In describing their living quarters to the Adjutant General, Merriam again spoke

---

[23] H. Rept. 1999, 56 Cong. 1 sess., p. 122.

[24] The same, p. 123.

[25] Testimony of James R. Sovereign in *Report of the Industrial Commission,* Vol. XII, p. 394.

[26] A famous trial arising out of the disorder was that of Paul Corcoran, secretary of the miners' union at Burke. William E. Borah, acting under a special appointment from Governor Steunenberg, prosecuted Corcoran, who had been arrested and charged with murder, arson, and conspiracy. The verdict was second degree murder, and Corcoran was sentenced to prison for 17 years. He was later pardoned. For an interesting account of the trial, see Claudius O. Johnson, *William E. Borah,* p. 75 ff.

[27] H. Doc. 2, 56 Cong. 1 sess., Pt. I, p. 40.

[28] The same, p. 34.

of the "abundance of hay."[29] Many complaints were made of the ill treatment of those in the "bull pen" by the soldiers, especially by the colored troops, eight companies of whom had been the first to arrive. Word reached the President that the prisoners had been denied counsel, but Governor Steunenberg branded the report an "absolute falsehood."[30]

For a period of three months few specific protests came to the President. On September 27, however, word came from Edward Boyce, president of the Western Federation of Miners, that the 100 prisoners remaining in the bull pen had been placed on a bread and water diet and were suffering extremely brutal treatment. Mc-Kinley thereupon sent the message from Boyce and the following brief command to the Secretary of War: "Important. Inquire of governor and military commander. This condition, if true, must be stopped."[31]

Elihu Root, who had succeeded Alger as Secretary of War, sent the message of Boyce to both Steunenberg and General Merriam. The Governor replied that the statement of Boyce was a "base falsehood in every particular."[32] General Merriam called upon Captain Edwards, then in command of the troops, for an explanation and received a somewhat different answer. Five of the prisoners were caught digging a tunnel through which to escape. Edwards ordered them to fill in the hole but they refused and their attitude was sustained by the other prisoners. The captain then directed an eight-day bread and water diet for all except the sick, during which time the bedding of hay, which was removed for "sanitary reasons," was not replaced.[33]

This incident prompted Root to ask that the civil guards be substituted for the troops so that the latter might be withdrawn. Steunenberg pleaded for more time, and it was not until the end of October that the soldiers were released from their task.[34] However, they

[29] The same, p. 58.
[30] The same, p. 59.
[31] The same, p. 64.
[32] The same.
[33] The same, p. 65.
[34] Root's letter was dated September 28. The long reply of the Governor was

were still stationed near Wardner at the time the congressional investigating committee reported in June 1900.[35]

Report of the congressional investigating committee. The committee which Congress established to investigate the affair brought a number of witnesses from Idaho and in the early months of 1900 amassed a great amount of evidence. Dividing on strict party lines, the Republican majority acquitted the administration on every charge while the Democrats submitted a short but scathing criticism. The impending presidential election undoubtedly greatly influenced this strict party division.

At the time of the committee's report, opponents of the President condemned his consent to the use of troops as one more demonstration of his subserviency to the industrial interests.[36] This criticism was based on telegrams introduced before the committee, illustrations of which follow:

Armed mob of strikers have destroyed our mill at Wardner, Idaho. Governor has appealed for Federal troops. Please do what you can for us and save immense damage and bloodshed.

As representative and treasurer of the Bunker Hill and Sullivan Mining Company, I earnestly endorse the request of the governor of Idaho to the effect that Federal troops be ordered to protect our property, now in course of destruction.

An armed mob has destroyed valuable property in Wardner, Idaho, in which Jack Hammond, James Houghtelling, and others of your [addressed to President's secretary] friends are interested. The governor has asked for Federal troops. Please lend your interest to this appeal with the President.[37]

The arrival of these telegrams coincident with the President's order for the use of troops is no reflection on McKinley. The "special interest" charge seems untenable. A formal request for help had come from a governor who was in the midst of a violent disturbance.

dated October 10. Actually, it was not written until October 24 or 25, after the Governor had visited Washington and talked with Secretary Root on three different occasions. Steunenberg admitted this before the congressional investigating committee. See *Congressional Record,* 56 Cong. 1 sess., App., p. 492.

[35] H. Rept. 1999, 56 Cong. 1 sess., p. 129.

[36] *Congressional Record,* 56 Cong. 1 sess., App. p. 464.

[37] H. Doc. 2, 56 Cong. 1 sess., Pt. I, pp. 53-54.

There was little time for an investigation inasmuch as serious violence had already occurred. In complying at once with the request of Governor Steunenberg, McKinley was doing exactly what his immediate predecessors had done under similar circumstances.

McKinley's failure to give careful supervision. On the other hand, from the available evidence of the congressional committee and the testimony taken by the Industrial Commission in July 1899, it seems clear that the President should have been more alive to the series of problems raised by the entrance of the federal forces. The point has been made, and rightly, that the administration is to be criticized for acts of omission rather than for acts of commission.[38]

McKinley's error in approving Merriam's questionable use of the General's own brand of martial law is an indication of the looseness and lack of supervision which characterized the use of the troops in the Coeur d'Alene. Had the soldiers been on duty for only a few days it would be difficult to place any blame on the President if, through the commander's misconception of his duty, the troops were not acting in a strictly legal manner. After many weeks, however, the soldiers were still acting in the capacity of prison guards, and in other respects serving merely as the agents of the state. Even then, unfortunately, McKinley conducted no investigation as to their need. For month after month federal troops assisted the state executive in the maintenance of complete domination over the entire mining region. Surely McKinley might have asked that the legislature give its approval of this extraordinary procedure. He might well have insisted that the state raise the small force necessary to police the area. Instead, at no time was there any suggestion from McKinley or any federal officer that the state legislature be convened. A little more attention on the part of the President would have saved the administration from a great amount of criticism and, of more importance, would have saved the people of the Coeur d'Alene from unnecessary suffering. By a prompt response to the Governor's request for troops McKinley was carrying out the national government's constitutional obligation to preserve the states from domestic violence. By permitting the troops to remain for such a long period, without conducting an adequate inquiry as

[38] Edward Berman, *Labor Disputes and the President of the United States*, p. 42.

to their necessity, and in view of the type of control established in
the area, the President was neglecting the like obligation to guarantee to every state a republican form of government.[39]

[39] To forestall violence, President Theodore Roosevelt also sent troops to the
Coeur d'Alene. In March 1906, Governor F. R. Gooding wrote to Taft, who was
then Secretary of War, stating that a disturbance was likely to result from the
forthcoming trial of several members of the Western Federation of Miners, who
were under indictment for the murder of ex-Governor Steunenberg. Gooding asked
that federal troops be placed under his orders. Taft explained that the military
forces of the United States must always act under the president, but that Roosevelt
had directed him to say that, upon proper application, troops would be furnished
to restore order.

On April 18, Roosevelt sent Taft the following confidential note: "What have
you done about getting some more troops quietly into Idaho—or even not quietly
if necessary?" Acting on Taft's instructions the Chief of Staff, J. F. Bell, ordered
two troops of cavalry from Fort Walla Walla, Washington, on a practice march
to the Boise Barracks. Five officers and 64 enlisted men left Fort Walla Walla on
April 23, traveled 310 miles, and "arrived in fine condition," May 4. Four days
later Captain William Yates reported that his men were "thoroughly rested and
ready for return march." However, he was ordered to hold the troops at Boise
until further notice. This order was repeated in the middle of June. War Department Archives, *Military Secretary's Office, 1112529, 1906.*

CHAPTER VIII

DISORDERS IN THE ADMINISTRATION OF
THEODORE ROOSEVELT

Professor Laski has observed that Theodore Roosevelt's "great verbal audacity" was "accompanied by a relative caution in action."[1] An examination of the instances when aid was requested of him lends considerable support to Laski's assertion. In his account of the famous Pennsylvania Anthracite Strike, Roosevelt intimates that he would ride roughshod over any group suspected of creating a disturbance.[2] When he was actually called on for assistance, how-

[1] Harold J. Laski, *The American Presidency, An Interpretation*, p. 93.

[2] "The method of action upon which I had determined in the last resort was to get the Governor of Pennsylvania to ask me to keep order. Then I would put in the army under the command of some first rate general. I would instruct this general to keep absolute order, taking any steps whatever that was necessary to prevent interference by the strikers or their sympathizers with men who wanted to work. . . . I had to find a man who possessed the necessary good sense, judgment, and nerve to act in such event. He was ready to hand in the person of Major-General Schofield. I sent for him telling him that if I had to make use of him it would be because the crisis was only less serious than that of the Civil War, that the action taken would be practically a war measure, and that if I sent him he must act in a purely military capacity, under me as commander-in-chief, paying no heed to any authority, judicial or otherwise except mine. . . . He answered quietly that if I gave the order he would take possession of the mines, and would guarantee to open them and to run them without permitting any interference either by the owners or the strikers or anybody else, so long as I told him to stay. I then saw Senator Quay. . . . [I asked him to arrange] that whenever I gave the word the Governor of Pennsylvania should request me to intervene; that when this was done I would be responsible for all that followed, and would guarantee that the coal famine would end forthwith. The Senator made no inquiry or comment, and merely told me that he in his turn would guarantee that the Governor would request my intervention the minute I asked that the request be made.

"These negotiations were conducted with the utmost secrecy, General Schofield being the only man who knew exactly what my plan was. . . . I was glad not to have to take possession of the mines on my own initiative by means of General Schofield and the regulars. I was all ready to act, and would have done so without the slightest hesitation or a moment's delay if the negotiations had fallen through." (Theodore Roosevelt, *An Autobiography*, pp. 474-75.)

A further illustration of Roosevelt's "great verbal audacity" is to be found in his account of the Morenci incident in the territory of Arizona: "The miners struck, violence followed, and the Arizona Territorial authorities notified me that

ever, he not only displayed considerable reluctance to send troops but was very vigilant that their use might not be unwarranted or unduly prolonged.

THE STRIKE AT TELLURIDE, COLORADO

Colorado found the period at the turn of the century an exceedingly troublesome one. In the metalliferous mining centers, labor outbreaks were common. Efforts to increase wages, to bring in the eight-hour day, or to effect unionization were stoutly resisted by officials of the large mining companies. Violence, either threatened or real, was such that, in the eleven years from 1894 to 1905, state militia were called out no fewer than nine times, several of which were for extended periods. The state auditor estimated the cost of transporting and maintaining the militia during these periods of military occupancy to be in excess of $1,000,000.[3]

On but one occasion was an appeal made to the federal government, and even then the desire to shift the policing cost was, perhaps, a larger factor than the disturbance itself. In September 1903, Governor James H. Peabody ordered a force of 1,000 militia into the Cripple Creek district on condition that the Mine Owners' Association provide the necessary funds pending action by the state legislature.[4] Rather than resort to this questionable procedure again, when a strike occurred at Telluride, Peabody called on

---

they could not grapple with the situation. Within twenty minutes of the receipt of the telegram, orders were issued to the nearest available troops, and 24 hours afterwards General Baldwin and his regulars were on the ground, and 24 hours later every vestige of disorder disappeared." (The same, p. 494.) It is true that within a very short time after the request was received, troops were ordered to Morenci. But Roosevelt had nothing to do with the order. He was in Cleveland at the time. His Secretary of War, Elihu Root, was at West Point. The President's assistant secretary, B. F. Barnes, received the message from Isaac T. Stoddard, Acting Governor of Arizona Territory. The Acting Secretary of War and the Acting Adjutant General were responsible for the orders to General Baldwin. Instead of the troops' reaching Morenci in 24 hours, they were delayed by a washout and did not arrive until June 12, 1903, almost three days after the order was sent from Washington. By the time of their arrival all disorder had ceased. War Department Archives, *Adjutant General's Office*, 488494, 1903.

[3] *A Report on Labor Disturbances in the State of Colorado from 1880 to 1904, Inclusive, with Correspondence Relating Thereto*, S. Doc. 122, 58 Cong. 3 sess., p. 360.

[4] The same, p. 175. See also *Statement of the Western Federation of Miners*, S. Doc. 163, 58 Cong. 2 sess., p. 29.

President Theodore Roosevelt. The dispute centered around the demand by the regular workers at the Telluride mill for an eight-hour rather than a twelve-hour day. No outbreak had actually taken place, but violence seemed imminent because of the company's decision to work the mines and mills with nonunion men.

On November 16, Peabody sent a short telegram to the President asking that General Baldwin, commanding the Department of the Colorado, be instructed "to furnish me such aid as I may call for."[5] After discussion of the question in the Cabinet meeting on the following day, Secretary of War Elihu Root was instructed to send a negative answer to the Governor's request. The controlling statute, Root pointed out, prevented the President from authorizing any action on the part of the military until proper application was made. He promised, however, that the government would act when a requisition was made in the manner "contemplated by law."

Before Root's reply reached the Governor, Peabody had sent a second, more urgent, message to the President. The state, he said, had "exhausted every means at its command to enforce the law, suppress lawlessness, and protect life and property there and elsewhere in the State. . . ."[6] The Governor concluded his plea by requesting that Baldwin be instructed to "furnish me such aid, immediately, as I may call for."

Again Roosevelt declined to take action, and this time Root sent a somewhat more detailed explanation of the law governing intervention by the national government. A disturbance, he pointed out, referring to section 5297 of the Revised Statutes, must amount to an insurrection against the government of the state. This fact, continued the Secretary, together with the state's inability to effect adequate control, must be demonstrated to the President before he can judge "whether the exigency has arisen upon which the Gov-

---

[5] The correspondence between Root and Peabody is to be found in S. Doc. 122, 58 Cong. 3 sess., pp. 9-11.

[6] The Governors' careful wording of this sentence, it was later revealed, protected him from the accusation of completely misrepresenting the situation. The militia were not on duty at Telluride but their use "elsewhere" had eaten up all available funds. In an interview Peabody admitted that his request was based on the fact that there was no money in the state treasury to pay the militia. The same, p. 195.

ernment of the United States is bound to interfere." The President, Root concluded, could not place the military forces at the disposal of the Governor, "but must himself direct their operations."

After twice refusing to assist the Governor, Roosevelt directed that an inquiry be conducted into the extent of the disturbance. Major General John C. Bates was appointed to make the investigation. In a letter of instructions to Bates, the Chief of Staff[7] concisely stated the government's position:

> . . . you will bear in mind that compliance with such a call as is here made is, under well established precedents, not to be ordered as a matter of convenience and for the suppression of a mere disturbance, but must in every instance be based upon urgent necessity proceeding from open, organized, and armed opposition to the execution of the laws of the State which the State authorities, civil and military, are clearly unable to overcome.[8]

Bates was also instructed to determine whether there were any violations of the laws of the United States.

The government's investigator reported that the disturbance had really amounted to an insurrection. The civil authorities, he said, had not maintained order, and the presence of state militia was necessary. However, Bates continued, unless there were further disorders, there was little need for federal troops. He was also of the opinion that there was no violation of the laws of the United States necessitating the intervention of the federal government.[9]

The report of Bates was dated November 29. Two days later Roosevelt received a different kind of request. Several men had been arrested and threatened with deportation from the district. William D. Heywood, secretary of the Western Federation of Miners, wired the President asking protection for these men under the civil rights statutes.[10] Both of Colorado's representatives in the

---

[7] Lieutenant General S. B. M. Young.
[8] S. Doc. 122, 58 Cong. 3 sess., p. 13.
[9] The same, p. 15. The Western Federation of Miners took offense at Bates's statement that the civil authorities had failed to maintain order. They pointed out that while on his tour of investigation Bates was the guest of the Mine Owners' Association. A United States naval captain, on the other hand, who had been in the district, had not only found no insurrection but had expressed his sympathy for the cause of the miners by a donation of $500. S. Doc. 163, 58 Cong. 2 sess., p. 34.
[10] The same, p. 32.

United States Senate interviewed Roosevelt at the behest of the Federation, but he declined to act on the ground that "he had neither the power nor the right to intervene."[11] The men threatened with deportation were merely fined, but in the early months of 1904, while state troops controlled the district under martial law, large numbers of men were forcibly ejected from Telluride.[12] Again the President was asked to intervene. John H. Murphy, general counsel for the Western Federation of Miners, wrote a long letter to Roosevelt entitled, "What is the Duty of the President?"[13] Murphy argued that the "driving away of men from their homes and preventing them from returning thereto" was a violation of the Fourteenth Amendment. The civil rights statutes were also pointed out as authorizing presidential action. Roosevelt, however, refused to intervene and the struggle continued as a local issue.

LABOR TROUBLES AT GOLDFIELD, NEVADA

The part played by President Theodore Roosevelt in the Goldfield, Nevada, labor disturbances demonstrates, in a commendable fashion, a temperate, decisive method of dealing with state calls for federal intervention. Deceived into sending troops by an urgent, though unnecessary, message of a governor, Roosevelt strongly asserted his presidential prerogatives and forced an unwilling state executive to take positive measures for policing troubled zones.

Cause of the strike. Located in Southern Nevada, Goldfield, in 1907, had an estimated population of from 15,000 to 20,000. Labor disputes were all too frequent. The incident which was shortly to bring federal soldiers to Goldfield arose over the manner of making wage payments. As a result of the financial panic of that year an acute currency condition caused the companies comprising the Goldfield Mine Operators' Association to make payment in the form of scrip.[14] Advertisements shortly appeared offering to cash the scrip at a discount. The miners set up the demand "that the employers

---

[11] The same, p. 33.
[12] S. Doc. 122, 58 Cong. 3 sess., pp. 200-06.
[13] There are numerous letters in the files of the Department of Justice asking federal protection against deportation. Letters to the President were referred to the Department of Justice.
[14] The miners referred to the scrip as "Christian Science money."

of labor shall back these checks with reasonable guarantee of their value as a medium of exchange."[15] The company employers' association thought this an unnecessary and unjustified request and, when no satisfactory agreement could be worked out, 1,900 miners went out on strike, November 27, 1907.

The governor's appeal for federal help to prevent violence. On the afternoon of December 4, the President received a telegram from Governor John Sparks stating that "in the *near* future . . . Nevada *may* expect serious labor troubles . . . which *may* result in violence and great destruction of property. . . . The sheriff of the county seems to be absolutely unable to cope with the situation."[16] Sparks also mentioned the state's impotence to maintain order because of the lack of an organized militia. He then requested that a "small detachment" of troops be stationed at Goldfield. Nevada's Senator, George Nixon, telegraphed from New York expressing the hope that the Governor's request would be granted.

The nearest body of soldiers was located at the Presidio Barracks in San Francisco, 18 hours away. Before answering the Governor's request the President ordered two companies of troops to make preparations for an immediate departure. He then notified Governor Sparks that before the troops could be moved, a call would have to be made in accordance with the constitution and statutes of the United States. Although Roosevelt indicated the laws governing the call, Sparks demonstrated a most amazing lack of care in drafting

[15] *The Evening Star*, Washington, D.C., Dec. 5, 1907, p. 1. Winfield Hogaboom's "The Last Stand at Goldfield," in the *Overland Monthly* for February 1908, gives a different version of the strike's cause. A brief summary of his article follows: The basic difficulty between the operators and the union was over the problem of "high grading," that is, the miners' lucrative practice of secreting ore of high grade in their clothes. Efforts of the operators to adopt change rooms were stoutly resisted by the miners, and the local officials would do nothing to help prevent the practice. The rich ore attracted the more unscrupulous members of the Western Federation of Miners and these troublemakers made conditions unbearable for the operators. The currency issue was, for the operators, the last straw, and they determined to beat the union.

Hogaboom may have overemphasized this factor. Certainly the immediate cause of the disturbance in question was over the issuance of scrip. Hogaboom admits as much. See p. 114. See also statement of the miners in the *Evening Star*, Dec. 7, 1907, p. 2.

[16] *Papers Relative to Labor Troubles at Goldfield, Nevada*, H. Doc. 607, 60 Cong. 1 sess., p. 3. Italics added.

his reply. His second request was based on one statute,[17] while the citations he gave were to two others.[18] As proof of the need for troops, the Governor listed such happenings as "unlawful dynamiting of property, commission of felonies, threats against the lives and property of law abiding citizens," and other crimes.[19] This recital was sufficient to satisfy the President, who was interested more in the substance than the form of the request, and he directed Acting Secretary of War Robert Shaw Oliver (Taft was in Europe) "to send a sufficient number of troops to be wholly adequate to meet any emergency. It is far better to avoid conflict by sending too many troops than by sending too few to run the risk of inviting bloodshed."[20]

Oliver instructed Brigadier General Funston, who was in command of the Department of California, to explain to the officer in charge of the troops that it was essential to consult with the governor of the state and the local civil authorities but that "in his acts, he will be guided solely by such instructions as he may receive from the President and from the commanding officer of the Department and by his own judgment of the military situation."[21] The Acting Secretary also notified Funston to send the following instructions to the commanding officer at Goldfield:

The President directs you to use utmost caution and good judgment in the very delicate and responsible situation which confronts you. Firmness and good nature are equally necessary. Anything rash or impulsive is to be avoided. So far as feasible, trouble is to be avoided, and the actions of the troops should make it evident to everyone that any difficulty that may arise has not been provoked by the troops but simply met when it has arisen. You should be especially conservative in speech, and say nothing whatever which is not absolutely necessary in fulfilling and carrying out your duty.[22]

The mere sending of the troops to Nevada did not, in the eyes of Roosevelt, constitute a cause for the issuance of a proclamation.

[17] R.S. 5299.
[18] R.S. 5297, 5298.
[19] H. Doc. 607, 60 Cong. 1 sess., p. 4.
[20] Roosevelt to Oliver, War Department Archives, *Adjutant General's Office,* *1310155F,* 1907. Hereafter cited as *A.G.O.*
[21] *A.G.O. 1310155K,* 1907.
[22] *A.G.O. 1310155J,* 1907.

One was prepared and dispatched to Funston with the request that he advise the War Department whether conditions were such as to warrant its issuance. The General replied at once recommending the publication of the proclamation, but apparently the President felt that the recommendation was not based on actual knowledge of the situation at Goldfield. As a result no action was taken. Two days later, December 9, after receiving the report of Colonel Alfred Reynolds, who was in immediate command of the troops, Funston advised that the issuance of the proclamation be deferred. Reynolds reported that the president of the miners' union had promised him that there would be no armed resistance to the execution of the law. The Colonel was instructed from Washington to telegraph the Adjutant General immediately whenever anything arose making the proclamation necessary.

Roosevelt insists that troops act only to preserve order. Nine companies of soldiers arrived in Goldfield on December 7. The next day the operators announced not only a reduction in wages but their determination no longer to employ any workmen affiliated with the Western Federation of Miners. This action naturally aroused considerable resentment and had it not been for the troops a clash might easily have followed. The operators admitted that they were responsible for the appeal to the President and this seemed, to the miners, to put the federal administration on the side of the mine owners.[23] Even General Funston seems to have had that impression. "It is my understanding," he wired the Adjutant General, "that if the Governor or his representative requests it the mines and those working them should be protected by troops."[24] This message, which Funston dispatched the evening of December 10, as he was preparing to leave for Goldfield, caused somewhat of a furor in Washington.

The next morning Roosevelt called to the White House J. F. Bell, Chief of Staff, Herbert Knox Smith, Commissioner of Corporations, and Lawrence O. Murray, Assistant Secretary of Commerce and Labor. In a memorandum to Oliver, Bell stated that in the presence of Smith and Murray, Roosevelt gave him a message,

---

[23] *Evening Star*, Dec. 6, 1907, p. 1.
[24] *A.G.O. 1310155V*, 1907.

"which the President himself wrote," to be dispatched immediately
to the commanding officer at Goldfield. Roosevelt's message, which
he instructed should be given to the public at Goldfield, follows:

> The troops are not sent to take the part of either side in a purely in-
> dustrial dispute, as long as it is kept within the bounds of law and order.
> They are to be neither for nor against either the strikers or the em-
> ployers. They are to prevent riot, violence and disorder, under and in
> accordance with the Constitution and the laws of the land. No man is
> to be interfered with so long as he conducts himself in a peaceful and
> orderly manner.

The President then directed that further instructions of a confidential nature be sent to Colonel Reynolds. Following is a translation
of the cipher telegram, a copy of which was also sent to General
Funston:

> Do not act at all until President issues proclamation. Notify Adjutant
> General at once whenever anything occurs making proclamation neces-
> sary, and then await further orders. Better twenty-four hours of riot,
> damage, and disorder than illegal use of troops.[25]

Reynolds was not supplied with a copy of the code and he did
not know the contents of the telegram until Funston arrived the
next day. The General, in the meantime, had received not only the
two telegrams given above, but a third message sharply informing
him that it was not the President's intention to use the troops for
guarding the mines or those working them, "or for any other purpose," until he gave further orders based on the reports of Funston
and Reynolds.

Apparently not satisfied with the manner in which the Acting
Secretary of War was handling the incident and because he wished
to take advantage of the wide experience of his Secretary of State,
Roosevelt requested Elihu Root to take charge of the Nevada
disturbance. On December 13, Oliver was directed to provide Root
with copies of all orders which the War Department had sent, and
"to do nothing without first submitting the proposed action" to the
Secretary of State.[26]

The President then asked Root to explain to Governor Sparks

[25] *A.G.O. 1310155X*, 1907.
[26] *A.G.O. 1310155A4* and *1310155A37*, 1907.

the steps that would be necessary before the federal government could take further action. Because of the importance of the statutes which had caused the Governor so much trouble, it seems advisable to include a considerable part of Root's explanation:

The calls upon the President on the part of the government of Nevada for the interposition of troops do not at present satisfy the requirement of the Constitution and the laws so as to justify orders that the military force now at Goldfield shall take any affirmative action. If such action should be desired under the Constitution and section 5297 of the Revised Statutes to suppress an insurrection a call must be made by the legislature of the State unless circumstances are such that the legislature can not be convened, and no statement or intimation has been made that the legislature of Nevada can not be convened. Action under 5298 of the Revised Statutes relates only to the enforcement of the laws of the United States. Action under section 5299 of the Revised Statutes is to be taken not upon the call of the government of a State, but upon the judgment of the President of the United States that some portion or class of the people of a State are denied the equal protection of the laws to which they are entitled under the Constitution of the United States. Action under this section requires the production of evidence of specific facts sufficient to sustain a judgment by the President that the condition described in the statute exists.

A mere statement of domestic disturbance would not seem to be sufficient.

The facts thus far stated in the telegraphic communication from the governor of Nevada, high and unimpeachable as is the source, do not seem sufficient to sustain a judgment that the condition described in section 5299 exists.

It therefore appears that the communications thus far received from the government of Nevada do not constitute or furnish the basis for authority on the part of the President to direct the use of the armed forces of the United States in the maintenance of public order at Goldfield.

I respectfully suggest that if in your judgment such interposition is needed you furnish further evidence of facts justifying action by the President under section 5298 or 5299, or cause the legislature of Nevada to be convened and to make the necessary call in accordance with the Constitution and section 5297 of the Revised Statutes.[27]

The Governor's reply to Root's message completely evaded the question of a legislative requisition. Somewhat irked by the action of Sparks and apparently suspicious that he had been deceived,

[27] H. Doc. 607, 60 Cong. 1 sess., pp. 6-7.

Roosevelt, on December 17, telegraphed the Governor that the troops would not be left indefinitely to perform "those ordinary duties of maintaining public order" which rest upon the government of the state.[28]

The President's investigating committee. In the meantime, in order to get a more complete picture of affairs in Goldfield, the President had appointed a three-man investigating committee.[29] On December 17, they conferred with the Governor and with General Funston, who had previously sent a report to Roosevelt upholding the Governor's call.[30] After hearing what must have been a rather terrifying account from these gentlemen, the investigating committee wired the President that conditions were "complex and probably critical" and requested him not to withdraw the troops. Within three days, however, their perspective had greatly changed. Where General Funston reported that the miners' union had driven 500 persons from the community in the last two years, the committee said the evidence sustained a maximum of only 25. They found no warrant for the assertion that civil authority had collapsed. On the contrary, none of the county authorities had been consulted before the troops were called. However, because of the more acute conditions brought about by the action of the operators in reducing wages and refusing employment to union men, the local authorities believed the troops should remain. Finally, the committee reported that notwithstanding the desire for continued federal protection, the Governor refused to convene the legislature or to take any steps of a military or police nature looking toward release of the federal troops.[31]

Withdrawal of federal troops threatened. The committee's report elicited from Roosevelt a sharp telegram reprimanding Sparks for calling on the national government before the state had made a serious effort to perform its duty. He announced that the troops would be withdrawn December 30. Sparks then sent a short but

[28] The same, pp. 7-8.
[29] The committee consisted of Assistant Secretary of Commerce and Labor Lawrence O. Murray, Commissioner of Labor Charles P. Neill, and Commissioner of Corporations Herbert Knox Smith.
[30] Frederick T. Wilson, *Federal Aid in Domestic Disturbances*, S. Doc. 263, 67 Cong. 2 sess., p. 310; *A.G.O. 1310155A5.*
[31] H. Doc. 607, 60 Cong. 1 sess., pp. 8-9.

very conciliatory message stating that he was preparing a letter on
the situation at Goldfield and suggesting that he would rather come
to Washington and give his explanation in person. "We are thankful to you," he concluded, "for the presence of the troops let their
stay be long or short."

The President's lack of enthusiasm for an interview with the
Governor is shown by his one-sentence reply: "I will await your letter and wire you after its receipt whether in my judgment it would
serve a useful purpose for you to come to Washington."[32] Because
of illness Sparks did not get the letter written, but on December
26 he sent Roosevelt a long telegram. At last he took up the question of convening the legislature. It was his opinion that the representatives were opposed to a special session. Furthermore, due to
the ten-day notice required by law, it would take at least three weeks
before they could be called together. All in all, the Governor
deemed it inadvisable to call a special session even though at the
same time he advocated the retention of the troops for "an indefinite period of time."

The President's advisers immediately drafted a reply to the arguments of Sparks. William Loeb, Jr., secretary to the President,
General Oliver, and Secretary of War Taft, who had just returned
from Europe, worked with Elihu Root in preparing the message.[33]
Roosevelt made certain modifications in the draft which, as it was
sent, amounted to an ultimatum. "If within five days from the receipt of this telegram," the message read, "you shall have issued
the necessary notice to convene the legislature of Nevada, I shall
continue the station of the troops at Goldfield during such period
of three weeks. If within the term of five days such notice has not
been issued, the troops will be immediately returned to their former
stations."[34]

Even this demand, couched in such peremptory language, did not
outwardly change the cheerful front essayed by Nevada's Sparks.

[32] The same, p. 10.
[33] The same, p. 12.
[34] The same, p. 13. See also Roosevelt, *An Autobiography*, pp. 376-77.

After four rather rough telegrams from the President, the Governor was still able to close his announcement that an extra session was to be called with "many thanks for your message."[35]

Report of the investigating committee. Meanwhile, the President's investigating committee, after a six-day stay in Goldfield, had returned to Washington. Their report, which was given to the President and the Secretary of State on December 30, was an elaboration of their earlier message. The committee felt that both the operators and the union were responsible for much unnecessary bickering in the mining area. However, with reference to this particular dispute, the committee agreed that "the action of the mine operators warrants the belief that they had determined upon a reduction in wages and the refusal of employment to members of the Western Federation of Miners, but that they feared to take this course of action unless they had the protection of federal troops, and that they accordingly laid a plan to secure such troops, and then put their programme into effect."[36] Instead of an era of violence and disorder before the arrival of the soldiers, the committee found that "the conditions did not support the general allegations in the governor's request for troops, nor were his specific statements established to any such extent as to justify his use of these statements for the purpose of getting federal troops."[37] The report stated further that because of the "violent tendencies" of some of the union's leaders and because of the action of the operators in reducing wages and refusing to hire members of the union, the possibility of disorder was very great. However, there was no reason, the committee agreed, "why the county of Esmeralda and the State of Nevada should . . . not assert their authority and power and enforce respect for law and order without support of federal troops."[38]

Roosevelt sent a copy of the report to Governor Sparks. The committee condemned the call for assistance in such unqualified terms that although the President agreed with their recommenda-

[35] H. Doc. 607, 60 Cong. 1 sess., p. 14.
[36] The same, p. 21.
[37] The same, p. 23.
[38] The same, p. 26.

tions and quoted parts of the report in his letter to Sparks, he practically wrote a defense of his own action in sending the troops at all. Once more the Governor was informed that sufficient evidence of disturbance must be produced before the President could act:

> "A mere statement of domestic disturbance" still less a mere statement of apprehension of domestic disturbance, is not sufficient, even though it comes from as high and unimpeachable a source as the governor of a State. Such communication from the governor or from the legislature warrants the President in taking immediate steps to put himself in readiness to act, in view of the probability of conditions arising which will require his action. I accordingly sent the troops to Nevada on your request, and I have now directed that they be kept there pending the assembling of the legislature.[39]

Withdrawal of the troops. On January 17, the legislature, without a dissenting vote in either house, asked that the troops be retained until provision could be made for a "State constabulary or other police force." Two weeks later the legislature requested the President to retain the troops for 60 days, from February 1 to April 1, 1908, pending the organizing, arming, and equipping of the Nevada State Police. The President's irritation at this delay was expressed in his telegram to Governor Sparks, February 4:

> Telegram received. It seems to me that it is quite unnecessary to delay sixty days. Surely with reasonable expedition the police force can be organized, armed and equipped in a tenth of that time. Certainly to allow a quarter of the time is ample. If there are any reasons why troops should remain beyond the fifteenth of this month I should like to hear them at once.[40]

The Governor immediately cut in half the estimate of the amount of time needed. He pointed out that the equipment had to be shipped from cities in the east but that 30 days would probably suffice to put the police force into actual operation. The President accepted this estimate saying, "I am sure you will understand that it is impossible for me again to defer the date of their return."[41]

[39] The same, p. 15.
[40] A.G.O. 1310155A27, 1907.
[41] A.G.O. 1310155A28, 1907.

Without at any time having been called on for active service, the troops were finally withdrawn on March 7.

There is little to criticize and much to praise about Roosevelt's part in the Goldfield incident. The mere presence of the troops, it is true, was all that the mine operators needed to break the strike. Yet the President's procedure was beyond reproach. He did not send troops until he was reassured by the flat statement of the Governor that a disturbance existed beyond the power of the state to control. Even then all that was done was to bring the troops to the scene. They were not to aid the Governor, nor to act on their own initiative. Roosevelt kept a tight rein on their activities. Through the reports of the investigating committee, he was better able to judge the value of the dispatches sent by the state officials and, for that matter, by the federal military as well. Finally, commendation is due the President for the firm and persistent manner in which he forced the state to adopt measures for its own protection against domestic violence.

CHAPTER IX

WILSON AND THE COLORADO COAL STRIKE

In the spring of 1914 bitter warfare broke out between the operators and the coal miners of Colorado. At the request of the governor, federal troops were called out in order to put an end to rioting and destruction and to stop the killing of miners and militiamen. In this the soldiers were highly successful. Their methods, sanctioned by President Wilson, were a novel, though perhaps necessary, departure from any previous practice.

EVENTS LEADING TO THE "LUDLOW MASSACRE"

The strike was not centered at any one town or at any one mine. Rather, it embraced the mines in many communities over a considerable area. Although there were a number of independent operators, the Colorado Fuel and Iron Company, a Rockefeller interest, was the recognized leader. The economic, political, and social life of the district was completely dominated by the operators, and it was in opposition to this domination, perhaps more than for any particular measure of relief, that the battle, in all its bitterness, raged.[1]

During the summer of 1913 officials of the United Mine Workers attempted to organize the district. A convention in Trinidad on September 15 voted a strike, to go into effect ten days later, unless the operators met the demands of the miners.[2] The managers refused to recognize this "mock convention," on the ground that the delegates were not representative of the miners but, on the contrary, had been hand picked by the union officials.[3] On the appointed day several thousand workers and their families moved out of their company-owned homes and established tent colonies.[4]

---

[1] For illustrations of political domination see *Report on the Colorado Strike Investigation*, H. Doc. 1630, 63 Cong. 3 sess., pp. 18-33.
[2] For a more complete account of the labor issues involved, see Edward Berman, *Labor Disputes and the President of the United States*, pp. 76-99.
[3] *Facts Concerning the Struggle in Colorado for Industrial Freedom*, Series I, p. 7.
[4] The managers contended that but 38 per cent of the miners joined the strike. They cited as proof the fact that in September 12,236 men were employed, whereas

Both sides prepared for violence. The purchase of arms by the miners was justified by the union officials under the clause of the Colorado Constitution which reads: ". . . the right of no person to keep and bear arms in defense of his home, person, and property . . . shall be called in question."[5] The operators hired large numbers of mine guards, set up machine guns, and secured a West Virginia detective agency to assist in defense measures.[6]

There were fatal outbursts at several points during October, and, at the request of the mining officials and the local authorities, Governor Elias M. Ammons called out the militia. At first the troops attempted to secure the arms of both mine guards and strikers, but this effort was only partially successful. For a time also they attempted to keep out strikebreakers, but protests from the operators caused the enforcement of this measure to be relaxed. The district was kept under a modified form of martial law and, as the strike wore on, the acts of the militia, some of whom had been recruited from the hated mine guards, became more distasteful to the miners.[7] However, for some months there was little violence and Governor Ammons began to withdraw the troops.

A detachment of about 40 men was left at Ludlow, where the largest tent colony was located. There were 21 nationalities represented in this group of 900 persons living in 179 tents.[8] On April 20, a minor incident quickly expanded into a serious conflict and resulted in what came to be known as "the Ludlow massacre." The miners were driven out of the colony and their tents burned. Both sides suffered losses, but the most tragic part of the struggle was the death, by suffocation, of two women and eleven children who had taken shelter in a pit dug beneath one of the tent floors.[9] This

---

in October 7,696 were still working. (The same, p. 9.) These figures are misleading, however, as numbers of strikebreakers had, in the meantime, been brought into the district.

[5] Art. II, sec. 13.

[6] George P. West, *United States Commission on Industrial Relations, Report on the Colorado Strike*, p. 102.

[7] H. Doc. 1630, 63 Cong. 3 sess., pp. 6-17.

[8] *New York Times*, May 2, 1914, p. 2.

[9] *Ludlow, Being the Report of the Special Board of Officers Appointed by the Governor of Colorado to Investigate and Determine the Facts with Reference to the Armed Conflict Between the Colorado National Guard and Certain Persons*

enraged the miners over the entire district and, in spite of additional guardsmen who were rushed into the strike zone, deeds of violence were common. The total death toll was estimated to be at least 50.[10] The disturbance seemed now completely beyond the state's ability to control. Furthermore, there were no funds to pay the militia.[11] To large numbers of Colorado's citizens, the only solution seemed to be federal aid. On April 25, Governor Ammons wired President Wilson for United States troops.[12]

EFFORTS TO EFFECT A PEACEFUL SETTLEMENT

The Governor's request was by no means Wilson's introduction to the disturbance. Even before the beginning of the strike a representative of the Department of Labor had endeavored to act as mediator but, on the ground that his interest was chiefly with the union, the operators rejected his offer.[13] Late in November, Governor Ammons asked the President to send Secretary of Labor William B. Wilson to assist in the dispute. The Secretary worked with Ammons for a ten-day period but with no result. To the operators it appeared that every proposal worked around to the question of recognition of the union and to that they were unalterably opposed.[14] Furthermore, they were afraid of the Secretary of Labor, who was himself a member of the United Mine Workers of America. "Behind the soft voice of Secretary Wilson," wrote one of the mine officials, "is the hand of Esau."[15]

Engaged in the Coal Mining Strike at Ludlow, Colorado, April 20, 1914, pp. 12-24. For a different account, see the testimony of one witness before the Commission on Industrial Relations, *Industrial Relations Final Report and Testimony Submitted to Congress by the Commission on Industrial Relations*, Vol. VII, pp. 6349-54. The coroner's jury found that death was caused by "asphyxiation or fire, or both." *Commercial and Financial Chronicle*, May 9, 1914, p. 1436.

[10] West, *Report on the Colorado Strike*, p. 135. A report from Denver in the *New York Times* of Dec. 9, 1914 (p. 18), placed the total deaths at 66.

[11] See testimony of Governor Ammons in *Industrial Relations*, Vol. VII, p. 6416.

[12] *New York Times*, Apr. 26, 1914, p. 15.

[13] See testimony of J. F. Welborn, president of Colorado Iron and Fuel Company in *Industrial Relations*, Vol. IX, p. 8426.

[14] By this time, early December, the managers were confident of breaking the strike. Plans were made to bring in a thousand men from outside and, in addition, the rigors of a Colorado winter were counted on to drive many from the tent colony back to their jobs and more comfortable housing. See letter of J. F. Welborn in *Industrial Relations*, Vol. VIII, pp. 7118-19.

[15] *Industrial Relations*, Vol. IX, p. 8426.

In addition to the work of the Department of Labor, whose efforts at mediation were in accordance with a statute passed earlier in the year,[16] the President also had been endeavoring to effect a peaceful settlement of the dispute. On three occasions in 1913 he wrote to company officials. His wish for "arbitration by an unbiased board" was backed by the threat of a congressional investigation, but he was no more successful than Governor Ammons or Secretary Wilson in reaching a settlement. The operators were fearful that the President would let his Secretary of Labor name the arbitration committee. The vice-president of the Colorado Iron and Fuel Company expressed his contempt for the President's proposal when he wrote to one of the Rockefeller staff in New York, "We prefer to let the President ask Congress to make the investigation and take our chances."[17] The investigation was made but its effect was negligible.

Apparently Wilson did nothing more until after the outbreak at Ludlow. Then, after Governor Ammons' first request, which was presented informally by the Colorado congressional delegation, the President called together the members of the investigating committee. Wilson and the Cabinet met with the committee chiefly for purposes of information rather than to act upon the Governor's request.[18] There seemed to be little time for domestic affairs. The entire attention of the President and his advisers was centered around the crisis with Mexico. Reparation was being demanded from the Huerta government for the Tampico incident. Thus, the Colorado disturbance was quickly disposed of by the decision to ask the committee to revisit the strike district.

Scarcely had the President arrived at this easy solution before a second request for troops was received from Governor Ammons. He had been in Washington at the time of the outbreak, but news of the riot sent him scurrying homeward. Upon reaching Denver his office was literally besieged by persons who demanded that he obtain federal aid. On April 25, one thousand women, including, so it was reported, prominent society leaders, descended upon the

---

[16] 37 Stat. L. 738.
[17] *Industrial Relations*, Vol. IX, p. 8426.
[18] *New York Times*, Apr. 26, 1914, p. 15.

Governor and virtually forced him to appeal directly to the President.[19]

Notwithstanding this second request, the President was slow to act. From Washington came word that there was doubt in his mind as to his power to send troops.[20] Ammons had called for a special session of the legislature to convene on May 4, and Wilson seemed disposed to wait until then. Furthermore, he was determined that troops should not be sent until every avenue for peaceful settlement was closed. On April 26, Representative Martin Foster, chairman of the House Committee on Mines and Mining and a member of the investigating committee, and Colorado's Senators and Representatives, were called to the White House for a conference. The only means left, short of intervention by the federal government, was an overture of peace by the mine owners. After the conference Wilson sent a personal appeal to John D. Rockefeller, Sr., asking him to intervene in order that further violence and bloodshed might be prevented. The elder Rockefeller replied that all his holdings in Colorado Fuel and Iron stock had been turned over to his son. However, he promised to ask the younger Rockefeller to consider the matter.[21] At Wilson's request Representative Foster went to New York for a conference with John D. Rockefeller, Jr., but like all previous efforts this one also was a complete failure.[22] Wilson expressed his regret at the result of the conference as follows: "It seemed to me a great opportunity for some large action which would show the way not only in this case but in many others. . . ."[23] Only after the return of Foster from his unsuccessful mission was the decision made to send the troops.

FEDERAL TROOPS SENT, BUT UNDER SPECIFIC INSTRUCTIONS

On April 28 detachments from Fort Leavenworth, Kansas, and Fort Russell, Wyoming, were ordered to the strike zone.[24] At the

[19] The same.
[20] The same, April 28, p. 6.
[21] The same.
[22] For Rockefeller's statement regarding the conference, see *Commercial and Financial Chronicle*, May 2, 1914, p. 1358.
[23] To John D. Rockefeller, Jr., Apr. 29, 1914. Quoted from Ray Stannard Baker, *Woodrow Wilson, Life and Letters, President 1913-1914*, p. 389.
[24] *New York Times*, Apr. 29, 1914, p. 1.

same time that the President issued a proclamation warning all persons engaged in "domestic violence and obstruction of the laws" to disperse,[25] he also sent to Governor Ammons a statement of the federal government's position in the disturbance:

I shall order *that no person or persons, natural or artificial, shall be permitted to do that which may give rise to disorder* . . . to the end that good order may be established and maintained. I shall not, by the use of the troops or by any attempt at jurisdiction, inject the power of the Federal Government into the controversy which has produced the present situation. The settlement of the controversy falls strictly within the field of State power. My duty, as I now see it is to confine myself to maintaining a status of good order until the State can reassert its authority and resume the enforcement thereof. . . .

The manifest disadvantage of having two military forces under separate sources of control, operating within the same localities, leads me to request you to withdraw your militia so soon as the troops of the United States have reached the scene and are ready to take over the necessary control.[26]

The President's letter to Governor Ammons, which was at once published, indicated plainly that the actions of the mining companies, as well as those of the strikers, were to be under the watchful eye of the military. The orders issued to the commanding officers on this point were very explicit:

If, in your judgment the conduct of any individual or corporation, either in their individual movements or in the prosecution of their business, is under the circumstances likely to lead to domestic violence and disorder, even if the said conduct is apparently lawful and would under normal conditions not be interfered with, you will immediately communicate your judgment to the department and await instructions unless the emergency is so grave that you are not justified in delaying action. You will act with the most extreme discretion and caution, so as not to cause what you are sent to prevent or allay.[27]

Although the troops were being sent to assist the state rather than to enforce federal law, little limitation was placed upon the scope of their activities:

The measure of your authority is what necessity dictates. State civil

---

[25] 38 Stat. L. 1994.
[26] *New York Times*, Apr. 29, 1914, p. 1. Italics added.
[27] Frederick T. Wilson, *Federal Aid in Domestic Disturbances*, S. Doc. 263, 67 Cong. 2 sess., p. 313.

functions and processes should not be displaced or interfered with when they can be successfully employed in the suppression of violence and the restoration of order. Persons arrested should ordinarily be turned over to the proper State authorities as soon as practicable. Should you find that State judicial procedure only results in the release and return to the scene of disorder of persons whose presence and conduct tend to prevent the restoration of normal conditions you may find it neccessary to retain in military custody those whom you arrest. Persons in military custody will be held under authority of the United States and a writ of habeas corpus issued from a State court should be met with a return declining to produce in court the body of the prisoner on the ground that he is held under the authority of the United States. In case of a writ issued from a United States court you will obey the writ, produce the body of the prisoner, and state in full the reason for restraint, reporting the fact direct by telegram to The Adjutant General of the Army.[28]

Governor Ammons set up no objection to the wide latitude given the commanding officers. On the contrary, he was delighted to be relieved of an exceedingly unpleasant problem. The 300 troops which arrived at Trinidad on May 1 were not, in the Governor's opinion, sufficient to patrol the whole area. He was not slow to ask for a larger force, and after due inquiry Secretary Lindley M. Garrison ordered 1,000 additional troops to the scene. Since most of the soldiers in posts adjacent to the strike zone had been sent to the Mexican border it was necessary to secure others from points far removed from Colorado. Over 800 of the last group were from Fort Oglethorpe, Georgia.

The arrival of the regulars brought a feeling of relief to the whole populace. There was no resistance at any point. At Louisville the strikers were out with a brass band to meet the troops. In accordance with the President's wishes, Governor Ammons withdrew the militia as soon as the regulars arrived to replace them. This took some time, as the whole area ultimately placed under the jurisdiction of the federal soldiers was 260 miles from north to south and 40 to 75 miles from east to west.[29] The Trinidad district alone comprised an area of about 400 square miles, in which were located nearly 60 mines.

[28] The same. Italics added.
[29] *New York Times*, May 4, 1914, p. 3.

FEDERAL CONTROL OF THE STRIKE AREA

Due to the geography of the area and to the necessity of scattering the troops so widely, no single officer was placed in command of the entire force. Instead, Secretary Garrison issued orders directly to the commanding officer of each locality. Before the troops arrived, Governor Ammons had again placed the district under martial law. The federal officers merely maintained in force some of the measures previously announced by the Governor, but with the difference that they actually enforced them. For example, Major Holbrook, commanding the Trinidad district, proceeded to enforce the already established embargo upon the shipment of arms. Saloons were closed and the importation of strikebreakers was forbidden. The rules laid down by the military gave considerable credibility to Secretary Garrison's answer to a commanding officer, who had suggested a federal declaration of martial law. "I do not know of anything," said Garrison, "that you can not do under existing circumstances that you could do any better if there was a written proclamation of martial law posted in your district."[30]

Disarmament. The widespread possession of arms among the strikers constituted an ever-present menace to the maintenance of good order. However, it was folly to suppose that the miners would surrender their weapons unless some assurance could be given that they need no longer fear the mine guards or, for that matter, the militia. The only solution was to effect a general disarmament. To bring this about Secretary Garrison, on May 1, sent a proclamation to each commanding officer. The proclamation was to be signed by

[30] On May 14, 1914, the Secretary of War wrote as follows: "It seemed to me that the first thing to do was to restore order; to endeavor to allay this absolutely abnormal tide of passion; and to produce conditions that tended toward normality. Many things which are perfectly lawful under normal conditions must, under such circumstances be temporarily suspended. For instance I have ordered all the saloons closed; I have forbidden the importation of any arms or ammunition into the State; I am taking away from those who possess them arms and ammunition; I am closing up shops which sell arms and ammunition. In the same spirit and for the same reason I am not encouraging the opening of mines which have for a long time been closed. We are having enough difficulty to maintain things in an equilibrium with the mines that are already running. All the mines that were running when we reached the ground are now running, and law and order is being preserved." S. Doc. 263, 67 Cong. 2 sess., p. 315.

each officer and published. It read, in part, as follows:

. . . I do by the authority of the President of the United States call upon and direct all persons not in the military service of the United States who have arms or ammunition in their possession or under their control to deliver them forthwith to the officer at the place herein designated. Receipts will be issued for all arms and ammunition so delivered. The above applies to individuals, firms, associations and corporations.[31]

This order was interpreted by Secretary Garrison to apply also to the state militia but,[32] since they were being withdrawn, Governor Ammons did not challenge the federal government's right to disarm the state troops.[33] Sheriffs' deputies and policemen were also included in the disarmament scheme.[34]

No effort was made to enforce the proclamation at once. Many of the miners could not speak English, and the army officers adopted the very commendable policy of allowing time for the foreign workers to understand the meaning of this extraordinary order. However, the quantity of arms turned in was so infinitesimal that on May 6 a second proclamation was issued which stated that the officers and soldiers of the United State Army "will at once disarm all persons . . . and take into their possession all arms, ammunition, or explosives which may be found upon the person of any individual.[35] At the time this command was issued Major Holbrook addressed one colony of strikers as follows: "When the United States speaks it is a matter of serious moment. The President of the United States must be obeyed. We have soldiers and officers here to see that he is obeyed."[36] In simple but very temperate language he explained why the government had issued such an order and when and where the arms were to be deposited. A second week passed before the soldiers were instructed to take active steps to disarm any-

[31] The same, p. 314.
[32] "The intent of the proclamation is that all persons of all factions or classes who have firearms are covered by and subject to the terms of the proclamation." Garrison to commanding officer at Canon City, Colo., War Department Archives, *Adjutant General's Office, 2154620, 1914.*
[33] *New York Times*, May 4, 1914, p. 3.
[34] The same, May 14, p. 19.
[35] S. Doc. 263, 67 Cong. 2 sess., p. 314.
[36] *New York Times*, May 7, 1914, p. 20.

one. Even then there was to be no searching of homes. A considerable quantity of arms was turned in but there was, of course, no way of accurately determining the amount not surrendered.[37] When the editor of *The Free Press*, the Trinidad union paper, charged that the Colorado Fuel and Iron Company had hidden machine guns and a wagon load of arms, Holbrook demanded a retraction. He asked also that proof be furnished for material appearing on the paper's front page.[38] The editor refused to retract although he did publish the fact that army officials denied the truth of his statement. He also refused to submit to what he called military censorship. The commanding officer, wisely, did not make an issue of the incident.

Exclusion of strikebreakers. To rid the district of as many troublemakers as possible, Garrison instructed the commanding officers to make a check on the strike settlements for the purpose of ferreting out every person who was not a legitimate member of the colony. Persons who had not been on the company pay roll within a certain period prior to the strike were subject to deportation. The same procedure was also applied to persons living on mining property. Strikebreakers who had been imported since April 21 were ordered to leave.[39]

The companies were not at all pleased with the policy of prohibiting their importation of strikebreakers. The rule was laid down that only those voluntarily seeking employment should be admitted.[40] The effectiveness of the plan, which was in force throughout the summer, was admitted by J. F. Welborn, president of the Colorado Fuel and Iron Company. On August 18, he wrote,

[37] From the Trinidad district alone, 2,678 firearms and 6,000 rounds of ammunition were surrendered. The strikers consented to turn over 300 rifles and 60,000 rounds of ammunition which were in transit. The same, May 14, p. 6.
[38] The same, May 11, 1914, p. 1.
[39] The same, May 12, p. 8. The first deportation occurred on May 12, when six strikebreakers under military escort were marched to the railway station and placed aboard a train for Denver. The same, May 13, p. 19.
[40] *Commercial and Financial Chronicle*, May 16, 1914, p. 1504. In September this rule was qualified by the further limitation that "miners who apply at the mines may be there employed provided they are residents of the state of Colorado, and have complied with the laws of Colorado relative to miners." Telegram of Secretary Garrison to a union official in Aguilar, Colo., Sept. 1, 1914. See Berman, *Labor Disputes and the President of the United States*, p. 91.

". . . no change has taken place in the policy of the Federal troops
with respect to the employment of men, although I do not think
their rules are as rigidly enforced as at the beginning. Our gain in
the number of men employed has not been material."[41] Earlier in
the month the operators, working through Congressman George J.
Kindel, had challenged the government's authority to prohibit the
importation of new workers. In a sharp, though not extraordinarily
able, reply, Secretary Garrison indicated the theory upon which the
administration was acting:

> The authority is that which is technically referred to as the police
> power, or power exercised where martial law prevails. I do not suppose
> it is necessary to point out that I am the constitutional organ of the
> President in issuing orders, and that the ultimate source of power is the
> President. Under the Constitution, where domestic insurrection over-
> throws the power of the State, the President is required to interfere
> if properly requested. When he interferes and sends the national forces
> into a State, he has full power and authority to do whatever he finds
> necessary to restore public order and maintain it.[42]

Federal control of the strike area met with great success. Apparently there was little friction between the miners and the 1,700
soldiers. In fact the presence of the troops was so greatly desired
by every group that the President could not withdraw them. When
the special session of the Colorado legislature was about to adjourn
without having made, as Wilson thought, adequate provision for
the state's resumption of control over the strike area, the President
wired Governor Ammons:

> Am disturbed to hear of the probability of the adjournment of your
> legislature and feel bound to remind you that my constitutional obliga-
> tions with regard to the maintenance of order in Colorado are not to
> be indefinitely continued by the inaction of the state legislature. The
> federal forces are there only until the state of Colorado has time and
> opportunity to resume complete sovereignty and control in the matter.
> I cannot conceive that the state is willing to forego her sovereignty or
> to throw herself entirely upon the Government of the United States and
> I am quite clear that she has no constitutional right to do so when it
> is within the power of her legislature to take effective action.[43]

---

[41] To J. J. McClement, in *Industrial Relations*, Vol. VIII, p. 7123.
[42] S. Doc. 263, 67 Cong. 2 sess., p. 315.
[43] *Commercial and Financial Chronicle*, May 23, 1914, p. 1573.

This message created quite a furor since it was interpreted as indicating the immediate withdrawal of the troops. Members of the state senate, the Colorado delegation in Congress, the United Mine Workers, and others, protested that if the federal forces were removed, anarchy would again reign. Governor Ammons asked for more time until money could be raised from a $1,000,000 bond issue which the legislature had authorized. The alarm created by the President's message died down only when White House officials gave assurance that Wilson intended to be reasonable about the question.[44]

Arguments for continued and more extensive control. In contrast with the President's belief that the state should settle the conflict, Governor Ammons, in a statement to the press on May 17, argued that because of the interstate relationships involved, national aid was essential. His basis for this new theory was a fourfold one: (1) the coal companies were owned largely by stockholders beyond the borders of the state; (2) the United Mine Workers was a national organization; (3) the newspapers which had so inflamed the public were controlled from without the state; (4) many "ultra-Socialistic, if not anarchistic" leaders had come to Colorado from other states.[45]

The Governor's proposal for national aid was seconded by Judge Ben Lindsey although on different grounds. In a conference with the President, Lindsey suggested that the Chief Executive should compel the contending parties to arbitrate. When Wilson asked by what authority this could be done, Lindsey replied that the Governor's call for federal troops was a confession that the state's sovereignty had broken down and that a republican form of government had ceased to exist. The President pointed out that the difficulty with such an argument was that according to the Supreme Court the states themselves were the judges of what was a republican form of government. The Judge then shifted his ground to argue that since Wilson had been called on as President to preserve law and order, he could take such measures as were necessary not only to maintain peace but to preserve the "bigger rights of the people

[44] The same.
[45] The same. See also *Industrial Relations,* Vol. VII, p. 6421.

under the Constitution." This proposal, according to Lindsey's account, appealed to Wilson, since already the Austrian and Italian ministers had protested that their citizens were not safe in Colorado. Wilson declared that he had done and wanted to do everything legally possible to bring about peace and order and that he would give further consideration to the Judge's proposal.[46]

Strike settlement and withdrawal of troops. Week after week passed while the state officials were trying in vain to dispose of the bond issue. In August, the President voiced his displeasure with the slow progress made toward relieving the federal troops. At the same time he expressed doubt as to his constitutional right to keep them there indefinitely. "I cannot believe," he wrote, "that the great state of Colorado will let the winter come without taking the steps necessary to obtain control of the situation."[47]

For a time, in early September, the strike seemed on the verge of settlement. In another effort at mediation Wilson sent to both the United Mine Workers and the operators a "Tentative Basis for the Adjustment of the Colorado Strike."[48] The union called a convention to consider the plan and it was at once accepted. Their representatives wrote the President that "the delegates to this convention convey to you their abiding faith in your integrity and your earnest and patriotic desire to be helpful in the present strike situation."[49] The operators, however, remained adamant, and the strike continued.

Although greatly disappointed, the President resumed his efforts. To the theories advanced by Governor Ammons and Judge Lindsey were now added other proposals by which the federal government could exercise complete control of the strike. The miners suggested that the government simply take over the operation of the mines.[50] The American Federation of Labor favored putting the mines in the hands of receivers.[51] Both of these proposals Wilson

[46] The same, Vol. VIII, pp. 7102-03.

[47] To Governor Ammons, Aug. 21, 1914. Quoted from Baker, *Woodrow Wilson, Life and Letters*, p. 390.

[48] The proposals were the work of two special investigators of the Department of Labor, W. R. Fairley and Hywel Davies.

[49] Baker, *Woodrow Wilson, Life and Letters*, p. 391.

[50] *New York Times*, Sept. 3, 1914, p. 9.

[51] The same, November 25, p. 12.

considered beyond the pale of the law. He did, however, give serious consideration to the plan of completely closing the mines, but Governor Ammons protested that there was no necessity for such an action.[52] According to the Governor, the Colorado National Guard was being rapidly equipped and, in a very short time, would be ready to maintain the peace.

By the middle of November Ammons was reported ready to *demand* the withdrawal of federal troops.[53] Wilson took little stock in this report and went ahead with his efforts to bring the strike to an end. "Merely to withdraw the troops and leave the situation to clear and settle itself," he wrote, "would seem to be doing something less than my duty after all that has occurred."[54] Again he appointed a commission,[55] and his message announcing his action expressed the "very earnest hope, that both parties may see it to be . . . a duty . . . to make use of this instrumentality of peace. . . ."[56] One week later the Executive Board of the United Mine Workers issued a report stating that "in view of this urgent request, coming as it does, from the Chief Executive of the nation, we deem it the part of wisdom to accept his suggestion and terminate the strike."[57]

On December 23 Wilson met with Colorado's governor and governor-elect, and plans were made for the gradual removal of the troops. By January 10, 1915, all of them had been withdrawn. No violence occurred, but the distrust engendered by such a long and bitter war made a permanent peace between miners and operators hard to achieve. However, in March 1916, the President's commission reported that new state legislation, a less arbitrary control on the part of the operators, and a public opinion more keenly alive to mining problems, were all helping to mitigate the injurious effects of the struggle.[58]

---

[52] The same, Oct. 30, 1914, p. 4.

[53] The same, November 23, p. 1.

[54] Baker, *Woodrow Wilson, Life and Letters*, p. 393.

[55] The members of the commission were Seth Low of New York, president of the National Civic Federation, Charles W. Miller, an eastern mine owner, and Patrick Gilday, a United Mine Workers official.

[56] *Commercial and Financial Chronicle*, Dec. 5, 1914, p. 1638.

[57] The same, December 12, p. 1716.

[58] *Labor Difficulties in the Coal Fields of Colorado*, H. Doc. 859, 64 Cong. 1 sess., p. 4.

WILSON'S ROLE IN THE STRIKE

In considering the President's part in the dispute, it is evident that he played two different roles. First, he endeavored to settle the strike, and his every action in this respect was strictly within the law. The Department of Labor, as Wilson early pointed out, was acting under a statute permitting intervention, but it had no actual authority to settle the dispute.[59] While the influence of the presidential office was brought to bear on both parties, yet at no time was an effort made to force a settlement.

The President's second, and more successful, role was that of preserver of the peace. Here, it would appear, his theory was similar to that of Judge Lindsey. The Governor, having confessed his inability to maintain order, had thereby surrendered the task to the Chief Executive who, thereafter, was subject only to the constitutional command to prevent domestic violence.

In great contrast to disturbances of a similar nature in the past, the military acted under federal orders only, with no pretense even of co-operation with state officials. It is quite probable that this procedure was one reason for the army's success. If the discredited officers of the state, after the dismal failure of the militia, had participated in formulating military policies, the strikers might have looked on the "regulars" as one more agent of the mine operators. As it was, the troops were able to maintain a strictly neutral position and, as a result, they retained the strikers' confidence. This was done, too, in spite of the unprecedented acts of the soldiers. Consider what they had done. Everyone not in the United States Army was ordered to surrender his arms and ammunition; the importation of arms was forbidden; stores selling arms were closed; saloons were kept closed for seven months; operators were prohibited from opening other mines and also from importing strikebreakers. Local government was practically at a standstill.[60] Never before had the federal officials exercised such extensive powers. Whether such a policy would have been successful in an area

---

[59] Baker, *Woodrow Wilson, Life and Letters*, p. 388.

[60] Not until ofter the withdrawal of the troops was an effort made to punish those involved in the April rioting. Nor was the feeling between the two sides made less bitter when it was found that of the 400 indictments returned, all of them were against the strikers. H. Doc. 859, 64 Cong. 1 sess., p. 4.

where the people were long accustomed to regulating their own affairs is an open question. In the Colorado strike zone, however, strife seemed ever present, and what local government there was acted chiefly as an agent of the operators. Under these circumstances an unbiased policing force, strict though it may have been, was heartily welcomed by the vast majority of the inhabitants. By virtue of the careful and responsible work on the part of the federal officers and soldiers, the President was eminently successful in carrying out his intention "that no person or persons, natural or artificial, shall be permitted to do that which may give rise to disorder."[61]

[61] See p. 141.

CHAPTER X

THE POSTWAR PERIOD

The World War was primarily responsible for a complete reversal of the policies which President Wilson had pursued during the Colorado strike. One reason for the change was the fact that the National Guard was drafted into federal service and the states were left without adequate protection against internal disorders. To compensate for this loss, Secretary of War Newton D. Baker gave instructions, May 29, 1917, that the commanders of the departments were to respond to gubernatorial calls for assistance. However, this order, which disregarded the intention of the statutes that the president only was to determine the need for troops, was modified within six months so that all requests were referred to the Adjutant General.[1] Thus matters stood until September 1919.

UNREST AFTER THE ARMISTICE

The period after the war was one of great restlessness. In his annual message to Congress, December 2, 1919, Wilson endeavored to explain the "various and complicated" causes of this unrest.

Broadly they arise from or are connected with the failure on the part of our Government to arrive speedily at a just and permanent peace permitting return to normal conditions, from the transfusion of radical theories from seething European centers pending such delay, from heartless profiteering resulting in the increase in the cost of living, and lastly from the machinations of passionate and malevolent agitators.[2]

One manifestation of this condition of unrest was widespread racial and industrial disorder. Since the law providing for the draft of the National Guard into federal service had made no provision for the Guard's return to its former status, the army was called upon frequently to preserve the peace. In the summer of 1919, there were a number of disturbances arising from racial quarrels.

[1] Edward S. Corwin, *The President: Office and Powers*, p. 172.
[2] *The Messages and Papers of Woodrow Wilson*, Vol. II, p. 1144.

Washington, D.C. One of these occurred at the President's very doorstep. On July 19, soldiers, sailors, and marines, on the hunt for a negro accused of attacking a white woman, invaded a colored residential district in Washington. This precipitated a four-day period of rioting. The *New York Times* of July 22 reported 4 dead and 70 wounded in the preceding day's fighting.[3] In one instance a band of negroes attacked the occupants of a streetcar. There was also a considerable amount of shooting both in the downtown area and in the outlying areas by negroes riding in automobiles. District authorities finally asked all persons who had no good reason for coming into the business district to stay away.

The Secretary of War gave orders that troops should be used to the extent necessary to maintain peace.[4] Cavalrymen, infantrymen, and marines were brought into the city in ever-increasing numbers. Members of the Military Intelligence Division, clothed in civilian garb, were scattered throughout Washington in an effort to pick up information of planned attacks. The police department added 1,000 special deputies and armed them with revolvers supplied by the army.

Major General William G. Haan, in command of the federal forces, established headquarters in the Municipal Building. In a general order, Haan made emphatic the fact that the function of the troops was to assist the police. The commanding officers of the reserves at the police stations were instructed to "render prompt assistance upon request of the police," while the reserves stationed at Camp Meigs, Potomac Park, and Marine Barracks were told to "act only under orders from these headquarters."[5] All told, 12,000 troops were brought to the city.[6]

Although he conferred with Secretary Baker, the President made no public statement about the rioting. Nor did he display any interest in the resolution introduced in Congress demanding a rule of martial law.[7] The only restrictive measure put into effect was an order that "persons will not be allowed to congregate in groups

[3] P. 1.
[4] The same.
[5] The same.
[6] The same, July 28, 1919, p. 4.
[7] The same, July 22, p. 2.

and everybody will be kept moving."[8] Within a short time order
was restored, and by July 28 all of the troops had been withdrawn.

Omaha, Nebraska. Two months after the riots in the nation's
capital, a serious outbreak occurred in Omaha, Nebraska. Throughout the city there was a feeling of resentment against the negroes,
large numbers of whom had been imported as strikebreakers. This
feeling crystallized into sudden action September 28, 1919, when
a negro was reported to have attacked a white girl. A mob estimated
to have been 5,000 strong surrounded the new Douglas County
courthouse in which the negro was held prisoner. When the authorities refused to surrender their charge, the mob rushed the sheriff
and his deputies, seized and lynched the negro, and set fire to the
courthouse. Mayor E. P. Smith appealed to the crowd but the
reaction of the mob was to attempt to lynch him also. Police reached
the Mayor only after he had already been suspended from a lamp
post.[9]

Secretary Baker immediately granted the request of state officials
for troops, and on the twenty-ninth of September 700 federal soldiers moved into the city. Machine guns were set up in the streets,
and an observation balloon was raised. Military headquarters were
established at the police station, and the police department was
placed under the orders of the commanding officer, Colonel J. E.
Morris.[10]

On September 30, General Leonard Wood, Commander of the
Central Department, arrived in Omaha. Wood conferred with the
governor, the city commission, the police department, and the
county authorities. By this time re-enforcements had increased the
number of troops to 1,300. The General made use of the large
number of troops to parade 1,000 of them through the business
parts of the city.[11] In addition, he established troop patrols in the

[8] The same, p. 1. No sooner had the disorders in Washington ceased than a severe
riot broke out in Chicago. The *New York Times* for July 30 (p. 1), reported
that a three-day period of rioting had resulted in 28 persons' being killed and 500
injured. Illinois troops restored order. Most of the states had no organized force.

[9] The same, Sept. 29, 1919, p. 1.

[10] The same, September 30, p. 1.

[11] The *New York Times* (September 30, p. 1) quotes General Wood as saying
there were 4,000 troops on duty. However, the *Annual Report of the Secretary of
War*, 1920, Vol. I, p. 69, states that only 70 officers and 1,222 men were in Omaha.

downtown streets and the negro sections. A large number of arrests were made and more than 50 persons were refused bond on the ground that they were military prisoners. In ordering the arrests, General Wood said:

> When you go to make an arrest, use no more force than is necessary, and use all the force that is necessary. Remember you are sent for a certain man. Come back with him. Bring him in alive if possible. But bring him in.[12]

Two days after his arrival, General Wood relaxed the restrictions which he had put into effect relating to public assemblages. The annual fall carnival, for example, which had been suspended for three days, was permitted to resume. Although there was no further violence, some of the troops remained in Omaha until the middle of November.[13]

Two days before the riot at Omaha, and during the famous western trip in which he urged the entry of the United States into the League of Nations, President Wilson suffered a nervous breakdown. As a consequence, troop movements during succeeding weeks were handled without his knowledge. Once again the power of the departmental commanders was increased. In an address at Cleveland, October 15, Secretary Baker explained the reason for the government's action.

> In our own country, we have been hearing a very great deal of post-armistice troubles. Sometimes it manifests itself as race riots, and mob violence. Sometimes it takes some form of industrial dispute. . . . if there be any doubt as to what the intention of the Government on the subject is, I can assure you that the timid can take heart.
> When the Omaha riot broke out not very long ago, I sent a telegram to every Governor in America, telling him that if civil disorder broke out in his State, which by reason of the demobilization of the National Guard, he did not have the power to suppress, he should communicate at once with the Department Commander and not go through the formality of telegraphing to Washington, and I sent a telegram to every Department Commander, telling him when the Governor of a State called on him for assistance, he should send troops at once to assist him.[14]

[12] *New York Times*, Oct. 2, 1919, p. 1.
[13] During the first week in October, 500 troops were sent to Elaine, Ark., to suppress a racial conflict. The same, October 2, 3, 5.
[14] The same, October 26, p. 3.

Gary, Indiana. Within a week of the Omaha riot, disorder broke out at Gary, Indiana. A nationwide steel strike began on September 22,[15] and on October 4, when a clash occurred between the strikers and the strikebreakers, state militia were sent to Gary. Two days later, when the strikers paraded in defiance of the mayor's orders, Governor James P. Goodrich requested the regular troops.

Anticipating such a call, General Wood, who had just returned from Omaha, had already stationed a provisional regiment of 1,000 men at Camp Sheridan, north of Chicago. Eighteen minutes after the call was received, troop trucks started the journey to Gary, and late that evening, October 6, the regulars arrived in the city.[16] Shortly after midnight General Wood issued a proclamation of "qualified martial law."[17] Public meetings were forbidden. The functions of the city government were to be carried on by the local authorities, but all law-enforcing agencies were to be under the supervision of the military. After the troops arrived, the state militia was transferred to other strike areas.

General Wood returned to Chicago leaving the troops, now numbering 1,600, under the command of Colonel W. S. Mapes. The Intelligence Department, working with agents of the Department of Justice, immediately set to work to round up all agitators. According to General Wood, there was a "dangerous and extremely active group of I.W.W. and red anarchistic elements" at Gary.[18] A large number of arrests were made and "a ton or more of anarchist and Bolshevist literature siezed."[19] The home of Paul Glaser, the attorney for the strikers, was searched, and Glaser himself was taken into custody and held for examination. The Intelligence Department announced that it had uncovered a plot "to involve the steel strike region in terrorism."[20] However, newspapermen who

---

[15] For an account of the strike see Edward Berman, *Labor Disputes and the President of the United States,* pp. 166-76.
[16] Testimony of Lieutenant Donald C. Van Buren, staff of General Wood in *Investigation of Strike in Steel Industries,* Hearings before the Senate Committee on Education and Labor, 66 Cong. 1 sess., Pt. 2, pp. 908-10.
[17] *Annual Report of the Secretary of War,* 1920, Vol. I, p. 69.
[18] *New York Times,* Oct. 11, 1919, p. 3.
[19] The same, October 8, p. 1.
[20] The same, October 16, p. 1.

attempted to get the details about the conspiracy were given no information.

The first mass meeting which the military authorities permitted was held on October 15. Colonel Mapes sat on the platform, and soldiers, with machine guns in readiness, were stationed on the outskirts of the crowd. Special agents in plain clothes circulated through the crowd.

There was no further disorder of any consequence. However, the many raids and arrests which had been conducted by the army caused the strikers to lose confidence in the troops and in the government. The soldiers lost their initial popularity. On several occasions automobiles carrying troops were stoned. The strike dragged on and part of the army stayed in Gary. Finally, after a clash between civilians and soldiers in a pool room on Christmas night, Mayor W. F. Hodges asked General Wood to withdraw the troops.

The Gary incident was perhaps the only one during the post-armistice period in which the military seems to have exerted itself to an unnecessary degree.[21] If President Wilson's manner of handling the Colorado coal strike is any criterion, it is highly probable that, had he not been ill, the military would have acted in a fashion less prejudicial to the strikers. It is probable also that the President would not have allowed the troops to remain so long that they were officially asked to leave. Another year elapsed, however, before the extraordinary power of the departmental commanding officers was curbed and they were once more made dependent upon the presidential determination of the need for troops.[22]

[21] During November and December 1919, as a result of the bituminous coal strike, the War Department announced that it would furnish 100,000 soldiers, if necessary, to protect the miners who wished to work. (The same, Nov. 29, 1919, p. 1.) Troops were sent into ten states, but in no instance was there a disturbance of any consequence. A summary of the troop movements is to be found in the *Annual Report of the Secretary of War*, 1920, Vol. I, pp. 68-69.

[22] On Dec. 7, 1920, corps area commanders were "advised that federal forces will not be sent upon the request of either legislatures or governors, made to the corp area commanders, without a reference of the request with all of the facts to the War Department for submission to the President for his information and instructions. . . . ("Employment of Military Forces to Maintain Civil Order and Obedience to Law," *Riot Duty Memo.*, p. 3.) Even these instructions, however,

It is evident that the government's policies during the post-
armistice period were a complete departure from customary practice.[23] Even though most of the states had no organized protective
force, and even though the President was ill, there would seem to
be little excuse for the action of the War Department in completely
abdicating its responsibilities. Instead of the governors' sending
their requests to the President, appeals went to departmental commanding officers, and upon them, rather than upon the President,
rested the decision concerning the necessity for troops. Notwithstanding the statutory requirement of a presidential proclamation,
this matter also was left to the discretion of the commanding officers. About none of these matters did the War Department exercise
any responsibility. The number and severity of restrictions upon the
inhabitants of the disturbed area, the policies to be pursued respecting arrest and detention, the length of time the troops were to remain—all of these problems, apparently, were left to the decision
of the individual commanders. Professor Corwin has aptly summarized this extraordinary situation by pointing out that the government's manner of handling disturbances immediately after the
World War represents the "most complete, sustained, and altogether deliberate neglect of the formalities required by Article IV
and the supplementary acts of Congress that has thus far occurred."[24]

WARFARE IN THE COAL FIELDS OF WEST VIRGINIA

Nine weeks after President Harding took office he was asked to
send the federal forces to the southern border of West Virginia.
Violence, which was nothing new to the coal fields of the state, had
again flared up, this time near the city of Williamson. There seemed
to be no end to the long and bitter struggle between the miners and
the operators over the question of unionization. The operators demanded the open shop, saying that to permit unionization would

---

were not strictly in accordance with the law. It was not until the first weeks of
Harding's administration that the Secretary of War directed that requests for aid
be sent straightway to the War Department rather than to the corps commanders.
New York Times, May 15, 1921, sec. 1, p. 3.

[23] During the Pullman troubles corps commanders were finally given the power
to decide upon the necessity for troops. See p. 104.

[24] Corwin, *The President: Office and Powers*, p. 172.

mean the loss of control over the entire industry.[25] The United Mine Workers of America, on the other hand, contended that to them also much more was at stake than the principle of collective bargaining. They stated that in West Virginia the relationship of the operator to the miner was that of master to servant and that by means of armed guards, private detectives, and deputy sheriffs, the miners were coerced and maltreated. According to Philip Murray, vice-president of the United Mine Workers, the operators of West Virginia constituted an "autocratic, industrial oligarchy," whose policies led to "industrial and civil warfare."[26]

Appeal by governors of two states. Neither the operators nor the miners were willing to accept the responsibility for having begun the shooting which broke out May 12, 1921, along the boundary line between West Virginia and Kentucky. Since West Virginia had never reorganized its National Guard after the World War and, as a consequence, had no organized force adequate for an emergency, Governor E. F. Morgan did not long delay in asking for federal help. His request was endorsed by Governor E. P. Morrow of Kentucky, who telegraphed the President:

> Lawless situation existing along Kentucky and West Virginia border line, Tug River boundary between Pike County, Ky., and Mingo, W.Va. Situation beyond the control of State forces at my command. Join in request of Governor of West Virginia made to me and proper military authorities that Federal troops be sent there to control the situation and restore law and order.[27]

Additional pressure was brought to bear upon Harding by a visit to the White House of West Virginia's United States Senator Sutherland, and a third request from Governor Morgan, asking, "Are we compelled to witness further slaughter of innocent law abiding citizens with no signs of relief from the Federal Government?"[28]

Refusal to send federal troops for state police work. Harding,

[25] Testimony of Harry Olmstead, representing the Operators' Association, Williamson Field, in *West Virginia, The Civil War in Its Coal Fields,* Hearings before the Senate Committee on Education and Labor, 67 Cong. 1 sess., Vol. I, p. 255.
[26] The same, Vol. II, p. 611.
[27] *New York Times,* May 15, 1921, sec. 1, p. 1.
[28] The same, p. 3.

however, was not to be stampeded. Although the troops at Camp Sherman, in Chillicothe, Ohio, were instructed to be in readiness, no move was made toward dispatching them until a corps area staff officer investigated the need for federal forces. Since requests had been received from the governors of both West Virginia and Kentucky, Harding, after conferring with Secretary of War John W. Weeks, signed a proclamation of martial law for each state.[29] Pending the results of the investigation, the proclamations were not issued. It was at this time also that the policy of allowing the corps area commanders to exercise control over any except emergency requests from the civil authorities was rescinded. Once again all requests were to be sent directly to the War Department for the information and decision of the President.[30]

In spite of renewed urging by Senator Sutherland to promulgate immediately the declaration of martial law and dispatch the troops, all thought of so doing was dispelled by the report of Major C. F. Thompson, the Fifth Corps Area staff officer who had been sent to investigate. Thompson simply stated that in his opinion, which proved to be correct, there was no necessity for troops.[31] After a Cabinet meeting on May 17, the President issued a declaration of policy in the form of a telegram from his secretary to Governor Morgan:

The President directs me to address to you the statement that the Federal Government is ever ready to perform its full duty in the maintenance of constituted authority, but he feels he is not justified in directing the military forces of the nation to enter the State of West Virginia, according to your request, until he is well assured that the State has exhausted all its resources in the performance of its functions. On the representations thus far made, the President is not convinced that West Virginia has exhausted all its own resources, and he awaits more definite assurances.[32]

Harding, it was explained, was opposed to the federal troops' acting as a police force. The New York Times, in speaking editorially of the "loose tendency . . . to appeal too quickly to Washington to do

[29] The same, p. 1.
[30] The same, p. 3. See note 22, p. 157.
[31] The same, May 17, 1921, p. 6.
[32] The same, May 18, p. 6.

police work, properly belonging to the States," commended the President for the position he had taken.[33]

The protest march to Mingo County. Left to his own resources Governor Morgan declared Mingo County under martial law. The enforcement of regulations laid down by the Governor was left to a small force of state constabulary and a newly organized Vigilance Committee. The United Mine Workers challenged the validity of the Governor's declaration, and the West Virginia Supreme Court of Appeals upheld the miners on the ground that there could be no real martial law so long as it was enforced by civil agencies. The Court held that a military force of sufficient size to hold the territory was essential under a declaration of martial law.[34] The Governor thereupon issued another proclamation of martial law and, in line with the Court's decision, called a part of the enrolled militia of Mingo County to active duty.

There were intermittent outbursts throughout the summer, but nothing of a really formidable nature occurred until the middle of August. Miners from the Paint Creek and Cabin Creek coal fields along the Kanawha River had assembled at Marmet for a march through Boone and Logan Counties to Mingo County. The March was to be staged as a protest against the martial law which had been in effect for over three months in the strike-ridden area.[35] New recruitments rapidly swelled the number at Marmet until on Au-

[33] The same, May 19, p. 14.

[34] *Ex parte Lavinder,* 88 W.Va. 713, 108 S.E. 428 (1921). For an account of this first phase of martial law, see Robert S. Rankin, *When Civil Law Fails,* pp. 126-33.

[35] *New York Times,* August 21, p. 10. "The object of the demonstration seems to be shrouded in uncertainty. One account has it that the miners intended to march to Mingo County, crossing Logan County in their path, and protest against the enforcement of martial law there and the abuses that they understood were being committed against their fellows. According to this version, what they really hoped for was to get Federal troops called into Mingo County as a better alternative than the regime then in force. Another story, credited to the operators and some residents of Logan County, is that they intended to seize the mines in Logan and compel the employers to recognize the union. A third is that theirs was a vague, leaderless uprising without deliberate purpose or objective. Whatever its motive, there is no doubt that it spread considerable terror among the inhabitants in its path, especially those in Logan County who were fearful of an attack." Winthrop D. Lane in *West Virginia, The Civil War in its Coal Fields,* Hearings before the Senate Committee on Education and Labor, 67 Cong. 1 sess., Vol. II, p. 1009.

gust 25, when the march began, 4,000 men were estimated to be participating in the "invasion."[36]

Once again Governor Morgan appealed for federal forces. Once again the War Department, with the President's approval, decided to investigate. This time two officers were sent, Major Thompson from the Fifth Corps Area staff and Brigadier General Henry H. Bandholtz, Commander of the District of Washington. The General lost little time in making his investigation. He arrived at Charleston at 3:15 A.M., August 26, and 45 minutes later was in conference with the Governor at the Capitol. Shortly afterward he talked with C. F. Keeney and Fred Mooney, president and secretary-treasurer of the local miners' union. According to a statement of Secretary Weeks, Keeney and Mooney were "briefly and courteously informed" that a condition bordering on insurrection existed, that the condition was due "to the action of members" of the district miners' union, "that leadership entailed responsibility as well as prerogatives," and that in the event a state of martial law was proclaimed the leaders would be held strictly accountable.[37]

At 5:30 Keeney and Mooney left the Capitol. By noon they had reached the advance guard of marchers and at 3:30 Bandholtz received word from the union leaders that the "movement had been checked and that the men had voted to return."[38] Keeney endeavored, without much success, to secure trains to expedite the homeward journey. The next day Bandholtz drove to Racine over the line of march and talked with a number of the miners. From the statements of Keeney and Mooney there is no indication that they resented the rather arbitrary position taken by the General. The action of Bandholtz so strongly urging, if not commanding, the dispersion of the miners was reported to have been decided upon "with the full cognizance of President Harding and his Cabinet."[39]

But neither did the General display much sympathy with the

[36] *New York Times*, August 26, p. 1.
[37] The same, August 30, p. 17.
[38] The same.
[39] The same, August 27, p. 5. The correctness of the report is attested by the telegram which Bandholtz sent to Washington: "I told the union leaders that a crisis had now arisen in the state of affairs, that they as leaders must be considered responsible to a great extent for the present situation and that in any event I should be reluctantly obliged to hold them responsible in case it might become necessary

position of Governor Morgan. On April 28, the legislature had passed an enabling act, to become effective July 1, providing for a National Guard. Yet up to the time of the march the Governor's only step had been to appoint an Adjutant General. Furthermore, in the opinion of Bandholtz, "the State had made only a feeble attempt to check the growth of the insurgent movement or to keep in reasonable touch with its progress."[40] On the basis of the General's report and also because of a letter from Governor Morgan stating that peace prevailed, the President and Secretary Weeks, in a conference on the afternoon of August 29, decided that it was unnecessary to send federal forces.

Outbreak of violence. Twenty-four hours later Harding issued a proclamation commanding the insurgents to disperse. Preparations were again made to dispatch troops. Conditions had suddenly changed and Governor Morgan had once more appealed for help. On the morning of August 30, the President conferred with Secretary Weeks, Major General James G. Harbord, the Assistant Chief of Staff, General Bandholtz, who had just returned, and a delegation of prominent West Virginians who urged the immediate dispatch of troops. After a second telephone call from Governor Morgan, and a second conference, it was decided to issue the proclamation.

The renewed calls for assistance were based on the fact that the miners had reassembled and there was fear that a regular battle might be waged in the "district of uncertainty" along the Boone-Logan border line. General Bandholtz, who was ordered to return to West Virginia, telegraphed from Charleston his explanation of what had happened to suddenly change the picture:

It is believed that the withdrawal of the invaders as promised by Keeney and Mooney (respectively President and Vice President of the district miner's union) would have been satisfactorily accomplished but for the tardy sending of trains and particularly but for the ill-advised and ill-timed advance movement of State constabulary on the night of Aug. 27, resulting in bloodshed.[41]

---

to resort to the drastic extreme required by my instructions." Cassius M. Dowell, *Military Aid to the Civil Power*, p. 198.

[40] *New York Times*, August 30, p. 17.

[41] The same, September 3, p. 2.

The Governor defended the constabulary with the statement that in attempting to serve warrants in the town of Sharples, the police had been fired upon and they had returned the fire. Two miners were killed and a like number injured. Philip Murray charged that the state had broken faith with the miners in that there was "a distinct understanding" that their lives were to be protected while they were following out the terms of the agreement to disperse.[42]

The President's proclamation, which was distributed by airplane, commanded all persons engaged in "unlawful and insurrectionary proceedings to disperse and retire peaceably to their respective abodes on or before 12 o'clock, noon, of the 1st day of September."[43] The effect of the proclamation was negligible, however, since the fighting had already begun. Harding quickly prepared a second proclamation, this one a declaration of martial law applying to five counties, Kanawha, Fayette, Boone, Logan, and Mingo. Bandholtz took the second proclamation with him, although there was no decision as to the time it should be issued. It was decided, however, that if the miners had not dispersed by the time designated by the President, they could be considered as having placed themselves in opposition to the United States and that the War Department would then be compelled to take action.

Sheriffs' deputies, state police, and volunteers to the number of approximately 1,200 were drawn up along the Logan County line while the miners and their followers were holding the Boone County side. Two army officers accompanied by representatives of the miners went into the trouble zone carrying letters from General Bandholtz and Governor Morgan asking the men to disband. The officers met with little success and, upon their return, the General telegraphed the Adjutant General for troops.[44]

The army takes charge. Two hours later the Adjutant General issued orders to dispatch the troops. The first contingent arrived at St. Albans, West Virginia, the evening of September 2. From Fort Benjamin Harrison, Indiana, Camp Sherman, Ohio, Camp Dix, New Jersey, and Camp Knox and Fort Thomas, Kentucky, came

[42] The same, p. 1.
[43] 42 Stat. L. 2247.
[44] *New York Times,* September 3, p. 1.

detachments of troops. Altogether 2,100 men were ordered into the trouble zone.[45] Eight one-pound guns, eight trench mortars, and a chemical warfare service detachment came from New Jersey; a complete radio outfit and 50 army mules from Kentucky. Even before Bandholtz had decided federal forces were necessary, the 88th Light Bombing Squadron consisting of 15 planes had been dispatched from Langley Field, Virginia.[46]

The arrival of the United States troops was welcomed by everyone. The leaders of the miners expressed the willingness of the men to "submit without objection to rules and regulations that might be laid down by the Federal authorities." They promised that "not a single shot will be fired on Federal troops *coming up from the rear of the miners' line*."[47] Governor Morgan was likewise pleased to be relieved of a very trying task. To insure the utmost cooperation with the federal authorities, he issued a proclamation of a very novel type:

> To all State and County Officers, Civil and Military, and Deputies, Assistants and Subordinates:
>
> Whereas, United States troops have, at my request, been ordered to this State for the purpose of quelling an insurrection, the peace officers of this State are ordered to cooperate with the United States troops to the end that there may be unity of action.
>
> The peace officers of this State will obey the direction of the officer commanding the United States troops, or his properly designated representative.[48]

The President and his Secretary of War were reluctant to issue the proclamation of martial law. For that matter, so was General Bandholtz.[49] Not only was there a natural unwillingness to declare martial law, there was also the fear that such a step was unwarranted in view of the decision in the Milligan case that "martial law can never exist where the courts are open and in the proper and un-

---

[45] The same, p. 2.

[46] The bombers were used for reconnaissance only. Four of the fifteen crashed before the squadron returned to Langley Field.

[47] *New York Times*, September 3, p. 1. Italics added.

[48] The same.

[49] To advise him on the proper legal procedure, the General was accompanied by Colonel W. A. Bethel, who had served as Judge Advocate General of the American Expeditionary Force in France.

obstructed exercise of their jurisdiction."[50] It was finally decided to delay as long as possible the issuance of the proclamation and to declare martial law only as a last resort.[51]

As a matter of fact Bandholtz had already received instructions which allowed him considerable discretion. He was advised, on the one hand, to act with the greatest discretion and caution, to countenance and support the civil officers, and to avoid interference with the civil functions and processes of the state. At the same time he was told that necessity was the measure of his authority and he was empowered to "make such dispensations as shall appear proper with respect to those who commit or may be about to commit physical violence," and to retain in military custody "so long as the necessity exists" persons whose presence at the scene of disorder "impedes the accomplishment of your purpose."[52]

Fortunately, the army met with no opposition whatever. Headquarters were established at Logan, behind the state and county forces, and at Madison behind the miners' lines. Bandholtz did not disperse the state and county forces but he made it plain that "they are now under the control of the Federal authorities and they will do just as they are told."[53] With the coming of the federal troops, however, they willingly left the scene. Bandholtz forbade any assemblies, either of "miners or other citizens," but it was evident that the federal commander did not intend to follow a harsh policy when he dismissed 400 miners who had surrendered to the army. They were taken by train to St. Albans and then allowed to go to their homes.

Within a very short time the miners had dispersed. The policy of the army was to disarm them, where possible, but to leave the question of punishment to the civil authorities. On September 6, a half week after their arrival, orders were given for the return of a large portion of the troops and within three months all of them were removed.

[50] *Ex parte Milligan,* 4 Wallace 2 (1866).

[51] No word other than insurrection, according to Secretary Weeks, properly described "the refusal of bands of armed men to comply with the presidential command to disperse." *New York Times,* September 3, p. 1.

[52] Dowell, *Military Aid to the Civil Power,* p. 200.

[53] *New York Times,* September 4, p. 1.

The sending of the army brought peace, but it did little to solve the issues in dispute. The President did nothing to effect a settlement, either before or during the period of crisis. His policy was simply to preserve the peace. It was not difficult to do this since the miners had no quarrel with the federal government. Indeed, they looked upon the troops as protecting them from the operators' force of mine guards and deputy sheriffs.

The President relied for advice almost exclusively upon the War Department. It is interesting to note that when the crisis was reached, nothing but the actual presence of the federal troops halted the fighting. General Bandholtz' daybreak pronouncement to the union officials seemed, for a time, to be all that was necessary. When, owing to unfortunate circumstances, the General's efforts failed, the President's proclamation was issued as a device, per se, to disperse the miners. When it was finally decided that nothing short of a demonstration of force would accomplish the desired result, the War Department wisely sent a considerable body of troops. Very wisely too, the troops were distributed in such a fashion as to reassure the miners of the impartial position of the federal government. With no military action whatever against the miners and without the drastic measures urged by the Governor and, for a time, considered by the President and his advisers, the disorder was abruptly ended.[54]

THE BONUS ARMY

In the summer of 1932, President Hoover faced one of the most trying problems imaginable, the presence in the nation's capital of

[54] The President's record for impartial action suffered considerably during the coal strike of 1922. Although at one time he refused to send troops into New Mexico until disturbances reached a point where the state was unable to maintain order, later he assured the governors of 20 coal-producing states of "the prompt and full support of the Federal Government whenever and wherever you find your own agencies of law and order inadequate to meet the situation." (Berman, *Labor Disputes and the President*, p. 222.) In a speech to the operators and miners, Harding invited both groups to resume operations. "It was understood," wrote Berman, "that the government would afford military protection for all operators who would undertake to run their mines with strikebreakers" (p. 222). The War Department instructed the corps commanders to be prepared for strike duty, but relatively few operators attempted to run their mines, and serious trouble did not develop.

thousands of needy veterans who were determined to force the immediate payment of the soldiers' bonus. From every part of the country, by almost every conceivable means of transportation, veterans flocked to Washington to demand that Congress relieve, by a flood of cash, the economic paralysis which had settled over the United States. Reminiscent of the followers of Coxey 40 years before, the veterans seized trains in East St. Louis and Baltimore and took temporary possession of the Pennsylvania Railroad yard at Cleveland. Their presence in Washington was described as a "supreme escape gesture."[55]

Arrangements for handling the Marchers. From the very first the task of providing for the Bonus Army proved to be a vexing one. The building program of the government on Pennsylvania Avenue was halted in order that shelter might be provided in a number of partially razed buildings. The main camp of the veterans was located across the Anacostia River where, in addition to a number of army tents, hundreds of shacks were erected from all sorts of materials. The problem of food was ever acute. The District authorities and especially the energetic superintendent of police, General Pelham D. Glassford, assumed the task of assisting the veterans in securing food and shelter.

The Patman bill, which called for immediate payment of the $2,400,000,000 represented by the veterans' adjusted compensation certificates, was passed by the House on June 15, by a vote of 209 to 176. The President, however, let it be known that he would not approve the bill and two days later, in spite of all the pressure which the veterans could muster, the bill was decisively defeated in the Senate, 62 to 18. Undaunted by this action, which they considered merely as a temporary setback, the Bonus Army determined to stay. They believed the Senate could be forced to reverse its decision.

However, a month of continuous agitation found the Marchers no nearer their goal. On July 16, Congress adjourned, having in the meantime, at the suggestion of President Hoover, passed a bill providing $100,000 to transport the veterans to their homes. The

[55] *New York Times,* June 9, 1932, p. 19.

money was to be distributed as a loan without interest and to be charged against the adjusted compensation certificates. Applications were to be made by July 15, but this date was soon extended ten days when the number applying for transportation proved to be such a small percentage of the total number of veterans. Even by July 22, only 3,200 had made application for transportation homeward. Police estimated that over 11,000 persons remained in the 24 separate camps throughout the District.[56] With the departure of one family, for many veterans had brought their wives and children with them, another group, veterans or not, attracted by the furor over the Bonus Marchers, would arrive.

During June and early July there were no disturbances of any consequence. The veterans were rather well organized and they realized very keenly the necessity of maintaining order. They had their own disciplinary body, which was active on several occasions in ejecting Communists from the camps. However, the presence of so many thousands of unattached and discontented men was a constant source of worry to local and federal authorities. As early as June 3, General Glassford had recommended that, in addition to special police precautions,[57] "preparations be made by the Commissioners to declare an emergency, and to provide for the use of the National Guard, or to place in effect 'The White Plan,' "[58] the War Department's official designation of the plan to be followed by the regular army in quelling internal disorders. The federal authorities were also active. The White House Guard was increased and 300 troops were secretly assembled "in the Munitions Building, to be used in the event of any disorder at the Capitol or White House."[59]

[56] The same, July 23, p. 2.
[57] Such as keeping a "heavy police reserve . . . out of sight in the crypt of the capitol building." Statement of General Glassford in the *New York American,* Nov. 3, 1932, p. 9.
[58] *New York Times,* Nov. 4, 1932, p. 2.
[59] Theodore G. Joslin, *Hoover Off the Record,* p. 264. On July 14, Vice-President Curtis, apparently in a moment of terror, asked that two companies of marines be sent to the Capitol. According to General Glassford, at the very time the marines were being moved he was in a meeting with General Mosely, General Miles, and several other officers, listening to General MacArthur explain the procedure for calling out federal troops. Glassford, Miles, and Admiral Butler, who had ordered the marines at the request of the Vice-President, went to the Capitol. At the request

On the day Congress adjourned an attempt to establish a picket line in front of the White House was frustrated by the police. Pennsylvania Avenue was closed and Lafayette Square was cleared. Again on July 20, a group of 200 marched to the White House where they were met and dispersed by 100 of the District police. Five days later a slight scuffle occurred when a third march by a somewhat smaller group was halted. By this time, in the opinion of General Glassford, the worst was over.[60] There were still, however, over 8,000 of the Bonus Expeditionary Force in the various cantonments.

Eviction from government buildings. In the meantime, Treasury authorities had indicated to the Commissioners their desire to resume work on the buildings undergoing demolition. Fearful of resistance, the Treasury asked that protection be given their agents in the task of repossessing the skeletonized structures. General Glassford was instructed by the Commissioners to furnish police protection. To give adequate warning of the intended repossession of the buildings, a formal notice to vacate was posted on July 23.[61] After the order to evacuate had been twice postponed, plans were made for repossessing the buildings on Thursday, July 28. This decision was reached after a long conference between the President, Secretary of War Patrick Hurley, Secretary of the Treasury Ogden Mills, and Acting Secretary of the Treasury Ferry K. Heath.

Late Thursday morning the Treasury employees, accompanied by a heavy police guard, acted to enforce the eviction order. The veterans resisted, and in the resulting clash the police killed one veteran and fatally wounded a second. Shortly after the riot, which lasted but a short time, the District Commissioners telephoned the White House asking that troops be dispatched to the scene. The President asked for a written request but, pending its arrival, he telephoned the Secretary of War, thus giving Hurley an opportunity to prepare for quick action. The letter of the Commissioners, which was promptly sent to the White House, concludes:

---

of Glassford, Butler ordered the marines to return to their base. *New York American*, Nov. 3, 1932, p. 9.
  [60] *New York Times*, July 26, 1932, p. 1.
  [61] *The Washington Herald*, July 24, 1932, p. 11.

. . . it is the opinion of the Major and Superintendent of Police, in which the Commissioners concur, that it will be impossible for the Police Department to maintain law and order except by the free use of firearms which will make the situation a dangerous one; it is believed, however, that the presence of Federal troops in some number will obviate the seriousness of the situation and result in far less violence and bloodshed.

The Commissioners of the District of Columbia, therefore, request that they be given the assistance of Federal troops in maintaining law and order in the District of Columbia.[62]

Buildings cleared by federal troops. The President at once instructed the Secretary of War to call out the troops. At 2:55 P.M. Hurley issued the following order to the Chief of Staff, General Douglas MacArthur:

The President has just informed me that the civil government of the District of Columbia has reported to him that it is unable to maintain law and order in the District.

You will have the United States troops proceed immediately to the scene of disorder. Cooperate fully with the District of Columbia police force which is now in charge. Surround the affected area and clear it without delay.

Turn over all prisoners to the civil authorities.

In your orders insist that any women and children who may be in the affected area be accorded every consideration and kindness. Use all humanity consistent with the due execution of this order.[63]

A tank platoon and a cavalry squadron from Fort Meyer, Virginia, and an infantry battalion from Fort Washington, Maryland, were selected to be sent into the District. Reserve troops from Fort Meade and Fort Howard, Maryland, and Fort Humphreys, Virginia, were ordered to concentrate at Fort Meyer. Altogether there were about 500 troops, with 1,000 more held in reserve.

Seldom has a major campaign witnessed such a display of military officialdom as participated in the movement against the Bonus Marchers. In addition to General MacArthur and General Perry L.

[62] For the complete text of the request see Joslin, *Hoover Off the Record*, p. 267. After the riot a long-drawn-out and very acrimonious debate developed between the Commissioners and General Glassford as to whether he had consented to the request for troops.

[63] The same, p. 268.

Miles, who was in immediate command of the troops, the army was accompanied by General Van Horn Moseley, the Deputy Chief of Staff. At 4:30 P.M. the order was given to begin the movement eastward on Pennsylvania Avenue. General Miles proceeded "on the theory that demonstration of overpowering force, accompanied by sufficient time to permit dispersion of the rioters, promised the surest, simplest and safest results in this situation."[64] The cavalry led the way, followed by tanks, machine gunners, and infantry, all headed toward the "fort" of the B. E. F.,[65] a skeletonized building at Third Street. After a half hour's wait the troops donned gas masks and in a few minutes of tear gas bombing completely cleared the "fort." The troops were deployed in such a fashion as to drive the Marchers away from the business area and toward the encampment at Anacostia. This was accomplished without the troops' firing a shot although, apparently, there was a considerable display of swinging cavalry sabres and prodding bayonets.

Demolition of Anacostia encampment. The troops did not stop after clearing out the area in which disorder occurred. Shortly after 9:00 P.M. they moved into the Anacostia encampment. General MacArthur reported that he ordered a temporary halt to give further time for the Marchers to withdraw from the camp. Presently, however, the troops were instructed to proceed. During the night and the following day the shacks which had been in the path of the troops were completely destroyed. The explanation of the Chief of Staff for the many fires was that the Marchers themselves had kindled the first flames, and that "reported subsequent burning of individual shacks by soldiers, if authentic,[66] was for the purpose only of hastening the destruction of the camp already doomed by the action of the Bonus Marchers themselves."[67]

The veterans were reported to have been "aghast at the failure of their confident prediction that no soldier would move into action against them."[68] Driven into the open, with their places of shelter

---

[64] Report of General MacArthur to President Hoover in Joslin, *Hoover Off the Record*, p. 269.
[65] Bonus Expeditionary Force.
[66] Newsreels demonstrated the authenticity of the report.
[67] Report of General MacArthur in Joslin, *Hoover Off the Record*, p. 273.
[68] *New York Times*, July 29, p. 1.

totally destroyed, there was nothing for them to do but leave the District. Penniless, homeless, and unwanted, their departure and ultimate dispersal marks a pitiful chapter in America's depression history.

On the day following the riot, the President replied to the Commissioners' request for assistance. "I complied with your request for aid from the Army to the police. . . . It is a matter of satisfaction," he wrote, "that, after the arrival of this assistance, the mobs which were defying the municipal government were dissolved without the firing of a shot or the loss of a life." He pointed out that since martial law had not been declared, responsibility for the maintenance of order "still rests upon your commission and the police." In a press conference statement the same day, the President made the oft-quoted declaration, "Government cannot be coerced by mob rule."[69]

Hoover placed the blame for the riot, not on the veterans, a large number of whom, he said, had gone home, but on the communistic and criminal elements who had led the remaining veterans into violence.[70] Attorney General William D. Mitchell was asked to make an investigation of the incident. On the eve of the national convention of the American Legion the President released Mitchell's report. It asserted that of the first 3,6000 men who had registered on the muster rolls of the Bonus Army, one fourth could not be identified, in either the War Department or the Veterans' Bureau, as having served in the World War.[71] The report also stated that of 4,700 men who had applied for transportation home, 22 per cent had police records. The President emphasized that the report should not be taken "to reflect upon the many thousands of honest, law abiding men who came to Wash-

[69] For the complete text of the quotations above see *The State Papers and Other Public Writings of Herbert Hoover* (William Starr Myers, ed.), Vol. II, pp. 244-45.

[70] The same, p. 242. On November 2, practically on the eve of the election, Glassford denied the charge that the Bonus Army contained an "extraordinary proportion of criminal, communist, and non-veteran elements." *New York American*, November 2, p. 17.

[71] Mitchell stated that the practice of registering the veterans was discontinued when it was learned that the muster rolls were being checked by the police. For the full report of the Attorney General see the *New York Times*, Sept. 12, 1932, p. 8.

ington with full right of presentation of their views to the Congress. This better element and their leaders acted at all times to restrain crime and violence, but, after the adjournment of Congress, a large portion of them returned to their homes and gradually these better elements lost control."[72]

Criticism of the President's action. The riot occurred just three months before a presidential election. This fact accounts, in part, for the unusually severe criticism to which Hoover was subjected. Why, the question was asked, did not the Treasury officials take legal action to rid the government properties of the trespassers? The argument was advanced that had the Bonus Marchers ignored an order of the court there would have been greater justification for the procedure which was employed. However, was there any reason to suppose that a court order would have commanded any greater respect than an eviction order signed by the Acting Secretary of the Treasury? Cleveland called out the troops more than once after he had tried in vain to stop various contingents of the Coxey Army by means of court processes.[73] In the case of the Bonus Marchers, the government of the United States had ordered an evacuation of its property. There was no moral or legal obligation to obtain a court order commanding the same thing.

The President was also criticised for not issuing a proclamation, as prescribed by law, announcing the coming of the troops. In view of the procedure used in calling the army, this criticism seems valid. His Cabinet officers, in writing of the incident, stated that the Commissioners had the "same right of call as the Governor of any State."[74] If this was the view of the President, and the steps taken in calling the troops would seem to indicate as much, then a proclamation should have been issued. However, in this instance, it is difficult to see what good the proclamation might have done.

Hoover's well-meaning biographers, in attempting to free him from all responsibility for the actions of the army, placed the President in an unfavorable light. In describing the events leading up to the movement of troops, the President's secretary wrote:

[72] *State Papers of Herbert Hoover,* Vol. II, pp. 274-75.
[73] See pp. 89-90.
[74] Ray Lyman Wilbur and Arthur M. Hyde, *The Hoover Policies,* p. 204.

I heard him ask Secretary Hurley that the troops should be moved into the trouble area without firearms. The request was not observed by the Army command. Now let it be stated that his responsibility was limited to acting on the request of the District Commissioners and to ordering the use of troops. That action having been taken, the responsibility thereafter rested with the military officials in charge. They could, and of course did, weigh his request. Then they made their decision. It was that soldiers use guns, not sticks.[75]

Such a description of the President's power is most misleading. It is incorrect to say that his responsibility was discharged once he had ordered out the troops. The statement obviously disregards his constitutional position as commander-in-chief of the armed forces. In asking that the troops use no firearms the President disregarded a principle the wisdom of which previous disorders had long since demonstrated, that, when troops are to be used *against* any group, less resistance is likely to be encountered and less injury to result from a demonstration of overpowering force.

The movement of the army into Anacostia was the one event most severely criticised. It was this act, rather than the more spectacular afternoon demonstration, which aroused so much resentment among the Marchers. To drive the Marchers out of their only places of shelter during the night was a harsh measure. On the other hand, had they been given time to organize their forces, a much more serious situation might have developed. Two members of Hoover's Cabinet afterwards claimed that the President's order to the Secretary of War specifying the area within which the troops were to operate was disobeyed.[76] This claim contradicted the report that the army's delay at Anacostia was because of a White House conference at which "Secretary Hurley and General MacArthur persuaded the President to allow the War Department's plans to be carried on without interruption."[77] In view of his position as commander-in-chief, and since, as his Secretary admitted, Hoover kept in close touch with all that was happening,[78] it seems inconceivable that any troop movements were carried out contrary to his express command.

[75] Joslin, *Hoover Off the Record*, p. 268.
[76] Wilbur and Hyde, *The Hoover Policies*, pp. 204-05.
[77] *New York Times*, July 30, p. 6.
[78] Joslin, *Hoover Off the Record*, p. 275.

Whether the President should have exercised an even greater patience and arranged for the removal of the Marchers to an area more remote from the city, or whether such action would simply have flooded the national capital with an ever-increasing number of unemployed is a matter for speculation. Any appraisal of Hoover's action must take into account the fact that for eight weeks the city's inhabitants had been annoyed by the presence of the thousands of Bonus Marchers. So long as Congress was in session, even though the Patman bill had suffered defeat weeks before, no untoward action was taken against this worrisome crowd of discontented men. Not until after the adjournment of Congress, when there was no longer any valid reason for their remaining, were the Marchers ordered to leave the property which they had appropriated. By refusing to obey the government's order and by defying the District police, the Marchers brought down upon themselves the armed forces of the United States. Owing to the efficient and orderly methods employed by the troops, the Marchers suffered relatively little physical injury. Whether a less harsh policy would in the long run have proved more satisfactory is a question, the merits of which, even a decade later, are extremely difficult to assess.

CHAPTER XI

THE STRIKE AT NORTH AMERICAN AVIATION

A sudden strike in the plant of North American Aviation, Incorporated, at Los Angeles, on June 5, 1941, precipitated President Franklin D. Roosevelt's first use of the regular troops. During his previous administrations, the President had disapproved every proposal to call out the troops.[1] In this instance, however, because of his belief in the urgent necessity for the continued production of fighting planes, he showed no hesitancy in making use of the armed forces.

STRIKE CALLED IN SPITE OF AGREEMENT

As a result of the defense program, production facilities at North American Aviation, Incorporated, had been rapidly expanded, and thousands of new workers had been added within a few months. A struggle for membership between rival union organizations had been settled in March 1941, when an election was conducted by the National Labor Relations Board. By a margin of only 70 votes the American Federation of Machinists was defeated by the Congress of Industrial Organizations' United Automobile Workers' Union.[2] In the period from March to June, over 4,000 additional workers were hired, and each union claimed a majority of the new employees. However, the CIO continued to be recognized as the bargaining agent of the aircraft workers.

The strike was called, ostensibly, in order to force an increase in wages. Seven weeks previously, the CIO Automobile Workers'

[1] For example, the Scottsboro trials in 1933. The defense counsel telegraphed the President for troops. The request was forwarded to the governor of Alabama and a statement was issued at the White House that "the Federal Executive has not interfered and cannot interfere in any case under the jurisdiction of the courts of a sovereign state." (*New York Times*, Nov. 21, 1933, p. 14.) The President was also requested to furnish troops during the San Francisco general strike in 1934 and during the automobile sit-down strikes in 1937. In one instance, the Rhode Island textile strike in 1934, preparations were made to send the army. See p. 194.

[2] *New York Times*, June 8, 1941, p. 37.

Union had demanded an increase from 50 cents per hour to 75 cents for beginners' pay, and a general increase of 10 cents per hour. The company balked at the thought of increasing by 50 per cent the wage paid to newcomers. Such a demand, in the opinion of the employers, was entirely out of line with the wage policies of other aircraft manufacturers.[3] After conciliation efforts had failed, the Secretary of Labor, on May 24, certified the dispute to the National Defense Mediation Board. Three days later the bargaining committee of the union and representatives of the company drew up an agreement before the Board, which was subsequently ratified by the union membership, to the effect that no "stoppage of work or interference in any way with production" would take place during the "pendency" of the case before the National Defense Mediation Board.[4] The company promised, providing there was no violation of the agreement, to make any benefits to the workers retroactive to May 1.

Notwithstanding this agreement, and without any authorization from the United Automobile Workers' Union or the CIO, leaders of the UAW Local 683 called the strike. They asserted that the National Defense Mediation Board was simply "stalling the workers."[5] Acting under the orders of local "strike captains," from 1,500 to 2,000 pickets barred the entrance to the plant Thursday morning, June 5, 1941. The company abandoned plans to continue operating, and the plant was closed. The shutdown affected 9,000 production workers and over 2,200 office and other employees.

Because of the tremendous emphasis which was being placed upon the production of fighting planes, and because of the important position which North American Aviation, Incorporated, held

[3] Though beginning wages in the aircraft industry may have been low compared with wages in other industries, the wage rates at North American were not different from those paid in most aircraft manufacturing plants. Indeed, the fact that they were no different is not without significance. Ryan, Republic, Northrup, Martin, Menasco, Fairchild, Curtiss Wright (St. Louis), Consolidated, and the Vultee plant in Tennessee, all paid 50 cents an hour as a beginning wage. After the strike at the Vultee, California, plant some months previously, the hiring rate had been set at 55 cents per hour. Lockheed paid 51 cents per hour, Douglas 52½, Brewster 55, and Boeing 62½. (Wage rates obtained at the office of the National Defense Mediation Board.)

[4] New York Times, June 6, 1941, p. 15.

[5] Statement of William P. Goodman, a spokesman of the striking workers. New York Times, June 6, 1914, p. 15.

in that production,[6] there was an immediate and widespread demand that the plant be opened without delay. Nationally recognized labor leaders were among the first to denounce the action of the local union. Representatives of the American Federation of Labor, the Congress of Industrial Organizations, and the Independent Railroad Brotherhoods, making up the Labor Policy Advisory Committee of the Office of Production Management, resolved that the strike was "in complete and irresponsible disregard of proper trade union practices.[7] Richard T. Frankensteen, national director of the aviation division of the United Automobile Workers, CIO, condemned the "irresponsible, inexperienced and impulsive action of local leaders" who had violated the agreement which they had themselves made to keep the plant in operation until the National Defense Mediation Board had completed its findings. Frankensteen asserted also that the strike demonstrated "the vicious manoeuvering of the Communist Party."[8] In a statement more conservatively worded than that of his assistant, Philip Murray, president of the Congress of Industrial Organizations, also advised the aircraft workers to return to their jobs.[9]

RUMOR OF FEDERAL INTERVENTION

The strike was called less than ten days after President Roosevelt had proclaimed that an "unlimited national emergency confronts this country." In his proclamation, the President called "upon all loyal citizens engaged in production for defense to give precedence to the needs of the nation," and he asked "workmen as well as employers to merge their lesser differences in the larger effort to insure the survival of the only kind of Government which recognizes the rights of labor or of capital."[10] The action of the aircraft workers seemed to be a direct challenge to the President's

[6] North American Aviation, Incorporated, produced about ten planes per day, or about 22 per cent of the nation's military aircraft production.

[7] *New York Times*, June 7, 1941, p. 8.

[8] The same, June 8, 1941, p. 37. Frankensteen said that he was "expressing the official position" of the Congress of Industrial Organizations and that he was speaking with the full knowledge and complete accord of President Philip Murray.

[9] The same, June 9, p. 10.

[10] *Federal Register*, May 29, 1941, Vol. VI, No. 105, p. 2617.

statement, made less than ten days before, that "this Government is determined to use all of its power . . . to prevent interference with the production of materials essential to our Nation's security."[11]

The strike was in progress a matter of hours, rather than days, before government officials, including President Roosevelt, were considering action of a drastic nature. On June 6, it was reported that the President's "first impulse" was to take over the plant.[12] A day later, Stephen T. Early, presidential press secretary, revealed that because of a proposed mass meeting of the strikers on Sunday, June 8, the President had given up plans to commandeer the plant immediately in the hope that the workers would themselves decide to terminate the strike. Mr. Early announced, however, that in the event the strike was continued, the President, with the unanimous approval of the Cabinet, would on Monday commandeer the plant and direct the army to operate it.[13] West Coast army units, it was indicated at the War Department, had been notified to be ready to move to the plant Monday morning.[14]

At the mass meeting on Sunday,[15] the strikers adopted a resolution giving a full vote of confidence to the negotiating committee.[16] Frankensteen, beset by what he claimed was organized booing, gave up the attempt to start a back-to-work movement. Nor did the threat of federal intervention have any effect upon the youthful strike leaders, several of whom were reported to have Communist connections.[17] Elmer Freitag, president of the local UAW union, who, earlier in the day, had sent a telegram to Early saying "Bombers can't be built with bayonets,"[18] told the strikers that a vote on

---

[11] Speech of May 27.

[12] *New York Times*, June 7, 1941, p. 1.

[13] The same, June 8, p. 1.

[14] The same, p. 36.

[15] Reports of the number in attendance varied considerably: 3,000 according to the *New York Times* (June 9, p. 1), 7,000 according to the *Los Angeles Examiner* (June 9, p. 1).

[16] *Los Angeles Times*, June 9, p. 5.

[17] With the exception of Wyndham Mortimer, assistant director of the CIO aircraft unionization drive, who was reported to have been the "motivating influence behind the strike," most of the strike leaders were quite young. Several of them were not only new to the union, but new to the factory also. Because he sided with leaders of the local union, Mortimer was dismissed by Frankensteen. For the reported Communist connections of Mortimer and Freitag, president of the local union, see the *New York Times*, June 9, pp. 1, 9.

[18] *Evening Star*, Washington, D.C., June 9, p. 2.

whether to return to work would be in violation of their constitution. He declared that a special meeting would have to be called and a secret ballot taken. William Bachman, one of the members of the negotiating committee, indicated that the threat of federal intervention was largely a bluff.

THE ARMY TAKES OVER

But the President was not bluffing! At the very time the mass meeting was in session, army trucks, loaded with approximately 2,000 troops of the Fifteenth Infantry from Camp Hunter Liggett, near Salinas, were rumbling toward Los Angeles.[19] Five hundred troops of the Third Coast Artillery at Fort MacArthur were ordered out shortly after midnight for duty "near North American." However, none of the soldiers arrived at the plant until after the clash Monday morning between pickets and police.

Reports that the plant would attempt to resume operation Monday morning brought pickets and a crowd of workers and onlookers to the plant before 6:30 A.M., Pacific Coast Time.[20] Fighting started when police attempted to open the picket lines in order to let workmen through. Tear gas bombs were hurled into the crowd, an action which Mayor Fletcher Bowron and Police Chief Arthur C. Hohmann later termed a mistake.[21] The troops arrived shortly after the initial clash and just in time to prevent a second outburst of disorder from becoming serious.

At the White House, awaiting word concerning developments at the North American plant, were President Roosevelt, Robert P. Patterson, Undersecretary of War, Sidney Hillman, Attorney General Robert Jackson, Harry L. Hopkins, and Stephen T. Early. The President was reported to have talked personally by long distance telephone to Lieutenant Colonel Charles E. Branshaw, who was in charge of the western district for the Army Air Corps, and who recommended that the troops take over the plant. Shortly

[19] Army officials refused to confirm the supposition that the troops were to be used for strike duty. Instead, Colonel Sidney H. Negotto, aide to Major General Ernest D. Peek of the Ninth Corps Area, said simply that the journey was to "give new soldiers training in night movements." *Los Angeles Times*, June 9, p. 5.

[20] The *Los Angeles Examiner* estimated that 10,000 persons were gathered near the gates of the plant (June 10, p. 3).

[21] *New York Times*, June 10, p. 14. At least five persons were treated for tear gas burns at the Venice Emergency Hospital. *Los Angeles Times*, June 10, p. 2.

after receiving Branshaw's report, the President issued instructions to the Secretary of War to "take charge of the plant and remain in charge and operate the plant until normal production shall be resumed."[22] In an accompanying executive order, the President emphasized how directly the government was concerned by the strike. Not only did North American Aviation, Incorporated, hold contracts with the United States, but part of the "aircraft in the course of production, raw material, machinery, and other property" was owned by the United States. The action of the strikers, the President declared, had seriously impaired the ability of the United States "to obtain aircraft essential to its armed forces and to the national defense.[23]

The President's order was transmitted to Colonel Branshaw by Undersecretary of War Patterson, and shortly afterwards the troops closed in on the plant. With rifles loaded and bayonets fixed, the troops formed a skirmish line and advanced slowly towards the crowd milling around the gates. Officers ordered the men to halt every 20 paces in order to give the massed picketers sufficient time to move back. A strike captain suffered the only injury, a bayonet-inflicted leg wound, because of his reluctance to move out of the path of the troops. Within a few minutes the roads were cleared and the danger of any large-scale disorder was ended. The plant gates were opened, and by 12:30 P.M. company officials announced that 1,200 of the 7,000 men on the day shift had returned to work. By sending the following telegram to the homes of over 8,000 North American employees, Colonel Branshaw let it be known that the army would not confine its activities to the immediate area of the plant:

I invite and request that all employees of the North American company return to their jobs at once. I guarantee to them absolute safety and protection while they are on the job, while they are proceeding to or from work or while they are in their homes.

Report for your regular shift.[24]

---

[22] Statement of the President accompanying the executive order, *New York Times,* June 10, 1941, p. 16.

[23] Executive Order 8773, June 9, 1941. *Federal Register,* June 10, 1941, Vol. 6, No. 112, p. 2777.

[24] *Los Angeles Times,* June 10, p. A. The President's executive order was sup-

With the assistance of the Los Angeles police, Branshaw proceeded to fulfill this all-inclusive pledge. When the day shift left
at 4:30, troops in "blitz buggies" convoyed the workers' cars to
the main highways. Later, patrols of army and police cars cruised
through the residential area where a large percentage of the
workers lived.[25] This policy succeeded in removing from the minds
of the workers the fear of violence at the hands of the more radical
strikers, with the result that by Tuesday evening nearly 90 per
cent of the night shift reported for work.

The troops experienced little difficulty with the striking workers.
At different times men were placed under military arrest and
escorted from the strike area, but no one was held for any length
of time.[26] Picketing was forbidden within a mile of the plant, the
sale of liquor was banned within the same area, and only residents
or workers bound for the plant were allowed passage into the
strike zone. Patrols were set up inside as well as around the plant
and a squad of soldiers remained on duty at either side of the main
gate. With order completely restored and production resumed, the
troops were withdrawn from the plant. Two thousand soldiers left
Inglewood on June 17 and the remainder, about 1,500, who were
bivouacked 1,000 yards from the plant, returned to their home
stations July 3. On July 2, the President signed an order terminat-
ing the government's possession of the plant.[27]

LEGAL BASIS FOR PRESIDENT'S ACTION AND PROBLEMS RAISED

The action of the President in ordering the War Department
to take over the plant raised a number of perplexing problems. The
first of these, of course, was the source of the President's power.
In his executive order President Roosevelt stated that he was act-

---

plemented by statements from Branshaw who, from time to time, explained to
the workers the policies which the government proposed to pursue.

[25] Twenty-five police cars were placed at the army's disposal to augment 18 army
combat cars. In addition, 24 armored scout cars were sent from Fort Hunter Liggett
on June 11. *New York Times,* June 12, p. 14.

[26] Confirmed by telephone conversation with Colonel Edward Greenbaum, legal
adviser to Colonel Branshaw.

[27] Executive Order No. 8814, July 2, 1941, *Federal Register,* July 4, 1941,
Vol. 6, No. 130, p. 3253.

ing in pursuance of the powers vested in him "by the Constitution and laws of the United States, as President of the United States of America and Commander-in-Chief of the Army and Navy of the United States."[28] Attorney General Robert Jackson upheld the President's action as an exercise of the "aggregate of the President's powers derived from the Constitution itself and from statutes enacted by the Congress." The Attorney General pointed out that Congress had appropriated money "to equip an enlarged Army and to provide for a strengthened Navy," and that as a consequence it was the duty of the President to find means to carry out the congressional intent. Jackson's statement concluded:

> There can be no doubt that the duty, constitutionally and inherently, rested upon the President to exert his civil and military as well as his moral authority to keep the defense effort of the United States a going concern.[29]

There were few who contended that the larger view of the President's powers, which Jackson had taken, was incorrect.[30] There was, however, no specific congressional authorization providing for federal intervention because of a labor dispute.[31] Although the Attorney General stated that "the situation at the North American plant more nearly resembles an insurrection than a labor strike," the President's declaration made no reference to the statutes authorizing federal intervention in time of insurrection.[32]

[28] *New York Times*, June 10, p. 16.
[29] *The Washington Post*, June 10, p. 3.
[30] One commentator, in referring to the Attorney General's "diaphanous" legal opinion, said: "Mr. Jackson's discovery that an 'aggregate of powers' enables a President to do what no one of his powers singly authorizes, transferred to our constitutional law the interesting proposition that two plus two equals five." I. F. Stone, "F.D.R. and the May Bill," *The Nation*, Vol. 153 (1941), p. 46.
[31] The Selective Service Act provided only for the seizure of plants whose management refused to manufacture arms or necessary supplies as ordered by the Secretary of War or the Secretary of the Navy. The Administration was said to have supported the Connally plant-seizure amendment to the Selective Service bill which passed the Senate on June 12 by a vote of 67 to 7. According to the *New York Times*, the bill symbolized popular support for the President's actions and also gave him definite statutory authority for similar action in the future. (June 13, p. 1.) Labor leaders strongly objected to the bill, and when a similar measure was under consideration in the House (the May bill) the President was reported to have told legislative leaders that he opposed its passage. (The same, July 9, p. 1.) The House subsequently killed the bill.
[32] Police Chief Arthur Hohmann undoubtedly had reference to the statutes

When the army took over, there was some question as to who would operate the plant providing the workers decided to remain on strike. Obviously, the soldiers knew little of the skills involved.[33] As one means of solving the problem, Brigadier General Louis B. Hershey, Acting Selective Service Director, telegraphed 6,500 local draft boards "to take the necessary action to reconsider the classification of all registrants who have ceased to perform the jobs for which they were deferred, and who are, by such failure, impeding the national defense program."[34] According to Secretary Stimson, the telegram was issued "with the express approval of the President."[35] This order, which made no distinction between strikes that were "called in strict observance of federal legislation" and those that were not,[36] was issued after local draft boards in the Los Angeles area had, on their own initiative, ordered a reclassification of the strikers.[37] As a matter of fact, the quick return to work of all classes of strikers demonstrated that Hershey's order was unnecessary.[38]

---

relating to insurrection when he declared that "the procedure is for the Mayor of the city to appeal to the Governor for the militia, and he in turn, if the State has no militia, asks the Federal Government to send in the Army." *Los Angeles Examiner*, June 10, 1941, p. 6.

[33] Frankensteen asserted that if the strikers refused to return, "our organization will cooperate with the Federal Government to supply skilled union members from organized plants throughout the nation." *New York Times*, June 10, p. 14.

[34] The same, p. 13.

[35] The same, p. 1. The *New York Times* pointed out that this action was very similar to that taken by President Wilson. On Sept. 13, 1918, Wilson told 5,000 striking machinists at Bridgeport, Connecticut, that refusal to accept the decision of the War Labor Board would mean that "each of you will be barred from employment in any war industry in the community in which the strike occurs for a period of one year. During that time the United States Employment Service will decline to obtain employment for you in any war industry elsewhere in the United States as well as under the War and Navy Departments, the Shipping Board, the Railway Administration, and all government agencies; and the draft boards will be instructed to reject any claim of exemption based on your alleged usefulness on war production." According to the *New York Times* the strikers returned to the plant on September 17. The same, p. 17. For the complete text of the President's letter see *The Messages and Papers of Woodrow Wilson*, Vol. I, pp. 515-16.

[36] Michael Straight, "Will Conscripted Labor Work," *The New Republic*, Vol. 104 (1941), p. 846. Phillip Murray, president of the CIO, referred to the Selective Service policy as a "flagrant abuse of the conscription law and an open breach of faith with labor." *Evening Star*, June 12, 1941, p. A7.

[37] *Los Angeles Times*, June 9, p. 1. Many of the workers had been classified as 2A because of their employment in a defense industry.

[38] That reclassification was not a proper weapon to use against strikes was

At the time the government took control of the plant, there was much speculation concerning the manner in which the army would manage the plant, what was to become of the stockholders' interest, and how the wage dispute would be settled. The almost immediate return of the workers resulted in an easy solution to problems, which, for a time, were very perplexing. Colonel Branshaw was placed in complete charge of the plant, but he made no effort to interfere with the normal supervision of production.[39] Although army officers forbade the return to work of a number of the strike leaders,[40] government "possession and operation" of the plant was largely a fiction. The mere presence of the troops was all that was necessary to ensure order and to enable production to be resumed.

The workers were paid the old wage rate pending further efforts to arrive at a satisfactory settlement before the National Mediation Board. Negotiations were resumed on June 17 with Frankensteen and a newly chosen negotiating committee representing the local union. An agreement was reached July 1, giving the 10 cents per hour increase which the workers had demanded, and establishing a graduated scale for trainees, starting at 60 cents and increasing automatically 5 cents each four weeks until 75 cents had been reached.[41]

APPRAISAL OF THE PRESIDENT'S COURSE

In attempting to assess the wisdom of the President's action in seizing the plant, it is necessary to bear in mind that the workers' grievances were not without foundation. They were working for a corporation which within a year had made a net profit of over $7,000,000 from sales amounting to about $37,000,000 and which

---

officially recognized by the government two months later. When local draft boards attempted to reclassify striking workers at the propeller plant of the Curtiss Wright Corporation in Caldwell, N.J., General Hershey sent the following order to state selective service headquarters: "Registrants will not be reclassified pending clarification of situation. Inform all local boards immediately." *Evening Star*, Aug. 9, 1941, p. A1.

[39] Conversation with Colonel Greenbaum, cited above.

[40] *Los Angeles Examiner*, June 11, 1941, p. 1.

[41] National Defense Mediation Board Release 4933. The new scale was obviously greatly out of line with that in other aviation companies. Douglas, Northrup, and Vultee subsequently adopted the 60 cents per hour beginning wage and made the new rate retroactive to July 1. *Evening Star*, Aug. 8, 1941, p. A19.

at the time of the strike had a backlog of orders valued at $200,000,000.[42] For weeks, the local union had been attempting to obtain an increased wage. To the committee, and no doubt to many of the workers, the company seemed to be making little real effort to arrive at a just settlement.[43]

Notwithstanding the merit of the workers' grievances, the leaders of the local union committed a threefold error in calling the strike. First of all, the strike was in defiance of the union's own national leaders. This fact tended to support the accusation that the strike was Communist inspired.[44] It has been pointed out that had the strike succeeded, it would have "dynamited the whole structure of collective bargaining,"[45] for collective bargaining can be carried on only where there is a responsible bargaining agent. In the second place, the strike was called while the National Defense Mediation Board was attempting a settlement and in spite of the fact that an agreement had already been reached making any benefits obtained retroactive to May 1. Certainly the record of the National Defense Mediation Board had not been prejudicial to the interests of labor. On the contrary, there was every reason for the workers to believe that they would receive favorable treatment. To defy the government agency which was set up for the specific purpose of adjusting labor disputes was, unquestionably, a major blunder.

[42] *New York Times*, June 7, 1941, p. 9. In a number of places a comparison was made between the corporation's profit of $7,000,000 and the plant and equipment cost of $3,777,000. (For example, see the *Congressional Record*, Vol. 87, No. 109, legislative day of June 10, 1941, p. 5119.) To contrast net profits with the volume of sales seems a much more fair basis for determining the company's position.

[43] During Frankensteen's speech exhorting the strikers to return to work, he said: ". . . the fact remains that a basic cause of the situation has been the inexperience and irresponsibility of the North American management which exhausted the patience of their workers through seven weeks of negotiations in which their response to a serious situation was a refusal to negotiate more than two hours each day." *New York Times*, June 8, p. 37.

[44] See pp. 179-80. "The distinction between loyal labor leaders and those who are following the Communist Party line is easy to observe. Loyal labor leaders fight for a settlement of labor grievances. Disloyal men who have wormed their way into the labor movement do not want settlements; they want strikes. That is the Communist Party line which those who have defied both the Government and their own loyal leaders to prevent a settlement of the strike have followed." Statement of Attorney General Jackson, *Washington Post*, June 10, p. 3.

[45] Freda Kirchwey, "Keep Cool on Labor," *The Nation*, Vol. 152 (1941), p. 714.

The local leaders erred also in calling the strike at a time when public feeling was strongly opposed to stoppage of work in defense industries. There was a widespread belief that, in view of the government's action in setting up special mediation machinery, disputes should be settled without impairing production.[46] As a consequence, the President's very decisive action was widely applauded.

Had the President not believed that a critical foreign situation made imperative the continued production of fighting planes, and had he not feared that a successful strike at North American might spread to other important defense plants, it is improbable that he would have acted with such suddenness. After all, the strike had been called only four days before the troops intervened. Furthermore, there had been no disorder. The rioting that occurred on Monday morning, June 9, came about because of the company's opening its gates. That action undoubtedly would not have been taken had it not been for the presidential ultimatum warning that the army would take over the plant unless production were resumed. In this instance, the minor disorder that occurred was a result of, rather than in spite of, the President's action.

It is true that in view of the circumstances surrounding the strike, there was a distinct possibility that severe rioting might occur. All fear of any large-scale disorder was removed by the President's action in sending the troops quickly and in sufficient number to insure control of any outburst. Roosevelt's primary object, however, was not the prevention of disorder. It was to prevent a tie-up of production for defense.

The President believed that the interests of the nation would be served best by decisive action on his part. Without proceeding, therefore, with the deliberation that has usually characterized the presidential use of troops, President Roosevelt moved suddenly, in a very determined and, as events proved, a very successful fashion to do the thing which he believed was of first importance for the nation's good.

---

[46] In a nationwide survey by the American Institute of Public Opinion (Gallup Poll), 76 per cent of the persons voting were in favor of forbidding strikes in "industries manufacturing materials for our national defense program." *New York Times*, June 11, p. 22.

CHAPTER XII

SOURCES OF PRESIDENTIAL AUTHORITY[1]

By virtue of the constitutional powers of the president and also because of the powers he has been delegated by Congress, the chief executive has a broad range of authority in relation to domestic disorders.

CONSTITUTIONAL PROVISIONS

The Constitution grants Congress the power:

1. To raise and support armies. . . .
2. To provide and maintain a navy;
3. To make rules for the government and regulations of the land and naval forces;
4. To provide for calling forth the militia to execute the laws of the Union, suppress insurrections, and repel invasions;
5. To provide for organizing, arming, and disciplining the militia and for governing such part of them as may be employed in the service of the United States. . . .
6. To make all laws which shall be necessary and proper for carrying into execution the foregoing powers, and all other powers vested by this Constitution in the Government of the United States, or in any department or officer thereof."[2]

The Constitution specifies that the president

1. . . . . shall be commander-in-chief of the army and navy of the United States, and of the militia of the several States when called into the actual service of the United States. . . .
2. . . . . shall take care that the laws be faithfully executed. . . .[3]

The Constitution also provides:

The United States shall guarantee to every State in this Union a

---

[1] In preparing this chapter the writer talked several times with Colonel Archibald King of the Judge Advocate General's Office. He also talked with Lieutenant Colonel A. L. Lerch and Colonel F. Granville Munson of the same office, Lieutenant Colonel C. A. Wickliffe of the National Guard Bureau, and Frederick Bernays Wiener of the Department of Justice. Needless to say, none of these gentlemen is responsible for any opinions expressed herein.

[2] Art. I, sec. 8.

[3] Art. II, secs. 2, 3.

republican form of government, and shall protect each of them against invasion, and on application of the legislature, or of the executive (when the legislature cannot be convened), against domestic violence.[4]

FEDERAL AID TO THE STATES

Congress, by statute, has supplemented the constitutional provisions enumerated above to give the president broad powers and great discretion in matters pertaining to the preservation of domestic peace. The first of these to be considered, section 5297 of the Revised Statutes, provides for federal assistance to the states.

> In case of an insurrection in any State against the government thereof it shall be lawful for the President, on application of the legislature of such State, or of the executive when the legislature can not be convened, to call forth such number of the militia of any other State or States which may be applied for as he deems sufficient to suppress such insurrection, or on like application, to employ for the same purposes such part of the land or naval forces of the United States as he deems necessary.[5]

The statute does not say that the president must obey the call of a state. It merely makes lawful his doing so. As the preceding chapters have demonstrated, the presidents have been rather reluctant to send troops in answer to such requests. Particularly in intrastate political contests there has been a definite tendency to avoid jeopardizing the delicate relationships between the state and national governments. Van Buren, Tyler, and Grant were asked to intervene in disputes of a political nature, and each one hesitated because of the possibility of "dangerous consequences to our republican institutions."[6]

One of the outstanding developments in the procedure for handling disturbances is the change in the federal government's position

[4] Art. IV, sec. 4.
[5] This act is an outgrowth of statutes passed in 1792, 1795, and 1807. See 1 Stat. L. 264, 424, and 2 Stat. L. 443.
[6] See p. 53. During Grant's second administration he was faced with an especially difficult problem in Arkansas. There were two claimants for the gubernatorial post, each of whom requested federal assistance. Followers of the two aspirants quickly organized, and had it not been for a small force of regular troops which took up a position between the opposing camps a major riot might have occurred. Grant subsequently proclaimed one of the governors duly elected. For the documents and an account of this disturbance see Frederick T. Wilson, *Federal Aid in Domestic Disturbances*, S. Doc. 263, 67 Cong. 2 sess., pp. 140-55, 263-69.

on the administrative problem of command. President Hayes repeatedly instructed his commanding officers to act under the orders of the governors who had requested aid. Obviously such an order gives the troops little discretion. They are unable, without the governor's consent, to take whatever action is necessary to preserve the peace. This faulty condition was recognized by General Hancock in the great railroad riots of 1877. The General wrote as follows to the Secretary of War:

My impression is that when the State governments declare their inability to suppress domestic insurrection through the ordinary channels and call upon the President of the United States to intervene to their assistance, he should not do it through the civil powers of the States which have already failed, but that it should be done by the intervention of Federal authority by military force and by the President exercising the control.[7]

This view gradually gained acceptance although as late as 1899, in Idaho, by virtue of McKinley's lack of careful supervision, the troops did about as the state adjutant general directed. However, by 1903, during the threatened disorders in Colorado, Elihu Root explained that the president could not place the military forces under the governor's management, "but must himself direct their operations."[8] In contrast to the position of President Hayes was the order given by the governor of West Virginia to his subordinates during the disturbances in the summer of 1921: "The peace officers of this State will obey the direction of the officer commanding the United States troops, or his properly designated representative."[9] This represents a complete reversal in policy from that of President Hayes a half-century before. In general it may be said that governors who have been compelled to call for help have had little disposition to assert control over the federal forces. On the contrary, they have been thankful to be relieved of a burdensome problem.

Two standard excuses have been used by presidents who have wished to avoid sending troops to states requesting aid. The first

[7] S. Doc. 263, 67 Cong. 2 sess., p. 276.
[8] See p. 124.
[9] *New York Times*, Sept. 3, 1921, p. 1.

is that, in the opinion of the president, the state has not yet demonstrated its inability to quell the disturbance. Van Buren refused the request of the governor of Pennsylvania at the time of the Buckshot War on this ground, and since then the same answer has several times been given.[10] A second common method of avoiding the sending of troops is the excuse that the governor's requisition is incorrectly drawn. For example, it is incorrect for a governor to make a request while the legislature is in session. The legislature itself should make the request. Another excuse which the president may give is that the parenthetical expression "when the legislature can not be convened" implies an obligation on the part of the governor to call the legislature into session. This was one of Pierce's arguments at the time of California's troubles with the San Francisco Vigilance Committee of 1856, and of Theodore Roosevelt's in the Goldfield, Nevada, disturbance. Again, the president's refusal may simply be based on the lack of a formal appeal. Hayes was very insistent that the governors' requests be worded formally, and he refused to honor those which were not. He expected a statement that disorder existed, that the state authorities were incapable of preserving the peace, that the legislature was not in session and could not be convened in time to meet the emergency, and that the appeal was for the purpose of protecting the state against domestic violence. In 1903, Theodore Roosevelt used the same excuse, that is, an improperly worded request, in declining to assist the governor of Colorado.

On April 1, 1941, Governor Julius P. Heil of Wisconsin sent President Franklin D. Roosevelt a telegram stating that the situation at the Allis Chalmers plant in Milwaukee was "absolutely out of control of all the peace officers available."[11] The Governor indicated his desire for federal intervention, but since he did not specifically ask for troops, the President took no action. The President's Secretary, Stephen T. Early, emphasized the necessity of a formal request.[12] For the most part, when a president does not wish to send troops, rather than openly refuse, he resorts to an

---

[10] See pp. 53, 69, 160.
[11] *New York Times*, Apr. 2, 1941, p. 1.
[12] The same, April 3, p. 12.

excuse similar to those above. When it is apparent that troops are needed quickly, in few, if any, cases has there been much quibbling over the wording of the application.

R. S. 5297 has been used reluctantly also because there is the fear, which, unfortunately, has in more than one instance been realized, that the armed forces of the United States will be used merely as policemen. As McKinley, Theodore Roosevelt, and Wilson learned to their misfortune, governors who succeed in obtaining troops are able to devise one scheme after another for keeping them. The United States not only bears the major cost of bringing disturbances to an end but, in addition, so long as the president can be persuaded that the presence of the troops is necessary, the federal government is saddled with a policing cost that rightly belongs to the states.

Increased speed in methods of communication and transportation has vastly improved the machinery for aiding the states. The procedure, briefly, is as follows. The governor sends a telegram to the president giving an explanation of the troublesome situation in his state and requesting assistance to prevent or curb violence. If the president is convinced troops are needed, the secretary of war is so informed. The secretary gives the order for the movement of troops to the adjutant general, and that officer, in turn, transmits the order to the corps area commander within whose territory the scene of the disturbance is located. Detachments of troops, ordinarily, are then dispatched from more than one army post, as the number at each garrison is usually rather small.

While this procedure may appear rather complicated, actually it is very simple. Once the president has made up his mind, it takes very little time to get the order to the corps area commander. There are, however, three points of possible delay. In the first place, local officials must convince the governor that outside aid is necessary.[13] Then, too, delay may occur in the president's office. He may desire to verify the accuracy of the governor's request. This has been a

---

[13] Although rather remote, there is also the possibility that the governor may be out of the state and that his subordinates are unwilling to assume responsibility. The absence of the governor of Pennsylvania was of great significance at the time of the railroad riots at Pittsburgh in 1877.

very common practice and, as events have proved, a very sound one. The president also frequently wishes to confer with some of his advisers. The secretary of war, the attorney general, and the chief of staff are commonly consulted, and in some instances presidents have brought state appeals before the whole Cabinet.

A third source of delay arises from the problems incident to the mobilization and transportation of the troops. For example, lack of proper understanding between railroad and army officials at the time of the West Virginia disturbance of 1921 meant that troop trains were sidetracked for passenger trains and the journey from Camp Dix, New Jersey, took 34 hours, almost three times the normal requirement.[14] The governor may assist in speeding mobilization by notifying the corps area commander of his request to the president. Thus, pending the president's decision, the commanding officer has an opportunity to make preparations for dispatching the troops. The president may also speed up the process by anticipating a governor's call and giving orders for the troops to be in readiness to move the moment a formal request is made. This practice has been common for almost a century. In 1842, at the time of the Dorr Rebellion, President Tyler strengthened the garrison at Fort Adams and ordered troops at other points to be prepared to move even though what he considered a correct requisition had not been received. In 1934, because of the textile strike in the same state, the War Department ordered the regular troops at several posts in the New England area to prepare for possible movement into the strike zone.[15] Both President Franklin D. Roosevelt and Secretary of War Dern visited the state, the latter to make an official study of the strike. Contrary to the wishes of the governor, the legislature refused to ask for aid.[16] Fortunately, the disorder was no greater than the Rhode Island National Guard could handle.

It was because of the post-World War reorganization of the National Guard, and not because of freedom from disturbances, that recent presidents have been relieved of the task of assisting the

---

[14] *New York Times*, Sept. 7, 1921, p. 17.
[15] The same, Sept. 14, 1934, p. 1.
[16] The same, September 16, p. 32; September 15, p. 1.

states to maintain order.[17] By virtue of the federal government's interest in increasing the personnel, supplying equipment, and establishing a training program, the National Guard was a much more potent force than the earlier militia bodies. However, the call of the National Guard into federal service in August 1940 raised again the problem of how the states were to cope with disorders of any consequence. Until such time as the National Guard is returned to the states, governors may be forced to rely upon federal assistance, for it is improbable that, without a considerable amount of training, the new State Guard organizations will be competent to handle a major disorder.[18] Once again an already overburdened chief executive may be faced with a problem which has proved ever difficult of solution.

ENFORCEMENT OF FEDERAL LAW

The second important law dealing with the power of the president in public disorders is *Revised Statutes*, section 5298:

Whenever, by reason of unlawful obstructions, combinations, or assemblages of persons, or rebellion against the authority of the Government of the United States, it shall become impracticable, in the judgment of the President, to enforce by the ordinary course of judicial proceedings the laws of the United States within any State or Territory, it shall be lawful for the President to call forth the militia of any or all the States and to employ such parts of the land and naval forces of the United States as he may deem necessary to enforce the faithful execution of the laws of the United States or to suppress such rebellion in whatever State or Territory thereof the laws of the United States may be forcibly opposed or the execution thereof forcibly obstructed.

It is upon this statute, or its antecedents,[19] that presidents have

[17] For a recent account of the development of the National Guard see Frederick Bernays Wiener, "The Militia Clause of the Constitution," *Harvard Law Review*, Vol. LIV (1940), pp. 181-210.

[18] By an act approved Oct. 21, 1940, Congress provided "that under such regulations as the Secretary of War may prescribe for discipline in training, the organization by and maintenance within any State of such military forces other than National Guard as may be provided by the laws of such State is hereby authorized while any part of the National Guard of the State concerned is in active Federal service." Public No. 874, 76 Cong. 3 sess.

[19] This statute is an outgrowth of laws dating from 1792. See 1 Stat. L. 264, 424; 2 Stat. L. 443; and 12 Stat. L. 281. R. S. 5301, which follows, although never brought into operation since the Civil War period, also vests great power in the President. The italics are added.

"Whenever the President, in pursuance of the provisions of this title [Insur-

relied to subdue resistance to the federal laws. The procedure for handling disorders is very similar to that already explained except that appeals to the president come from the civil authorities of the United States rather than from state officials.[29] The similarity extends to even the question of command. As late as the Pullman strike in 1894, General Schofield rather heatedly reminded his officers that under no circumstances were they to take orders from the federal marshals. In a General Order, Schofield pointed out that ". . . the troops are employed as a part of the military power of the United States, and act under the orders of the President, as commander-in-chief, and his military subordinates."[21] This principle has been accepted and is a part of the present-day Army Regulations. Whether the troops are sent in response to a state request or whether they are upholding federal laws, they "cannot be di-

rection], has called forth the militia to suppress combinations against the laws of the United States, and to cause the laws to be duly executed, and the insurgents shall have failed to disperse by the time directed by the President, and when the insurgents claim to act under the authority of any State or States, and such claim is not disclaimed or repudiated by the persons exercising the functions of government in such State or States, or in the part or parts thereof in which such combination exists, and such insurrection is not suppressed by such State or States, or *whenever the inhabitants of any State or part thereof are at any time found by the President to be in insurrection against the United States, the President may, by proclamation, declare that the inhabitants of such State, or of any section or part thereof where such insurrection exists, are in a state of insurrection against the United States;* and thereupon all commercial intercourse by and between the same and the citizens thereof and the citizens of the rest of the United States shall cease and be unlawful so long as such condition of hostility shall continue; and all goods and chattels, wares and merchandise, coming from such State or section into the other parts of the United States, or proceeding from other parts of the United States to such State or section, by land or water, shall, together with the vessel or vehicle conveying the same, or conveying persons to or from such State or section, be forfeited to the United States."

[20] As a matter of fact the President's action is not dependent upon an appeal.

[21] See p. 102. Confusion had arisen because of the lack of familiarity with the Posse Comitatus Act of 1878 (20 Stat. L. 152). Prior to the passage of the act troops had been used as a part of the marshal's posse. The statute specified, however, that ". . . it shall not be lawful to employ any part of the Army of the United States, as a posse comitatus, or otherwise, for the purpose of executing the laws, except in such cases and under such circumstances as such employment of said force may be expressly authorized by the Constitution or by act of Congress. . . ." Shortly after the passage of the act Attorney General Charles Devens ruled that by Revised Statutes 5298 and 5300, the military forces, *under the direction of the President,* could be used to assist a marshal. 16 *Atty. Gen. Op.* 162.

rected to act under the orders of any civil officer."[22] This does not mean that they are to act in complete disregard of local officialdom. On the contrary, since their purpose is to restore peace, "their action, should, . . . as far as practicable, be in concert with the action or views of the duly constituted authorities."[23]

In enforcing federal law, as in aiding distressed states, the president's determination as to the need for troops has, since the Whiskey Insurrection, been exclusive and final. At that time judicial notification was necessary before the president could call forth the militia.[24] This provision of the law was subsequently changed to make the president the sole judge of the exigency.[25] In the case of *Martin* v. *Mott*, growing out of the War of 1812, Justice Story, speaking for the Supreme Court, stated that "the authority to decide whether the exigency has arisen, belongs exclusively to the President, and that his decision is conclusive upon all other persons."[26] The factors incident to the presidential determination are summarized as follows by Frederick Bernays Wiener in his able book on martial law: "The extent of the disturbance which will induce him to act, the evidence necessary to move him to action, the persons on whom he will rely for testimony or counsel—all these are matters entirely confided to his discretion and his alone." Wiener believes that these problems pertain not to law but to statesmanship, "for the solution of which there is no formula or magic sesame."[27]

In spite of the generally accepted doctrine of conclusiveness, there is ground for the argument that the president's decision as to the necessity of troops is not necessarily final. In the Pullman strike at least three governors, in addition to Altgeld, protested against Cleveland's policy, but none of them took the matter to the courts. In numerous cases prior to 1932, the judiciary had upheld the finality of a *governor's* decision to use armed force,[28]

---

[22] *AR* 500-50, Apr. 5, 1937.
[23] Cassius M. Dowell, *Military Aid to the Civil Power*, p. 206.
[24] 1 Stat. L. 264.
[25] 1 Stat. L. 424.
[26] 12 Wheaton 19 (1827).
[27] *A Practical Manual of Martial Law*, p. 54.
[28] See *Sterling* v. *Constantin*, 287 U. S. 378, 399 (1932).

but in that year the Supreme Court wrought a decided change in the picture. In *Sterling v. Constantin* the Court, speaking through Chief Justice Hughes, placed very definite restrictions on the military activities of a governor in instances where there was in fact no disorder or apparent necessity for armed force.[29] State governors, however, have made bold use of their military prerogatives, whereas the sobering presidential office has caused the domestic military power to be handled more seriously. Against a president who was not so affected by his office, the restrictions of *Sterling v. Constantin* might be applied.

PRESERVATION OF CONSTITUTIONAL RIGHTS

In addition to the two statutes already considered there is a third measure, one that has received singularly little attention. Section 5299 of the Revised Statutes provides:

Whenever insurrection, domestic violence, unlawful combinations, or conspiracies in any State so obstructs or hinders the execution of the laws thereof and of the United States as to deprive any portion or class of the people of such State of any of the rights, privileges, or immunities or protection named in the Constitution and secured by the laws for the protection of such rights, privileges, or immunities, and the constituted authorities of such State are unable to protect or from any cause fail in or refuse protection of the people in such rights, such facts shall be deemed a denial by such State of the equal protection of the laws to which they are entitled under the Constitution of the United States, and in all such cases, or whenever any such insurrection, violence, unlawful combinations, or conspiracy opposes or obstructs the due course of justice under the same, it shall be lawful for the President, and it shall be his duty, to take such measures, by the employment of the militia or the land and naval forces of the United States, or of either, or by other means, as he may deem necessary for the suppression of such insurrection, domestic violence, or combinations.[30]

Writers dealing with the subject of domestic disturbances have done little more than recognize the existence of this statute. Even Professor Corwin, in referring to "the vague powers conferred by this measure," merely points out that "it still remains on the

[29] The same, 403, 404.
[30] The measure was approved Apr. 20, 1871 as the third section of "An Act to Enforce the Provisions of the Fourteenth Amendment," 17 Stat. L. 13. The wording of the revised statute enlarges the scope of the act of 1871.

statute books a potential threat to lynchers and their ilk."[31]

/Into the hands of the president is placed the power of determining whether, by insurrection, domestic violence, unlawful combinations, or conspiracies, any portion or class of the people of a state is being deprived of the "rights, privileges, or immunities, or protection, named in the Constitution and secured by the laws. . . ." If the president finds the existence of such a deprivation within a state, that state will be deemed guilty of denying the equal protection of the laws. Under such circumstances the president is authorized to use the military forces of the United States to correct the evil. The president can intervene, not to prevent conspiracies, unlawful combinations, domestic violence, or insurrection, as such, but to guard the "rights, privileges, or immunities or protection named in the Constitution and secured by the laws for the protection of such rights, privileges, and immunities."

The problem, obviously, is in determining what those rights, privileges, and immunities are. In the Slaughter House cases the Supreme Court enumerated certain ones "which owe their existence to the Federal government, its National character, its Constitution, or its laws."[32] Referring to *Crandall* v. *Nevada*, the Court said that it is the right of citizens of the United States "to come to the seat of government."[33] Others mentioned were the right to peaceably assemble and petition for redress of grievances, the privilege of the writ of habeas corpus, the right to use the navigable waters of the United States, and the right to become a citizen of any state by a bona fide residence therein.[34] Other rights, such as freedom of speech, are "secured to all persons, without regard to citizenship by the due process clause of the Fourteenth Amendment."[35]

Although no definite classification has been made of the "rights, privileges, or immunities, or protection named in the Constitution and secured by the laws" to all the people of the United States, it

---

[31] Edward S. Corwin, *The President: Office and Powers*, p. 171.
[32] *Slaughter House Cases*, 16 Wallace 36, 79 (1873).
[33] In *Twining* v. *New Jersey* the expression was "to pass freely from State to State." 211 U. S. 78, 97 (1908).
[34] *Slaughter House Cases*, 16 Wallace 36, 79 (1873).
[35] *Hague* v. *C. I. O.*, 307 U. S. 496, 519 (1938).

would seem that the president's right to intervene in the event of domestic violence or insurrection within a state is considerably broadened by this statute.[36] The Supreme Court has said that "there is a peace of the United States."[37] It may be argued that the protection of such a peace is an obligation resting upon the government which R. S. 5299 delegates to the president. Thus a "general condition of disorder . . . might . . . furnish basis for Presidential intervention, even in lack of an application from the state authorities for aid against 'domestic disorder.' "[38]

Since the publication of the Revised Statutes,[39] no president has based his action in handling a disturbance exclusively on R. S. 5299.[40] It has not gone unrecognized, however. It was cited by President Cleveland as one of the laws authorizing his action in the Pullman strike[41] and its meaning was explained to the governor of Nevada by Secretary of State Elihu Root at the time of the Goldfield disorder.[42]

The courts have never given an interpretation of the statute.

[36] At the time of the sit-down strikes in 1937, Senator Borah, although denying the President's right to end the strikes under R. S. 5299, said that "in order that the President may have authority to proceed under that section [5299] it would have to be shown that rights, privileges, and immunities guaranteed by the Constitution of the United States or some law of the United States have been infringed or broken or violated." Again Senator Borah said, "If the national rights of the citizens, if the national immunities and the national privileges of the citizen as guaranteed by the Constitution are interfered with, the National Government does not have to wait upon the government of the State." *Congressional Record*, 75 Cong. 1 sess., Vol. 81, Pt. III, p. 3063.

[37] *In re Neagle*, 135 U. S. 1, 69 (1890).

[38] Edward S. Corwin, "Martial Law, Yesterday and Today," *Political Science Quarterly*, Vol. XLVII (1932), p. 102.

[39] June 22, 1874.

[40] Under authority of the original act, President Grant, in 1871, sent troops into several counties of South Carolina to suppress the Ku Klux Klan. Wilson, S. Doc. 263, 67 Cong. 2 sess., p. 103.

[41] Grover Cleveland, *The Government in the Chicago Strike of 1894*, p. 20. Cleveland quoted only the last of the statute referring to obstruction of the laws of the United States.

[42] "Action under section 5299 of the Revised Statutes is to be taken not upon the call of the government of a State, but upon the judgment of the President of the United States that some portion or class of the people of a State are denied the equal protection of the laws to which they are entitled under the Constitution of the United States. Action under this section requires the production of sufficient evidence of specific facts sufficient to sustain a judgment by the President that the condition described in the statute exists." *Papers Relative to Labor Troubles at Goldfield, Nevada*, H. Doc. 607, 60 Cong. 1 sess., pp. 6-7.

In one instance, in Ohio, the federal district court was asked to certify to the president the existence of a state of insurrection making troops necessary. The judge declined, however, on the ground that "this court should not undertake to make in advance a decision of that which is solely for the determination of the President of the United States."[43]

In view of the broadened interpretations of the powers of the federal government, it is rather improbable that any large-scale disorder would not, to some degree, violate the laws of the United States and thereby make possible, if the president so wished, intervention under R. S. 5298. However, R. S. 5299 is an additional weapon in the president's hands to guard against the dangers of widespread and unchecked oppression of minority groups.[44]

THE PRESIDENTIAL PROCLAMATION

In addition to the statutes authorizing the President to employ the armed forces to aid the states (R.S. 5297), to enforce federal law (R.S. 5298), and to maintain the rights of persons in the United States (R.S. 5299), there is a fourth statute (R.S. 5300), which is linked with each of the others:

Whenever in the judgment of the President, it becomes necessary to use the military forces under this title [Insurrection], the President shall forthwith, by proclamation, command the insurgents to disperse and retire peaceably to their respective abodes, within a limited time.

This statute has been a part of the national law since 1792.[45] Practically every president who has been faced with an internal disturbance has placed a different interpretation upon its use. The

---

[43] Consolidated Coal and Coke Co. v. Beale et al., 282 Federal Reporter 934 (1922).

[44] There is still another basis for presidential action, that stemming from the Neagle case, namely, that the President's duty to take care that the laws be faithfully executed "is not limited to the enforcement of acts of Congress or of statutes of the United States according to their expressed terms, but includes the rights, duties, and obligations growing out of the Constitution itself, our international relations and all the protection implied by the nature of the Government under the Constitution." (The Constitution of the United States, Annotated (1938), p. 401.) This basis is similar to Attorney General Robert Jackson's "aggregate of the President's powers." See p. 184.

[45] The wording is slightly changed. For the original law see 1 Stat. L. 264.

measure had been in effect less than six months before Washington utilized it in an effort to quell the discontent in Pennsylvania arising out of the excise tax on liquors. The President admonished the inhabitants of the western counties "to refrain and dissent from all unlawful combinations," he exhorted them to obey the law, and he warned that "all lawful ways and means will be strictly put in execution for bringing to justice the infractors thereof."[46] In the summer of 1794 renewed opposition caused Washington to issue a second proclamation commanding the insurgents to disperse and announcing his determination to take measures for calling forth the militia. This threat was not enough, however, and six weeks later he issued a third proclamation announcing the fact that a force "adequate to the exigency is already in motion to the scene of disaffection."[47] The President's anxiety to avoid a clash caused him not only to comply fully with the statute relating to the proclamation but to add a special requirement of his own. General Henry Lee, the commanding officer of the militia, was instructed to issue an additional proclamation inviting the citizens to "join the standard of the United States."[48]

Five years later when the Fries Rebellion broke out in eastern Pennsylvania, President Adams issued but one proclamation. He summarized the incidents of opposition to the law, announced his determination to use force, commanded the insurgents to disperse, and warned against "aiding, abetting, or comforting" those opposing the laws of the United States.[49] Following the earlier practice, General William McPherson published a proclamation at the time his troops arrived at the scene of the disturbance.

Jefferson was the first to depart from the requirements of the statute. As a part of the complicated system of enforcing the embargo law, Jefferson permitted the governor of Vermont to decide when the proclamation, which Jefferson had already prepared, should be issued. The proclamation accused the people living near Lake Champlain of "forming insurrections against the authority of the United States."[50] The accusation was vehemently denied by the

[46] See p. 5.
[47] See p. 12.
[48] See p. 15.
[49] 11 Stat. L. 757.
[50] See p. 32.

inhabitants of the area, who pointed out the distinction between evasion of the law by individuals and a general insurrection. Increased opposition to the law and the necessity for additional action by the military force justified the issuance of further proclamations, but Jefferson's unhappy experience on this occasion caused him, thereafter, to refuse.

Few succeeding presidents have followed any consistent plan. At the time of the nullification excitement in South Carolina, Jackson endeavored by his 9,000-word proclamation of December 10, 1832, to prevent a recourse to arms.[51] On the other hand, at the time of the colored uprisings in 1831, troops were ordered out on several occasions, but at no time was a proclamation issued.[52] .

Like Jefferson, Tyler prepared a proclamation to be issued at the discretion of a presidential representative. During the Dorr Rebellion, after being four times importuned for aid by Governor King of Rhode Island, the President was finally persuaded that federal intervention was necessary. The Secretary of War was instructed to proceed to Rhode Island and to issue the proclamation, given him by the President, upon a proper request from the state authorities. The Secretary was also authorized to call the troops upon the issuance of the proclamation. The rebellion had collapsed, however, even before Tyler issued his instructions.

A variant of this procedure occurred during the administration of President Buchanan. When word was received of John Brown's seizure of the arsenal at Harper's Ferry, Buchanan signed a proclamation which was then given to Lieutenant Robert E. Lee. Probably without thinking of the proclamation, in view of the great excitement which prevailed at the West Virginia village, Lee attacked the arsenal. After most of Brown's party had been killed and the remainder taken prisoner, Lee felt there was little need of the proclamation and it was never published.[53]

During the reconstruction era there was constant disorder. Military government prevailed for years. In the latter part of his administration, Grant made considerable use of the proclamation,

---

[51] See p. 43.
[52] See note 58, p. 50.
[53] Wilson, S. Doc. 263, 67 Cong. 2 sess., pp. 84-85.

especially where disorder seemed imminent as a result of controversies between gubernatorial aspirants.[54]

In the industrial disputes since the Civil War in which federal
troops were involved, the proclamation has been used more spar-
ingly. In the great riots of 1877, President Hayes complied with
all proper state requests, but he felt obliged in each case to announce, by proclamation, his decision to send federal troops. In
some instances troop movements were not preceded by a presidential proclamation, but the activities of the soldiers were limited
to the protection of federal property and, less frequently, to enforcing the processes of the United States courts. Hayes believed
that under such circumstances a proclamation was unnecessary.
Actually, as Cleveland was shortly to demonstrate, enforcing the
process of the United States courts might prove very embarrassing.

Although in his first administration Cleveland had twice issued
a proclamation in relation to disturbances in the Territory of Washington, he neglected to do so in the Pullman strike until he was
aroused by the sharp criticism of Oregon's Governor Pennoyer.
The President may simply have ignored the statute as a result of
Attorney General Olney's belief that a proclamation was unnecessary.[55] After Pennoyer's statement, however, Cleveland lost no
time in issuing proclamations covering the use of troops not only
in Illinois but in the western states as well.

When troops were first sent to Idaho's Coeur d'Alene in 1892,
President Harrison did not issue a proclamation until four days
after the troops were ordered to the troubled mining area. By that
time all rioting had ceased. Seven years later, when a disturbance
of much larger proportions occurred, federal troops were used to
round up the troublemakers and then, for several months, to act
as police officers. At no time, however, was a proclamation issued
by President McKinley. He believed that none was necessary since
there was no actual rioting at the time of the arrival of the troops.

Theodore Roosevelt made a distinction between sending troops
to a troubled zone and their actual use while there. During the
mining disturbances in Goldfield, Nevada, in 1907, Roosevelt

[54] The same, pp. 103, 128, 132, 151, 157.
[55] Henry James, *Richard Olney and His Public Service*, p. 205.

ordered several companies of troops to the disturbed area, but he forbade them to act before a proclamation was issued. The commander was instructed to "notify the Adjutant General at once whenever anything occurs making proclamation necessary, and then await further orders. Better 24 hours of riot, damage, and disorder than illegal use of troops."[56]

During President Wilson's first administration the troops were ordered to Colorado and Arkansas. In each instance their movement was preceded by a presidential proclamation. After the National Guard had been called into federal service, however, the states were left without any organized body of troops to draw upon in disturbances too large for local police to handle. Regulars were used about thirty times in little more than a year. In no instance was a presidential proclamation issued.

When President Harding was asked to send troops into the troubled mining region of West Virginia, in 1921, he, reverting to Washington's practice, tried to bring peace by issuing a proclamation and then waiting to determine its effect. Harding found, as did the first president, that a proclamation unsupported by troops had little effect.

Proclamations usually apply to a rather limited area.[57] This has given rise to the question of the proclamation's legal effect, especially whether or not it establishes martial law. In 1880 Secretary of War Alex Ramsey referred to a proclamation of President Hayes as a declaration of martial law. He was quickly disabused of this idea by William Evarts, Secretary of State, who, specifically denying the assertion of the Secretary of War, pointed out that a proclamation "does not suspend or authorize the suspension of the writ of habeas corpus. . . ."[58] There is nothing to indicate that any president ever thought that his proclamation was a declaration of martial law. Certainly Washington did not attribute any special significance to his proclamations. During the Whiskey Insurrection he continually emphasized the subordination of the military to the civil power. When Lincoln proclaimed martial law, he used the

[56] See p. 129.
[57] An illustration to the contrary is Cleveland's second proclamation during the Pullman strike. It specified seven states and two territories.
[58] Wilson, S. Doc. 263, 67 Cong. 2 sess., p. 180.

expression, "martial law."[59] Except for his two Civil War declarations the words "martial law" have never appeared in any presidential proclamation.

Edmund Randolph spoke of the proclamation as a "merely humane and prudent caution," the purpose of which was "to prevent if possible, bloodshed in a conflict of arms, and if this cannot be done, to render the necessity of it palpable, by a premonition to the insurgents to disperse and go home."[60] This observation made at the time of the Whiskey Insurrection is still very apt. It is doubtful if any proclamation ever had the effect President Fillmore feared, of defeating the efforts of the federal forces by notifying "persons intended to be arrested that they would be enabled to fly or secrete themselves."[61] Troops do not, after all, move that rapidly. The proclamation simply announces the intervention of the president and of the armed forces. Far from telling too much, it does not sufficiently explain what the government intends to do. As a result the commanding officer may and, if possible, should indicate in a supplementary announcement the policies which the government intends to pursue and the responsibilities of the inhabitants in the area of the disturbance.

USE OF TROOPS IN EMERGENCIES

Notwithstanding the statutes providing for the president's use of the troops, there is the possibility that, for some reason, such as an impaired means of communication or a sudden and unlooked for disorder, there may be no opportunity for the chief executive to make a decision. Since 1878, army regulations have provided for such a contingency.[62] The present regulation follows:

In case of sudden and unexpected invasion, insurrection, or riot, endangering the public property of the United States, or of attempted or

---

[59] Lincoln's proclamation of Sept. 24, 1863 specified that all those "affording aid and comfort to rebels against the authority of the United States, shall be subject to martial law and liable to trial and punishment by courts martial or military commission." (13 Stat. L. 730.) On July 5, 1864, he proclaimed martial law in the state of Kentucky. The same, p. 743. See also James G. Randall, *Constitutional Problems under Lincoln*, pp. 169-74.

[60] *Pennsylvania Archives*, 2d series, Vol. IV, p. 229.

[61] James D. Richardson, *Messages and Papers of the Presidents*, Vol. V, p. 105.

[62] See G. Norman Lieber, *The Use of the Army in Aid of the Civil Power*, p. 28n., also pp. 45-46.

threatened robbery or interruption of the United States mails, or of earth-quake, fire, or flood, or other public calamity disrupting the normal processes of government, or other equivalent emergency so imminent as to render it dangerous to await instructions requested through the speediest means of communication, an officer of the Army may take such action before the receipt of instructions as the circumstances of the case and the law under which he is acting may justify, and will promptly report this action, and the circumstances requiring it, to the Adjutant General, by telegram if possible, for the information of the President.[63]

Under normal circumstances there would be no reason for any troop action without proper authorization from the president. This regulation is to cover such contingencies as the Wall Street bomb explosion of 1920 when a battalion of infantry from Governor's Island rushed to the scene to protect the Sub-Treasury.[64] Action initiated by a local commander should be confined "to defensive measures . . . until receipt of instructions from higher authority."[65]

Aside from the regulation providing for emergencies, every positive troop action to aid the civil authorities, state or federal, must be decided upon by the chief executive.[66] There is nothing in the statutes to indicate that this power may be delegated. The intention of the laws was plainly disregarded in 1919, when, because of the lack of a National Guard, requests for aid were so numerous that departmental commanders were authorized to "take necessary action . . . without reference to the War Department."[67] Except in the most extreme case of sudden and widespread disorder, when the very volume of requests would make impossible a satisfactory determination by the president, there would seem to be no necessity for departing from the procedure prescribed by law. Then

---

[63] *AR* 500-50, Apr. 5, 1937.

[64] Wiener, *A Practical Manual of Martial Law*, p. 56.

[65] War Department, Basic Field Manual, *Military Law, Domestic Disturbances*, p. 7.

[66] That Congress did not intend the important and far-reaching power of calling out the troops to be delegated is indicated, it is argued, by the law requiring a presidential proclamation (R.S. 5300): "Since making a presidential proclamation is by custom and law a personal function, it is inferable that Congress intended the employment of troops to be a personal function also." "Employment of Military Forces to Maintain Civil Order and Obedience to Laws," *Riot Duty Memo*, p. 1 (memorandum prepared by Judge Advocate General, June 1922, Office of Judge Advocate General).

[67] The same, p. 2.

would come into effect the corps area commander's exercise of the emergency power, which he already possesses, to move troops within the territory under his jurisdiction. Quite often, as the preceding chapters have indicated, the mere presence of troops is sufficient to prevent disorder.

THE PRESIDENT AND MARTIAL LAW

Whenever disorder occurs and federal troops are sent into a disturbed area, a dispute invariably arises over the extent of the president's authority to institute controls over the civil population. The argument has been advanced that under Revised Statutes 5297 and 5298, since there is nothing in the law as to *how* the president shall suppress the insurrection, the determination of the methods to be employed is wholly within the president's discretion:

> But when power is given by a statute to do a thing and the manner in which it is to be done is not prescribed, the means necessary to do it and to accomplish the purpose for which the power is given is clearly implied.

The indefiniteness of the statutes concerning the extent of the president's action is said to be especially significant since American law generally requires the strict observance of civil liberties. The statutes enjoin the suppression of the insurrection, and whether it is necessary to rescind civil liberties, for the moment, it is argued, is a matter of secondary importance.[68]

This argument obviously has one vital weakness. No statutory power can abridge the provisions of the Constitution.[69] The constitutional guarantees against interference with freedom of speech and of assembly, for example, could scarcely be disregarded on the grounds that such disregard was merely an exercise of the powers implied from Revised Statutes 5297, 5298, and 5299. The courts have never decided what measures may be taken under these statutes. It is reasonable to suppose, however, that some restrictions might be effected without their being considered as unduly curtailing the constitutional guarantees. If such an undue abridg-

[68] The same, p. 7.
[69] Art. VI.

ment of the liberties guaranteed in the Constitution is to be justified, the justification must come from the necessity for martial law. Although a theoretical discussion of the subject of martial law is outside the scope of this study, it is entirely pertinent to review, briefly, the extent to which the presidents have made use of this device in handling public disorders.[70]

Martial law has been defined as "the public law of necessity."[71] "[It] is the public right of self defense against a danger threatening the order or the existence of the state."[72] To eliminate some of the confusion surrounding the expression, writers in recent years have favored the use of two terms, "absolute martial law," and "qualified martial law."[73] By the first is meant the complete displacement of civil agencies by the military. By the second is meant a condition where the military does whatever is necessary to preserve the peace, although civil agencies continue to function, in whole, or in part.

There is little basis for the popular notion that where the troops are, there is martial law. There are at least two circumstances, for example, in which troops might be used in a domestic disturbance where by no stretch of the imagination could even qualified martial law be said to exist. One of these is when troops are sent to a disturbed area with specific instructions to take no action until authorized to do so by the president.[74] The second is when troops are ordered to protect government property. It is obvious that positive action by the military authorities is a first requirement of any form of martial law.

In no instance of domestic peacetime disturbance has any president ever declared martial law.[75] The subject was discussed by Hayes and his Cabinet during the great railroad riots of 1877, but

[70] For extended discussions of the subject of martial law see Wiener, *A Practical Manual of Martial Law;* Charles Fairman, *The Law of Martial Rule;* and Robert S. Rankin, *When Civil Law Fails.*
[71] Wiener, *A Practical Manual of Martial Law,* p. 16.
[72] The same, p. 17.
[73] Punitive and preventive martial law have the same meaning as absolute and qualified martial law. See Fairman, *The Law of Martial Rule,* p. 25; Wiener, *A Practical Manual of Martial Law,* p. 12.
[74] For example, Theodore Roosevelt's command in the Goldfield incident: "Do not act at all until President issues proclamation." See p. 129.
[75] On Lincoln's wartime proclamations, see note 59, p. 206.

no action was taken. It was considered also at the time of the mining disturbances in West Virginia in the summer of 1921. Harding, in fact, prepared a proclamation of martial law but because of doubt as to its constitutionality and also because the troops met with no resistance, the proclamation was never issued.[76]

Qualified martial law was twice declared, however, by federal military officers in the period after the World War when presidential control of troop activities was so greatly relaxed. According to the report of the Secretary of War, as a result of the race riot in Omaha, Nebraska, General Leonard Wood "took personal charge of the situation, and on October 1, 1919, proclaimed the city under qualified martial law."[77] Five days later, because of the danger of violence in Gary, Indiana, during the steel strike, General Wood, after conferring with the municipal authorities, placed that city also under qualified martial law.[78]

There have been other instances where the modified form of martial law existed in fact, though undeclared. General Merriam placed restrictions on travel into and out of the mining camps of Idaho's Coeur d'Alene in 1899.[79] In the Colorado disturbance of 1914, saloons were closed (a common practice), the sale of arms was forbidden, arms and ammunition were seized, and the opening of mines was forbidden as was also the importation of strikebreakers.[80] Public assemblies were forbidden and arms were taken in the West Virginia strike zone in 1921.[81]

It is apparent that in spite of any lack of a presidential proclamation of martial law, the military does take steps beyond those of ordinary police. To the commanding officer at the scene of the disturbance it may seem necessary to demand that people remain in their homes, that places of amusement be closed, that assemblies be forbidden, that arms be surrendered, and that other measures be taken to lessen the chance of outbursts of violence. Whether some of these restrictions are justified as being implied in Revised

[76] See pp. 165-66.
[77] *War Department Annual Report*, 1920, Vol. I, p. 69.
[78] The same.
[79] See p. 114.
[80] See pp. 143-44, 150.
[81] See p. 166.

Statutes 5297, 5298, and 5299, the courts have never decided. In view of the necessity for maintaining order, however, it seems very probable that extraordinary military measures, if at all reasonable, would be upheld, either as an exercise of implied power under these statutes, or as an exercise of qualified martial law. Since the Milligan decision,[82] not only has a president never declared martial law, but no attempt has been made without a declaration to put absolute martial law into effect. Under conditions of absolute martial law the commanding officer may establish military courts to punish those who disobey the orders of the military. That this device is considered unnecessary for handling any civil disturbance is indicated by the present-day Army Regulations:

> Persons not normally subject to military law, taken into custody by the military forces incident to the use of troops contemplated by the regulations in this part should be turned over to the civil authorities. *Punishment in such cases belongs to the courts of justice and not to the armed forces.*[83]

Martial law, either declared or de facto, has great potential dangers. Yet, as the Court remarked a century ago, "All power may be abused if placed in unworthy hands." The acts of the presidents in cases of domestic disorder have borne out the Court's further observation that the high responsibilities of the elevated office of the president "appear to furnish as strong safeguards against a willful abuse of power as human prudence and foresight could well provide."[84]

[82] "Martial rule [absolute martial law] can never exist where the courts are open, and in the proper and unobstructed exercise of their jurisdiction." *Ex parte Milligan,* 4 Wallace 2 (1886).

[83] *AR* 500-50, Apr. 5, 1937. Italics added. Persons held in custody under the authority of the United States cannot be released by a writ of habeas corpus issued from a state court. (*A Digest of the Opinions of the Judge Advocates General of the Army* (1912), p. 268.) "It does not follow that a prisoner arrested and detained by the military authorities under martial law or otherwise in aid of the civil authorities would necessarily be released or turned over to the civil authorities for trial at the hearing of the writ, for the courts usually hold such arrest and detention to be lawful in such situations upon reasonable showing of military necessity, even where no specific crime is charged. War Department, Basic Field Manual, *Military Law, Domestic Disturbances,* p. 9.

[84] *Luther* v. *Borden,* 7 Howard 1, 44 (1849).

CHAPTER XIII

CONCLUSION

From the study of the instances of disorder considered in the preceding chapters it is possible to arrive at certain conclusions regarding the character of the disturbances, to assess the degree of success which the army has met in handling disorders, and to summarize the differing practices of presidents confronted with domestic strife.

CHARACTER OF THE DISTURBANCES

The domestic disorders in which the presidents have been involved are divisible into two broad categories, those directed against government, and those arising out of social and industrial conditions in which the authority of government is interposed between the contending parties in order to preserve the peace.[1]

Prior to the Civil War the major instances of disorder were occasioned by opposition either to a state government or to the national government. Washington, Adams, and Jefferson were each faced with the task of upholding the federal laws by force of arms. In each case the origin of the conflict, although economic in nature, was directed against the government itself. Since the reconstruction period, on the other hand, disorders necessitating federal intervention have arisen chiefly as a result of industrial conditions. Groups have been arrayed against one another rather than against any unit of government.

In the disorders since 1875 in which the presidents have intervened to enforce federal law, opposition to the statutes has usually been merely incidental to the main dispute. Court orders, by making a federal issue out of an industrial disturbance, for a time were a particularly fruitful source of trouble. In the early stages of the Pullman strike, for example, there was not the slightest opposition to the federal government. Not until the district court's sweeping

[1] Legally, disorders are divided into two categories also: those in violation of state law and those in violation of federal law.

injunction was issued did the Cleveland administration become deeply involved. It is obvious that a too hasty decision to enforce a court order could be just as embarrassing to the president as a like decision to assist a state governor. Since 1932 there is less likelihood of a president's being called upon to enforce the court processes, as the Norris-LaGuardia Act of that year greatly restricted the court's use of the injunction in labor cases.[2]

The time element is also a factor distinguishing the early instances of disorder from succeeding ones. The nature of the opposition to the excise law enabled Washington to move very slowly. Indeed, the nature of our military establishment was such that he had no choice. The railroad riots of 1877, on the other hand, called for the utmost expedition on the part of the president. Neither before nor since has any civil conflagration spread with such amazing speed. Compared with Washington, Hayes had no time to deliberate on matters of procedure. Whereas the first president had an opportunity to devise the best means of exacting obedience to the law, later presidents have been required to take positive steps within a short span of time to quell disturbances which threatened or were actually in progress.

ARMY PARTICIPATION

The history of domestic disturbances in the United States demonstrates that the inhabitants of a disturbed area have little to fear from an army which is properly trained, equipped, and commanded. All three are essential. No president was ever more zealous to preserve the civil rights of the inhabitants and to pre-

---

[2] 47 Stat. L. 70. That the danger still exists, however, is indicated by the action of Judge Arthur J. Tuttle of the federal district court in issuing a temporary order restraining the United Automobile Workers—C.I.O. from interfering with employees of the Ford Motor Company who wished to enter or leave the company plant at Dearborn. (*New York Times*, Apr. 4, 1941, p. 1.) In April 1914 a federal court order enjoined interference with the Bache-Denman Coal Co. in Arkansas. The company was later placed in receivership. When violence occurred in November, President Wilson issued a proclamation announcing the employment of the military forces in "protecting property in charge of the courts of the United States." Troops remained until the middle of February 1915. This is probably the most recent use of the troops to enforce court process. See Edward Berman, *Labor Disputes and the President of the United States*, pp. 99–100n; Frederick T. Wilson, *Federal Aid in Domestic Disturbances*, S. Doc. 263, 67 Cong. 2 sess., pp. 317, 321.

vent excesses by the troops than was Washington. Yet, as the first chapter indicates, it was impossible to effect complete control of the inadequately trained and equipped body of soldiers which marched into western Pennsylvania. In contrast to Washington, President Adams paid little attention to matters of discipline. The number of troops marching into eastern Pennsylvania was much smaller, but again a great portion of them had little training. Due in part, perhaps, both to the activities of the troops and to the character of the inhabitants of the area, "on the march of the Army, neither Man, Woman, nor Child could be seen at the Doors of most of the Houses to view them as they passed. . . . A Panic has uniformly preceded the Army on all its Route. . . ."[3] With the exception of the laxness displayed by General Merriam, and for that matter by President McKinley, during the Coeur d'Alene troubles of 1899, the regular troops have given no cause for complaint. On the contrary, their conduct has been such as to command a high degree of respect among the inhabitants of the zones of disorder.

The amount of actual fighting which the troops have been called upon to do in time of disorder has been infinitesimal. With the exception of the Pullman strike, in which there were probably more casualties than in any other disturbance, the soldiers have encountered little active opposition. On most occasions the mere presence of a small body of troops has been sufficient to prevent any disturbance.

An evidence of the success of the troops is the ease with which small detachments have been able to cope with rather serious situations. This was especially noticeable in the great railroad riots of 1877, when the large number of disorders and the limited supply of available troops made the force sent to any one area pitifully small.

With the increased size of the army there has been a tendency to use larger bodies of troops, on the theory that a demonstration of overpowering force acts as a deterrent on those who would provoke violence. Acting upon this theory, General MacArthur au-

[3] Report of Samuel Sitgreaves, *Pennsylvania Insurrection*, Library of Congress Mss.

thorized the parade of tanks down Pennsylvania Avenue at the time of the Bonus Riot. This theory, of course, is not new. It is simply a reversion to the policy of President Washington, who sent a force westward which "according to all human calculation would be prompt and adequate in every view, and might perhaps, by rendering resistance desperate, prevent the diffusion of blood."[4]

There is still some confusion as to what measures the troops may employ to ensure the peace. Throughout the nation's history the principle has always been recognized that a special technique is required to handle civil disorder properly. Wanton killing for the purpose of terrorizing the inhabitants into submission has ever been foreign to the United States. From the very first, also, there has been respect for the principle that no more severe steps should be taken than are absolutely essential to end the disorder. Notwithstanding the advocates of "blood and thunder" theories of martial law,[5] the commanding officers have followed policies of a relatively temperate nature and have never attempted to put into effect a state of complete military control. The policy has always been to preserve, not to displace, the civil authority. Restrictions placed upon the inhabitants of a disturbed area have not been onerous or of long duration. Nor has there usually been any reason for severe restrictions. Where the troops have been sent as impartial preservers of the peace they have been given a friendly welcome.

Every disturbance considered in the preceding pages indicates the necessity for the government and its armed forces to maintain an attitude of complete impartiality. When the administration has sided definitely with one of the disputants, as was done in the Pullman strike, the troops were placed in an embarrassing, if not a positively dangerous, position. An excellent illustration of the manner in which the troops handled a difficult problem without bias is to be found in the West Virginia mining troubles of 1921.

[4] See p. 18.
[5] ". . . Whereas the advocates of a blood and thunder theory of martial law are usually civilian lawyers, with perhaps a smattering of military training, the calmest heads on the whole are the professional soldiers, including the compilers of the Army Regulations. In law, as in actual combat, the most belligerent spirits are generally found well to the rear." Frederick Bernays Wiener, *A Practical Manual of Martial Law*, p. 2.

The soldiers were drawn up behind the lines of both the state and county forces and the forces of the miners. They acted neither for nor against either group, yet, in a short time, they effected the peaceful dispersion of both groups. Where the United States troops have acted in an impartial manner to preserve the peace, not only has their presence been welcome but they have received the respect and co-operation of practically every person.

PRESIDENTIAL PRACTICE

As Professor Herring has pointed out, "to treat the powers of the Chief Executive without reference to the individual incumbent is to ignore the chief determining factor."[6] For this reason and, what is also important, because of changed circumstances, no two presidents have handled disorders in the same manner. Indeed, there is little to indicate that during the first century of the Republic any president ever gave serious study to the procedures established by his predecessors. Consider, for example, the actions of the first two chief executives. During the Whiskey Insurrection Washington sent emissaries to attempt a settlement and to determine the need for troops, he co-operated fully with the state officials, and he made a resolute effort to exercise strict control of the troops. Adams, on the other hand, five years later, made no effort at a peaceful settlement of the dispute; he conducted no investigation; he issued merely a summary notice to the governor to call out the militia; and he made no attempt to control any of the three classes of troops which marched into the area opposing the house assessment.

Just as the practices of succeeding presidents have varied greatly, so also have the practices of one president, faced with a different kind of disturbance and a different set of circumstances. When Jackson confronted the hostile state of South Carolina in the controversy over nullification, he moved with great caution. When faced with a possible race riot, on the other hand, he gave little thought to the matter but dispatched troops immediately. Circumstances likewise made the greatest difference imaginable between the first and second administrations of Woodrow Wilson. The fact

[6] Pendleton Herring, *Presidential Leadership*, pp. 10-11.

that after the World War the states had no National Guard but had to rely on the army, plus the fact of the President's sickness, caused a complete inversion of the policy established in 1914 during the mining troubles in Colorado.

Where it is at all possible it would seem wise for a president to attempt a peaceful settlement of a controversy before making use of the army. At present, in any industrial situation of sufficient gravity to demand presidential intervention, preliminary efforts at a settlement would already have been made by the Conciliation Service of the Department of Labor and the National Defense Mediation Board.[7] In the event all negotiations fail, however, and widespread violence threatens but has not broken out, the president still has the opportunity to use the prestige of his office and his person to bring the parties in dispute to an understanding.

After the efforts of the state and local governments to preserve the peace have proved unsatisfactory, and whenever violence has already taken place or is undeniably imminent, the inhabitants of the troubled zone welcome the arrival of federal forces. In such a circumstance not only is the work of the troops made easy but there is a general feeling throughout the country that the president has done the right thing. When the president acts too quickly, however, before the public is convinced strong measures are necessary, there is likely to be, as Adams and Cleveland found, an unfavorable popular reaction.

Once having made the decision to use force, there is every reason for the president to co-operate with the state and municipal authorities. From a legal standpoint there may be no necessity for co-operation when a federal question is involved, but the Cleveland-Altgeld controversy demonstrates all too well the repercussions likely to be encountered when the state governor is completely ignored. Washington's conduct in this respect is a model which every president can profitably study. In view of the seriousness of any problem which demands the use of the army for its solution, there would seem to be little excuse for not attempting to secure the full co-operation of state and local officials, in order that the dislocations caused by military intervention be kept at a minimum.

[7] Established by executive order, Mar. 19, 1941.

In few disturbances is the president's task an easy one: his job is not done until the troops have been returned to their posts. An important duty of the chief executive is to keep in close touch with the activities of the troops and their commanding officers. It is to the president that the people petition for relief from excesses by the military. To him also the military looks for relief from extended service. There is a tendency for governors to keep the troops as long as the president permits. In contrast, for example, with McKinley's lack of attention to the activities and length of stay of the troops in the Coeur d'Alene are Theodore Roosevelt's and Wilson's continued urging of the governors of Nevada and Colorado to organize state defense bodies so that the regular troops might be relieved. In every instance of disorder where the troops have been called out there is need for a presidential awareness of what is going on.

In addition to the task of keeping himself informed, the president faces also the problem of how much information to give the inhabitants of the disturbed area. It was partly for this purpose that the very first law pertaining to civil disorders required a presidential proclamation. The present law contains the same requirement. However, a proclamation in itself is not always enough. Whenever, by authority of the president, the commanding officer places restrictions upon the activities of the inhabitants, those restrictions should be sufficiently publicized to prevent their being violated through ignorance of their existence.

Where violence seems imminent, the chief executive is besieged by individuals and various pressure groups who desire him to intervene. Obviously, he cannot send the army to every spot where disorder threatens. Not only would he be assuming a function which has always been recognized as the prerogative of the states but he would, by constant use of the troops, endanger popular respect for the armed forces of the United States. The presidents, therefore, have usually resisted the importunities of those who look for federal assistance at the first indication of violence.

There are many factors responsible for the reluctance of the presidents to use the armed forces. The personality of the president, the circumstances surrounding a given disturbance, the effect of a too hasty decision upon public opinion, the delicacy of federal-state relations—all these affect in greater or less degree the president's policy. Nor is the effect of the presidential office upon the incumbent to be ignored. The responsibilities imposed by the office have acted as a very definite brake upon impulsive action. Washington, Jackson, Wilson, and the Roosevelts, all famed for their strong leadership, have acted for the most part with extraordinary care in matters involving the domestic use of the armed forces.

Rarely, if ever, has the exercise of extraordinary care been in error. Civil disorders are seldom caused by trifles. Whenever any dispute has reached a point where consideration is being given to the use of the military forces of the nation, there is need for an unusually high degree of vigilance on the part of the chief executive. Unless there is some special reason which seems to make imperative the immediate use of the troops, or until all efforts to effect a peaceful settlement have failed and violence threatens of a nature beyond the ability of the local and state governments to control, the president is wise to avoid recourse to force. To use the troops only when no other solution seems possible has been the most frequent presidential practice—a practice the value of which is attested by the fact that it has met with complete success.

SELECTED BIBLIOGRAPHY

UNITED STATES GOVERNMENT PUBLICATIONS

GENERAL

American State Papers. Documents, legislative and executive, of the
Congress of the United States. Washington, 1832-1861.

Annals of the Congress of the United States. Washington, 1834-1856.

Army Regulations. Washington, 1937.

Congressional Globe. Washington, 1834-1873.

Congressional Record. Washington, 1873-   .

Constitution of the United States.

Constitution of the United States, Annotated. Washington, 1938.

Debates in Congress. Washington, 1833.

Fitzpatrick, John C. (ed). *The Writings of George Washington from
the Original Manuscript Sources,* 1745-1799. Washington, 1931-
1938.

Official Opinions of the Attorneys General of the United States.

Register of Debates.

*Report of the Industrial Commission on the Relations and Conditions
of Capital and Labor Employed in the Mining Industry.* Washington, 1901.

Richardson, James D. *A Compilation of the Messages and Papers of
the Presidents,* 1789-1897. Official Edition, Washington, 1896.

Riot Duty Memo, Employment of Military Forces to Maintain Civil
Order and Obedience to Law. Judge Advocate General's Office,
1922.

Statutes at Large of the United States.

United States Federal Register.

United States Reports.

War Department Annual Report. Washington, 1920.

*War Department, Basic Field Manual, Military Law, Domestic Dis-
turbances.* Washington, 1941.

SPECIAL REPORTS (LISTED BY CONGRESSES)

*Message from the President of the United States Transmitting Copies
of the Proclamation and Proceedings in Relation to South Carolina.*
Senate Document 30, 22 Cong. 2 sess. (1832-33).

Correspondence—Governor of Pennsylvania. House Document 28, 25
Cong. 3 sess. (1838-39).

Interference of the Executive in the Affairs of Rhode Island. House Report 546, 28 Cong. 1 sess. (1843-44).

United States Troops in Rhode Island. House Document 225, 28
Cong. 1 sess. (1843-44).

Report of the Secretary of War. Senate Executive Document 5, Pt. II. 34 Cong. 3 sess. (1856-57).

Vigilance Committee in San Francisco. Senate Executive Document 43, 34 Cong. 3 sess. (1856-57).

Vigilance Committee in California. Senate Executive Document 101, 34 Cong. 1 and 2 sess. (1856).

Report of the Secretary of the Navy. House Executive Document 1, Pt. III. 45 Cong. 2 sess. (1877-78).

Report of the Secretary of War. House Executive Document 1, Pt. II. 45 Cong. 2 sess. (1877-78).

Report of the Secretary of War. House Executive Document 1, Pt. II. 52 Cong. 2 sess. (1892-93).

Fees and Expenses of U. S. Marshals. Senate Executive Document 120, 53 Cong. 2 sess. (1894).

Report on the Chicago Strike by the United States Strike Commission. Senate Executive Document 7, 53 Cong. 3 sess. (1894-95).

Report of the Secretary of War. House Executive Document 1, Pt. II. 53 Cong. 3 sess. (1894-95).

Appendix to the Annual Report of the Attorney General for the Year 1896. House Document 9, Pt. II. 54 Cong. 2 sess. (1896-97).

Coeur D'Alene Labor Troubles. House Report 1999, 56 Cong. 1 sess. (1899-1900).

Report of War Department. House Document 2, 56 Cong. 1 sess. (1899).

Statement of the Western Federation of Miners. Senate Document 163, 58 Cong. 2 sess. (1903-04).

A Report on Labor Disturbances in the State of Colorado, from 1880 to 1904, Inclusive, With Correspondence Relating Thereto. Senate Document 122, 58 Cong. 3 sess. (1905).

Papers Relative to Labor Troubles at Goldfield, Nevada. House Document 607, 60 Cong. 1 sess. (1907-08).

Report on the Colorado Strike Investigation. House Document 1630, 63 Cong. 3 sess. (1915).

Industrial Relations, Final Report and Testimony Submitted to Congress by the Commission on Industrial Relations. Senate Document 415, 64 Cong. 1 sess. (1916).

Labor Difficulties in the Coal Fields of Colorado. House Document 859, 64 Cong. 1 sess. (1916).

Investigation of Strike in Steel Industries. Hearings before the Committee on Education and Labor, Pt. II, United States Senate, 66 Cong. 1 sess. (1919).

West Virginia Coal Fields. Hearings before the Committee on Education and Labor, United States Senate, 67 Cong. 1 sess. 2 vols. (1921).

Wilson, Frederick T., *Federal Aid in Domestic Disturbances*. Senate Document 263, 67 Cong. 2 sess. (1922).

BOOKS

Adams, Charles Francis, ed. *The Works of John Adams*, 10 vols. Boston, 1856.

Adams, Henry, ed. *The Writings of Albert Gallatin*, 3 vols. Philadelphia, 1879.

Baker, Ray Stannard, *Woodrow Wilson, Life and Letters, President 1913-1914*. New York, 1931.

Baldwin, Leland D., *Whiskey Rebels*. Pittsburgh, 1939.

Bancroft, Hubert Howe, *Popular Tribunals*. 2 vols. San Francisco, 1890.

Barnard, Harry, *"Eagle Forgotten," The Life of John Peter Altgeld*. New York, 1938.

Bassett, John Spencer, ed. *Correspondence of Andrew Jackson*, 7 vols. Washington, 1926-35.

Benton, Thomas Hart. *Thirty Years View*. 2 vols. New York, 1864.

Berman, Edward. *Labor Disputes and the President of the United States*. New York, 1924.

Biennial Message of John P. Altgeld, Governor of Illinois, to the 39th General Assembly. Springfield, 1895.

Boucher, Chauncey S. *The Nullification Controversy in South Carolina*. Chicago, 1916.

Brackenridge, Hugh H. *Incidents of the Insurrection in the Western Parts of Pennsylvania in the Year 1794*. Philadelphia, 1795.

Browne, Waldo R. *Altgeld of Illinois, A Record of His Life and Work*. New York, 1924.

Buck, Solon J., and Elizabeth H. *The Planting of Civilization in Western Pennsylvania*. Pittsburgh, 1939.

Channing, Edward. *A History of the United States*. 6 vols. New York, 1905-1925.

Chitwood, Oliver Perry. *John Tyler, Champion of the Old South*. New York, 1939.

Cleveland, Grover. *The Government in the Chicago Strike of 1894*. Princeton, 1913.

Corwin, Edward S. *The President: Office and Powers*. New York, 1940.

Cummings, Homer Stille, and Carl McFarland. *Federal Justice*. New York, 1937.

Dacus, Joseph A. *Annals of the Great Strikes*. Chicago, 1877.

Davis, William Watts Hart. *The Fries Rebellion*. Doylestown, 1899.

Dowell, Cassius M. *Military Aid to the Civil Power*. Fort Leavenworth, Kansas, 1925.

Facts Concerning the Struggle in Colorado for Industrial Freedom. Series I.

Fairman, Charles. *The Law of Martial Rule.* Chicago, 1930.

Farrand, Max. *The Records of the Federal Convention of 1787.* 3 vols. New Haven, 1934.

Federal Cases, Comprising Cases Argued and Determined in the Circuit and District Courts of the United States. St. Paul, 1896.

Federal Reporter, Cases Argued and Determined in the Circuit Courts of Appeals and Circuit and District Courts of the United States. St. Paul, 1898.

Findley, William. *History of the Insurrection in the Four Western Counties of Pennsylvania.* Philadelphia, 1796.

Fitzpatrick, John C., ed. *The Diaries of George Washington, 1748-1799.* New York, 1925.

Flick, Alexander C. C., ed. *History of the State of New York.* 10 vols. New York, 1933-37.

Ford, Worthington Chauncey. *The Writings of George Washington.* 14 vols. New York, 1889-1903.

Gresham, Matilda. *Life of Walter Quintin Gresham.* 2 vols. Chicago, 1919.

Hamilton, John C., ed. *The Works of Alexander Hamilton.* 7 vols. New York, 1850.

Herring, Pendleton. *Presidential Leadership.* New York, 1940.

Hittell, Theodore H. *History of California.* 4 vols. San Francisco, 1895-1897.

Holst, Hermann Eduard von. *The Constitutional and Political History of the United States.* 8 vols. Chicago, 1881-1892.

Houston, David Franklin. *A Critical Study of Nullification in South Carolina.* New York, 1896.

James, Henry. *Richard Olney and His Public Service.* New York, 1933.

James, Marquis. *Andrew Jackson, Portrait of a President.* New York, 1937.

Jones, Charles Henry. *Memoir of William Rodman.* Printed privately, 1867.

Joslin, Theodore G. *Hoover Off the Record.* New York, 1934.

Laski, Harold J. *The American Presidency, An Interpretation.* New York, 1940.

Lieber, G. Norman. *The Use of the Army in Aid of the Civil Power.* Washington, 1898.

Ludlow, Being the Report of the Special Board of Officers Appointed by the Governor of Colorado to Investigate and Determine the Facts with Reference to the Armed Conflict Between the Colorado National Guard and Certain Persons Engaged in the Coal Mining Strike at Ludlow, Colorado, April 20, 1914. Denver.

McCabe, James Dabney (Edward Winslow Martin). *The History of the Great Riots*. Philadelphia, 1877.

McElroy, Robert. *Grover Cleveland, The Man and the Statesman*. New York, 1923.

McMaster, John Bach. *A History of the People of the United States from the Revolution to the Civil War*. 8 vols. New York, 1927-29.

Miller, Alphonse B. *Thaddeus Stevens*. New York, 1939.

Mowry, Arthur May. *The Dorr War*. Providence, 1901.

Myers, William Starr, ed. *The State Papers and Other Public Writings of Herbert Hoover*. New York, 1934.

Nevins, Allan. *Letters of Grover Cleveland*. Boston, 1933.

———. *Grover Cleveland, A Study in Courage*. New York, 1934.

Ogg, Frederic A. *The Reign of Andrew Jackson*. New Haven, 1920.

Pennsylvania Archives, second and fourth series. Harrisburg, 1874-1935.

Randall, James G. *Constitutional Problems under Lincoln*. New York, 1926.

Rankin, Robert S. *When Civil Law Fails*. Durham, 1939.

Records of the Governor and Council of the State of Vermont. 8 vols. Montpelier, 1873-1880.

Report of the Trial of the Honorable Samuel Chase, Associate Justice of the Supreme Court of the United States. Baltimore, 1805.

Rippy, J. Fred. *Joel R. Poinsett, Versatile American*. Durham, 1935.

Rhodes, James Ford. *History of the United States from Hayes to McKinley, 1877-1896*. New York, 1919.

Roosevelt, Theodore. *An Autobiography*. New York, 1925.

Schofield, John M. *Forty-Six Years in the Army*. New York, 1897.

Sears, Louis Martin. *Jefferson and the Embargo*. Durham, 1927.

State Papers on Nullification. Boston, 1834.

Thorpe, Francis Newton. *The Principles of American Statesmanship*. New York, 1909.

Two Trials of John Fries. Philadelphia, 1800.

Tyler, Lyon G. *The Letters and Times of the Tylers*. 2 vols. Richmond, 1884.

Vincent, Henry. *The Story of the Commonweal*. Chicago, 1894.

Washington, H. A., ed. *The Writings of Thomas Jefferson*. 9 vols. New York, 1861.

West, George P. *United States Commission on Industrial Relations, Report on the Colorado Strike*. Washington, 1915.

Wharton, Francis. *State Trials of the United States*. Philadelphia, 1849.

Wiener, Frederick Bernays. *A Practical Manual of Martial Law*. Harrisburg, 1940.

Wilbur, Ray Lyman, and Arthur J. Hyde. *The Hoover Policies*. New York, 1937.

Williams, Charles Richard, ed. *Diary and Letters of Rutherford Bir-chard Hayes.* 3 vols. Columbus, 1924.

Williams, Mary Floyd. *History of the San Francisco Committee of Vigilance.* Berkeley, 1921.

Wilson, The Messages and Papers of. 2 vols. New York, 1924.

ARTICLES

Allen, Charles C. "Injunction and Organized Labor," *American Law Review,* Vol. XXVIII (1894), pp. 828-59.

"Autobiography of William Michael, Part II," *Historical Papers and Addresses of the Lancaster County Historical Society,* Vol. XXV (1921), pp. 69-77.

Ayres, W. O. "Personal Recollections of the Vigilance Committee," *The Overland Monthly,* Vol. VIII, 2d series (1886), pp. 160-76.

Coleman, W. T. "San Francisco Vigilance Committee," *The Century Illustrated Monthly Magazine,* Vol. XXI, new series (1891), pp. 133-50.

Corwin, Edward S. "Martial Law, Yesterday and Today," *Political Science Quarterly,* Vol. XLVII (1932), pp. 95-104.

Egle, William. "The Buckshot War," *The Pennsylvania Magazine of History and Biography,* Vol. XXIII (1899), pp. 137-57.

Field, David Dudley. "The Army Bill," *Albany Law Journal,* Vol. XVI (1877), pp. 198-201.

Hogaboom, Winfield. "The Last Stand at Goldfield," *The Overland Monthly,* Vol. LI (1908), pp. 111-19.

Howe, George Frederick. "President Hayes's Notes of Four Cabinet Meetings," *The American Historical Review,* Vol. XXXVII (1932), pp. 286-89.

Kirchwey, Freda. "Keep Cool on Labor," *The Nation,* Vol. 152 (1941), pp. 713-14.

Lindsey, Almont. "Paternalism and the Pullman Strike," *The American Historical Review,* Vol. XLIV (1939), pp. 272-89.

"Letters on the Nullification in South Carolina, 1830-1834," *The American Historical Review,* Vol. VI (1901), pp. 735-65.

Miller, William. "The Democratic Societies and the Whiskey Insurrection," *The Pennsylvania Magazine of History and Biography,* Vol. LXII (1938), pp. 324-29.

Scott, Thomas A. "The Recent Strikes," *North American Review,* Vol. CXXV (1877), pp. 351-62.

Sherman, W. T. "Sherman and the San Francisco Vigilantes," *The Century Illustrated Magazine,* Vol. XXI, new series (1891), pp. 296-309.

Stead, W. T. " 'Coxeyism,' A Character Sketch," *Review of Reviews,* Vol. X (1894), pp. 47-59.

Stone, I. F. "F. D. R. and the May Bill," *The Nation*, Vol. 153 (1941), pp. 46-47.

Straight, Michael. "Will Conscripted Labor Work?" *The New Republic*, Vol. 104 (1941), pp. 846-48.

Wiener, Frederick Bernays. "The Militia Clause of the Constitution," *Harvard Law Review*, Vol. LIV (1940), pp. 181-220.

MANUSCRIPTS

Adjutant General's Office. War Department Archives.

Cleveland Papers. Library of Congress.

Hayes Papers. Hayes Memorial Library, Fremont, Ohio.

Papers of Brigadier General Josiah Harmar. William L. Clements Library, Ann Arbor, Michigan.

Pennsylvania Insurrection. Library of Congress.

Policing of Labor Disputes in Chicago. (Thesis of Howard Barton Myers) University of Chicago, 1929.

St. Clair and Harmer. Orderly Book. Library of Congress.

NEWSPAPERS

Aurora General Advertiser (Philadelphia, 1799)

Chicago Socialist (Debs's reply to Cleveland, August 27, 1904)

Claypooles' American Daily Advertiser (Philadelphia, 1799)

Commercial and Financial Chronicle

Evening Star (Washington, D.C.)

Los Angeles Times

Los Angeles Examiner

National Republican (Washington, D.C., 1877)

New York American

New York Times

Niles National Register

Washington Herald

Washington News

Washington Post

INDEX